W9-CKH-330

BUSINESS DEPARTMENT
BIRMINGHAM PUBLIC LIBRARY
2100 PARK PLACE
BIRMINGHAM, AL 35203

21ST CENTURY MANUFACTURING

Creating Winning Business Performance

Thomas G. Gunn

HarperBusiness
A Division of HarperCollins*Publishers*

BUSINESS DEPARTMENT
BIRMINGHAM PUBLIC LIBRARY
2100 PARK PLACE
BIRMINGHAM, AL 35203

658.5

21st CENTURY MANUFACTURING. Copyright ©1992 by Thomas G. Gunn. All rights reserved. Printed in the United States of America. No part of this book may be used or reproduced in any manner whatsoever without written permission except in the case of brief quotations embodied in critical articles and reviews. For information address HarperCollins Publishers, Inc., 10 East 53rd Street, New York, NY, 10022.

HarperCollins books may be purchased for educational, business, or sales promotional use. For information, please call or write: Special Markets Department, HarperCollins Publishers, Inc., 10 East 53rd Street, New York, NY 10022. Telephone (212) 207-7528; Fax: (212) 207-7222.

FIRST EDITION

Library of Congress Cataloging-in-Publication Data

Gunn, Thomas G.
   21st century manufacturing : creating winning business performance
/ by Thomas G. Gunn.
     p.   cm.
   Includes bibliographical references and index.
   ISBN 0-88730-546-6
   1. United States–Manufactures–Management.   2. Industrial
management–United States.   I. Title II. Title: Twenty-first
century manufacturing.
   HD9725.G846   1992
   658.5–dc20   91-38149
                                                               CIP

92 93 94 95 96 PS/HC 10 9 8 7 6 5 4 3 2 1

CONTENTS

iii

For my children: Benjamin, Leslie, and Julia. May they experience the joy of learning and productive work, and the pleasure of life and love while contributing to a world of peace and prosperity.

ACKNOWLEDGMENTS

No book is an individual effort, and this one is no exception. Thanks first and always to my wife Sandra—my best supporter and critic—who has added her skills and keen business insight to my work. Thanks also to my comrades at EDS—Will Clark, Hank Johnston, Hiten Varia, and especially Mike Glynn, among so many others—for their support, advice, and encouragement. Jim Childs, my editor, has been a constant source of support, advice and sound judgment. Finally, thanks to my clients for the richness of learning and experience we have shared together.

INTRODUCTION

A valued professional associate of mine remarked recently that the 1980s was the decade of learning about all the buzzwords of the modern manufacturing world—computer integrated manufacturing (CIM), total quality management (TQM), and just in time (JIT), and all their components, for example—and that the decade of the 1990s would be the decade of implementing these and other competitive advantage enablers.

My consulting experience leads me to believe otherwise. Yes, the manufacturing community has heard most of the buzzwords and perhaps read a few articles or books on these subjects, but from what I have seen in the course of my work, manufacturing management still has much to learn. Why do I reach this conclusion?

I find that the learning that has taken place over the last decade is for the most part rather superficial and has occurred sporadically, in rather narrow segments. Manufacturing executives say they know about all that (buzzword) stuff; they want to hear something *new*. Yet in the next breath they'll say, "Sure, I know all about JIT—that's an inventory reduction technique where you get your suppliers to keep all your inventory," or "Yeah, we're 'doing' TQM. Didn't you see our SQC charts? We've gotten rid of all our inspectors." Some say either "nobody knows what CIM is," or "sure, we have a 'CIM' cell on our plant floor." The latest catchphrase is, "We've just empowered all our workers."

One doesn't have to look too far beyond these dialogues to find that most manufacturers' business performance hasn't improved significantly in the past few years. Most of them are far behind the curve of world class manufacturing performance. Some companies have made excellent progress in one or two narrow areas, but only a few have made progress on a broad front functionally or (even more importantly) cross-functionally or *as a corporation* toward world class business performance. What's needed is a different, more holistic approach toward the entire business of manufacturing. Manufacturing managers must display a much greater sense of urgency toward the goal of quantum performance improvement. Benchmarking may show us in an absolute sense what other manufacturers are doing, but as a snapshot it cannot convey their rate of improvement. The rate of improvement of world class performing companies is staggering. Those companies in the lower 50 percent of the performance spectrum will never know what hit them. Those in the top 50 percent may survive if they move more quickly and effectively than they ever have.

The intensity of global competition and the breathtaking pace of technological change in materials and information technology is propelling change at a rate far beyond most executives' comprehension. As I write this, the information technology revolution has come full circle to devastate the computer industry—the very people who are supposed to know all about the implications of their own technology!

The one thing most manufacturing companies need is vastly improved performance—for survival, growth, and prosperity. This book provides a big-picture guide to achieving major performance gains in the business and science of manufacturing. Not only will it present the reader with steps he or she can take today to improve their company's operations, but it also demonstrates how the manufacturing business will be conducted in the future by those companies that survive today and those that emerge tomorrow.

Read closely, think big, think "must do" in addition to "can do," get inspired, and take action now! As David Lloyd George once said, "Don't be afraid to take a big step if one is warranted. You cannot cross a chasm in two steps."

1

Becoming a World Class Manufacturing Company

Even the most casual observer of business and society knows that the world is changing at an ever increasing pace. In particular, senior managers in every facet of business are reminded on a daily basis of the need for them to make sure that their companies keep pace (at a minimum) with this dramatic rate of change if they are to survive, prosper, and grow.

The Globalization of Business

Today we live in a global environment. Jet air travel and the effects of television and other forms of communication, such as the phone and fax machine, have shrunk the globe. The intensity of global competition today means that there are few protected niches left in which manufacturers can play. Two illustrations serve to make the point.

The U.S. aerospace and defense industries used to think that they were immune to foreign competition, but as of November 1989, 20 foreign-owned U.S. firms were cleared for secret security agreements and were working on 325 classified contracts or subcontracts. By March 1990 these contracts were worth over

$1.3 billion.[1] One may say that this is a small part of the total defense budget, but this figure is bound to increase in the future as defense procurement changes to allow more standard civilian market products to substitute for products that previously had to have a "mil spec."

As early as 1987, I was in a Midwest manufacturer's bakery, where its managers were quite proud of a new food-processing line they had just installed. In those days, particularly, when U.S. food manufacturers wanted new processing equipment, they obtained the production machinery from one or two U.S. manufacturers or from more traditional sources in Germany, Switzerland, or Italy. This particular food line was making a breakfast roll filled with jelly and coated with frosting. The line my client had installed was from a major Japanese producer of food equipment. So here in the American Midwest was a Japanese food line making an item not found in the Japanese diet!

But today competition from the Far East comes not only from Japan, but also from the "four tigers"—South Korea, Taiwan, Singapore, and Hong Kong—as well as, more recently, from Thailand, the Philippines, and Indonesia. Increasingly sophisticated competition in aircraft comes from Brazil and in leather goods from Brazil and Argentina. China and India are gradually becoming more competitive for certain goods in global markets, and we cannot ignore some of the world's best manufacturers from western Europe, as well as the gradual rebuilding of manufacturing companies in the newly opened eastern Europe.

In the past 15 years, many U.S. manufacturers have moved some or all of their manufacturing operations offshore, primarily to Mexico and the Far East. They did this, of course, to lower costs, as direct labor in some foreign countries was only one-tenth the cost of direct labor here in the United States. But the companies that did this often found that things didn't go as planned. First, direct labor in many cases was less than 10 percent of their manufacturing costs, so the move to cheaper labor had a much smaller effect than expected. Second, because of the problems associated with traditional cost accounting methods, U.S. cost systems did not directly reflect the increased overhead costs of doing business overseas—the extra and more expensive people needed to arrange for procurement, track shipments, and communicate engineering needs or engineering changes. Furthermore, supply pipelines became longer, forecasts for part and component demand had to be made further out (which decreased their accuracy), and inventories went up, to reflect not only the longer lead times, but also mistakes from forecast errors, quality problems, or being behind the engineering change curve. Computer systems became even more fragmented, telecommunications were slow, and entire operations were run by fax. Often, the quality of parts received was below standard, and extensive testing or rework was necessary at a U.S. location to rectify the problem. Management travel costs increased as executives, engineers, and procurement people suddenly became extensive world travelers. Of course, attention to matters overseas for a given management team usually meant less time for attention to matters at home.

In most cases, moving out of the United States was a reactive move by U.S. manufacturers who were avoiding their real problems and trying to take the easy way out. Their high costs were caused by poor quality and business processes that usually contained about 90 percent waste. On top of that, there was a certain cachet to having international operations, being a "global" manufacturer, and having to go on all those exciting overseas trips. But, for the most part, moving offshore only postponed the inevitable—the company's continued decline as a competitive force in their marketplace.

Some U.S. manufacturers established Maquiladora operations along the Mexican border in order to take advantage of cheap Mexican labor. This was no panacea either. In most cases they found a scarcity of workers, very high labor turnover (in the 8 percent to 10 percent per month range), and the need for extensive education and training to teach the work force the fundamentals of quality and how to meet production schedules. Education costs often ran 15 percent to 18 percent of payroll costs in Mexico (admittedly on a lower base), against a 1 percent average in the United States.[2] In addition, U.S. workers were required to kit materials and take them through customs and back in and out of Mexico. Again, supply lines were long, lead times went up, inventory went up, and quality went down.

Let me give a typical example. The management of a small plant (less than $20 million) in Texas spent two years putting together and selling to its corporate management the idea of establishing their own Maquiladora operation in Reynosa, about 400 miles away. They were going to produce some of their standard high-volume products in this new operation, which would be headed by a manager from their current operation. The ostensible reason for this move was to lower costs and gain much-needed space.

However, the current operations in their Texas plant were a disaster. There were few, if any, managers in the plant who had sufficient knowledge of operations, production and inventory control systems, JIT, or quality improvement. Overall inventory turns were about three, the shop floor was packed with WIP (work in progress), the average part was handled 44 times in traveling 1200 feet in a 65,000 square foot facility, and lead times were three to five weeks when competitors' were two to three weeks. Sales per employee were only $75,000. Because of the excessive lead times, the company often had to give an additional 2 to 4 percent discount to get an order, thus eroding their gross margin well below plan. On the other hand, many of their customers were willing to pay a premium to get one- or two-day delivery on their orders! Furthermore, given their conventional cost system, they had failed to anticipate what would happen when they pulled their high-volume standard parts out of their current plant. This meant that the product costs in the Texas plant would go up dramatically, since its overhead would be spread over a much lower production volume of specials and "cats and dogs."

The current plant's management was having trouble operating one plant effectively. How did it ever expect to run two plants so that the total was even more competitive? On top of that, they failed to recognize that their main problem (from the customers' viewpoint) was lead times, not costs. Moving to a second operation would increase their asset base (buildings, machinery, people, and inventory), spread their already thin management even thinner, exacerbate the lead time issue, and vastly complicate their scheduling and material management problems.

We were able to show them that an equivalent investment of about $2.5 million in improving their U.S. plant would produce far more dramatic results than the Maquiladora would and, more importantly, solve their major customer problem of excessive order-to-delivery lead times.

Unfortunately, there is considerable evidence that many U.S. corporations have had to learn the above lesson the hard way, both with respect to operating Maquiladora operations as well as moving their operations to the Far East. Motorola, Lionel Toys, Zycom, and many others have finally seen the light, closed some or all of their offshore operations, and concentrated on making their U.S. operations better performers—in some cases world-class manufacturers.[3]

As we have seen, the temporary use of these offshore operations might buy a company in dire straits some time in the marketplace until it dramatically improves its plants at home. But this should be an emergency measure only, complete with time limits and a plan to improve the home operations.

There are valid reasons to set up manufacturing operations in other parts of the globe. The foremost of these is to be near key markets, to stay closer to customers and their unique cultures in other parts of the world. Mazda and Nissan, for instance, have established automotive design studios in California in order to be "closer" to the U.S. automotive marketplace.[4]

Another valid reason to set up global operations is to be near key suppliers, particularly if the products bought from them are bulky and costly to ship, or if products may degrade when shipped over long distances and times. Finally, legal or political reasons may dictate the establishment of manufacturing operations in other than your company's home country. There may be local labor content laws or international trade offsets to comply with; the latter require that for every dollar (or mark or yen) taken out of the country by a company selling its products, that company must put a certain amount of money back into the country in investment and wages or goods purchased. These reasons are legitimate ones to go overseas, whereas chasing cheap labor is not. In addition to the reasons noted above, sources of cheap labor continually move around the globe as different countries go through their economic development cycles.

Ted Leavitt set the business world on its ear with his seminal *Harvard Business Review* article "The Globalization of Markets."[5] Since then, we've learned that what Leavitt espoused therein can be taken too far. Most of the world is not ready for a truly global single product—a composite of global consumers' taste. Experience has shown that products still have to be tailored to their local consumers' taste or to legal requirements.

But instead of a manufacturer having ten completely different models of a product it manufactures and sells around the world—ten different product designs produced with possibly ten different production processes—it makes far more sense to have global product "platforms" that can be quickly tailored to each local market's needs. These product platforms are based on one standard global product and process design, are usually modular in nature, and are established with groups of options that allow them to be easily adapted to customer needs or desires in different parts of the world. Sony, Apple, and Sun are examples of companies that excel in the design and production of these standard global product platforms. Because of existing investments in process equipment in different areas of the world, it is sometimes not possible to have one global production process; but two is better than ten. With fewer processes, quality improves, more learning takes place, and skills are more transferable between operations. The best long-term solution is one fundamental product employing one process.

Strategic Differences in Plant Designs

Companies that already own plants around the world and are trying to sort out their future options must recognize strategic differences in plant design and configuration and how these differences affect different stages in their global expansion, in accommodation of new or growing markets, and in global plant production loading. Exhibit 1-1, adapted from Robert Reich's article "Who Is Us?"[6] shows different types of modern plants.

Type of "Plant"	Functions In "Plant"	Intellectual Content	Labor Content	Nature of Products	Required Investment	Production Tech Used	Sourcing Decision	Typical Countries
1. Full operation Integrated co-located	Prod Design Proc Design Production Purchasing	High	Low	State of art High tech	High up to $600 Million	High Proprietary	Same loc	U.S. Japan Germany
2. Production complex	Component Fabrication & Assembly	Some	Medium	Engineered Med Tech	Medium	Medium Older (Std) Processes	Mixed Most hdqtrs Some local	Taiwan So. Korea
3. Assembly operation	Assembly	Low	High	Mature Standard Low tech	Low to Med	Low / old	may buy local but buy decision made at hdqtrs	Thailand Singapore Malaysia Indonesia
4. Import operation	No prodn Sales Marketing Distribution	---	---	Any	Very low	----	----	----

Exhibit 1-1 Four types of typical plants.
(Source: Robert Reich, "Who Is Us?" *Harvard Business Review*, January–February 1990, pp. 53–64.)

The exhibit shows that there are four basic types of plants, ranging from a full operation to an import operation only. The point is that each of these plants requires a different investment and staffing, and each is suited for different global competitive conditions. Observe how, as the intellectual content of the product and process design increases, the labor content decreases. Note too the critical positioning of the sourcing function, especially in modern less vertically integrated manufacturing companies. Configuring your company's global operations network effectively is a key to obtaining and sustaining competitive advantage. The taxonomy shown in Exhibit 1-1 provides a useful framework for thinking about the problem.

Becoming a Global Corporation

No one interested in conducting business on a global basis should be unfamiliar with the writings of Kenichi Ohmae, McKinsey's top consultant in Japan. His latest book, *The Borderless World*,[7] contains a superb description of the stages a company goes through in becoming a global company, summarized in Exhibit 1-2.

Most U.S. companies aren't even at stage 1 of this diagram. Of the minority of U.S. companies that export, most are somewhere around stage 3, with the largest companies perhaps at stage 4. Sony and Honda are two of Ohmae's examples that have reached stage 5; they are models for the rest of the world's corporations to emulate.

Being a successful global competitor is much more difficult than just limiting your operations to one country, but it brings opportunity and growth if managed successfully. Management has to "think big," but, more than ever, it must also decide how to quickly achieve world class business performance to take advantage of global opportunity.

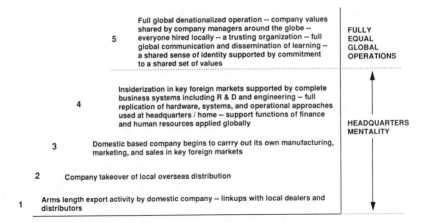

Exhibit 1-2 Ohmae's five stages toward global operation.
(Source: Kenichi Ohmae, *The Borderless World* [New York: Harper Business, 1990].)

The New Manufacturing Environment

Manufacturing has become an increasingly complex business to manage for at least five reasons.

• *First, manufacturing has become global in scope.* Design expertise and product components are sourced globally. Subassembly work may be done on three different continents while final assembly is accomplished on a fourth. Distribution must accommodate the customer, whatever the customer is—another industrial company, a retailer, or an individual consumer—wherever it may be in the world.

• *Second, all business activity is moving at a faster pace.* Time and distance are being compressed by the electronic movement of information in all forms—from television's influence on consumer desires and global politics, to electronically connected financial trading markets, to the influence of fax machines and portable telephones on executives' management styles. Business activities that used to take weeks now take a day, or are even performed in "real time."

• *Third, increasing consumer sophistication and more sophisticated marketing* have led to a proliferation of products to target more diverse tastes and accommodate special market niches. This growth in stock keeping units (SKUs) compounds manufacturing complexity exponentially, especially in light of customer demand for higher quality and shorter lead times.

• *Fourth is the increased emphasis by all customers on higher quality.* Customers can't afford to buy unreliable products. Their lifestyles and schedules leave no time for getting products serviced or returning defective ones to their supplier. The conventional wisdom that zero defects is unachievable has been debunked by a flood of products that seem to work perfectly.

• *Finally, in many parts of the world* manufacturers face increasing pressure for regulatory compliance under a variety of environmental, health, safety, and consumer information statutes. Not only do these regulations add a bewildering maze of complexity to management's challenge, they also add cost to the operations.

In spite of these tough challenges, some manufacturing companies from all parts of the globe have established themselves as leaders in the business of manufacturing—as world-class performers. Yet for the most part, the managers of manufacturing companies—particularly in the United States, Europe, and Latin America—still don't know or haven't been able to implement the concepts and tools necessary to perform on a world-class basis and thus ensure their survival, prosperity, and growth in the years ahead. Are manufacturers collectively doing better than five or ten years ago? The answer is yes, in some areas. Is each manufacturing company doing *sufficiently* better on an overall basis? No.

Some companies with enlightened management—no more than 5 percent of the United States' 355,000 manufacturing companies (125,000 with over 20 employees)[8]—have shown good progress toward world-class performance levels in the past decade. Probably no more than 25 percent of these companies—less than 1.5 percent of the total—have moved fast enough to achieve these goals. Only a few companies are doing everything possible within the limits of today's technology and human learning to steadily propel themselves to dominance in the business of designing and manufacturing goods for their world markets; these companies are the vanguard of world-class manufacturing.

Consider that world-class manufacturing performance means the following quantum leaps relative to today's averages:

- Quality—increased by a factor of 100 to 1000
- Costs—decreased by 30% to 50%
- Inventory turns:

  Work-in-process (WIP) turns increased by a factor of 4 to 10
  Overall turns increased by a factor of 3 to 5

- Productivity—increased by a factor of 2 to 4
- Order-to-delivery lead times—reduced by a factor of 5 to 10
- New product and process design lead times—decreased by a factor of 30 percent to 60 percent

These improvements are only the beginning. They become a moving target as progressive companies led by enlightened management and an empowered workforce improve these and other measures of performance even more every day.

Why the Lack of Progress Toward World Class Performance?

What explains the lack of better progress by the vast majority of manufacturers? We hear an endless litany of excuses. The excuses are generally characterized by the following labels and built on the following themes:

- **The Doubters.** "We don't believe those world-class performance numbers cited above. They are impossible for any manufacturer to achieve! They may be possible in other industries (or countries), but not this one! You don't understand our industry, or how unique our company is. On top of that, inventory turns don't matter to us; we get progress payments for materials from the U.S. government. That defective parts per million quality stuff doesn't apply to us. We only make a few dozen products a year!"

- **The Mañana Gang.** "Sure, a few companies may be achieving those numbers, but there's no hurry for us. You can't push this stuff too fast you know. We're doing all right—our sales were up 5 percent this year while we took 2 percent off our costs. We all got our bonuses for last year, but wow, this year looks really tough. We'll have to cut some corners in our new product line to get it out in time to make our numbers again."

- **The Poorboys.** "We can't afford to be a world-class performer like those big global companies. We don't have the money or staff or time to make all those changes! Can you believe a major consulting firm assessed our operations and reported to us that our cost of poor quality was in excess of 25 percent of sales?"

- **The Luddites.** "We don't believe in computers around here—too many companies have been ruined by them. We do things the old-fashioned way—with smart and hardworking people. Boy, are they getting hard to find, though, especially design engineers! We've got to hire more help because we're drowning in paper and no one seems to know how things work around here anymore."

- **The Generals.** "Our work force is too slow and dumb for us to ever be world-class performers. You can't find anyone who's willing to work today. Can you believe that when we tell these new young people what to do, they don't want to do it! Our employee turnover gets higher every year. On top of that, the high school or college graduates we hire don't seem to know anything. Our schools really do a lousy job today. Where's some old-fashioned street smarts and discipline?"

- **The Fatcats and the Reticent.** "Yeah, we all know that we have to get this company moving. But who's going to tell that to our senior management and board? They're isolated in their headquarters and don't even understand manufacturing anyway. On top of that, they only seem to care about satisfying Wall Street, enjoying their big compensation plans, and flying around in their corporate jets. Several of us were talking the other day about moving on before this company and our careers fall even further behind."

- **The Provincialists.** "We don't believe all this stuff about global markets and competitors. There's no need for us to be expanding internationally. One of our local competitors tried that a few years ago and lost its shirt. Some of our customers did say those foreigners were around asking them questions about their needs and about us. But there's no way those guys will ever figure out how to beat our distribution system."

- **The Whiners.** "Those Japanese have access to cheap capital. If we could get capital at the same low cost, we'd be that good too. Yeah, our return on assets has been way down the past few years. We have to carry too much inventory to keep our increasingly demanding customers happy these days. I don't understand why they expect us to carry most of the inventory now!"

- **The Bailout Crowd.** "We're waiting for our government to do something to protect us. Then we can get back to business as usual."

- **The Perplexed.** "We're trying to do more to become a world-class manufacturer, but we're confused about what to do with our limited resources first, how to plan properly for a successful implementation, and how to get all of our workforce behind our program. We're really not even sure how much we have to improve to sustain leadership in our industry. I can't get an objective view from my people as to where we stand today. Besides we have no idea of how much we should be spending on educating and training our people."

Thus it goes as manufacturers in America and many other parts of the world gain speed but lose altitude in a nosedive toward mediocrity or business failure. Needless to say, this state of affairs need not be. Not only is manufacturing vitally important to the commercial base of any country, but the overall steps that a company must take to move toward world-class manufacturing performance have been demonstrated by a number of companies around the world. Furthermore, most of the techniques necessary to imitate these world-class performers have been written about extensively, though usually on a narrow basis as a stand-alone subject. The approach in this book mirrors the approach manufacturers must take—a broad and all-encompassing assault upon becoming a world-class business performer.

The Importance of the Manufacturing Industry to the United States

Consider the importance of manufacturing in the United States. Manufacturing as a percentage of gross national product has grown slightly in the last 10 to 15 years, averaging about 22 percent to about 24 percent in the most recent year measured.[9] It still provides for some 18 percent of total jobs, employing some 19 million people.[10] Manufactured goods represented about 80 percent of all exports from the United States in the year 1988.[11]

Much has been written about the current trend toward services and away from manufacturing. Most of the new jobs created in the past decade have indeed been service jobs, and many of the traditional white-collar jobs in manufacturing companies can be considered service jobs—those such as engineering, travel, legal work, purchasing, maintenance, and so forth. The flow of manufactured goods around the globe today is dwarfed by the flow of monetary funds. But these factors do not diminish the importance of manufacturing as an industry that directly or indirectly creates many of those service jobs. One study has shown that, for every 1000 manufacturing jobs created, 700 nonmanufacturing jobs are created.[12] Manufacturing's value added is vital to maintaining any nation's prosperity, competitiveness, and independence.

The Progress of Leading Manufacturing Companies

When considered within any one company, industry, or even country, progress toward world-class performance in all aspects of a manufacturing business might seem slow. However, when progress is evaluated from a cross-functional, cross-company within an industry, cross-industry, and global basis, the picture becomes clearer and more heartening, for then a pattern emerges of the total effort required to make the enormous leap from today's mediocrity to tomorrow's excellence.

Where are we on the journey to world-class manufacturing business performance? It is not where we thought or hoped we'd be a decade ago. We've found that it is not just a matter of throwing money or technology at the problem. We cannot accomplish the job by implementing the teachings of a single guru or by implementing just one of a variety of competitive advantage enablers like just-in-time (JIT), computer-integrated manufacturing (CIM), or total quality control (TQC). We've found that we cannot achieve it only with computers and elaborate information systems. On the other hand, we have learned that we can't do it *without* computers and effective information systems. Most business executives now share the realization that there is no "magic wand" solution for achieving world-class performance in any manufacturing company.

So we're moving toward the goal. But, unfortunately for most companies and for many countries, we're moving too slowly to keep up with those industry leaders who are more strategic in intent, more adept at technology adoption and more accomplished at educating and motivating people to work together in diligent pursuit of a common vision. Moreover, their progress as leaders in the world-class performance race only moves the goal posts farther away for companies that have fallen behind and may be trying to catch up.

There is no question that U.S. manufacturing executives are not exhibiting sufficient management leadership. In company after company on a global basis, there is a considerable body of evidence that where management is enlightened their companies can equal or exceed the performance of the world's best manufacturing companies. This is as true in the United States as it is in any other region of the globe. Whether it is Motorola with its "Bandit" pager plant in Florida, Hewlett-Packard with its design of inkjet or laser printers, the Allen Bradley Division of Rockwell International with its motor contactor plant in Milwaukee, John Deere or Caterpillar excelling with their heavy equipment design and manufacturing capability, Ford Motor Company in its diligent pursuit of designing quality and low cost into its products and processes, Boeing with its use of solid modeling computer-aided design (CAD), or Cypress Semiconductor and Intel with their leading computer-aided design and engineering (CAD/CAE) software, U.S manufacturers have shown that they can maintain or even set the global pace in manufacturing excellence.

What's the lesson here? First, management leadership is essential to inspire, motivate, and strategically lead a manufacturing company toward world-class business performance. I do not mean administrative or even management skill (these too are needed), but leadership. My purpose in this book is not to establish what constitutes this skill so uniquely manifested in but a few people, but to acknowledge its need and value above administrative and management expertise.

Second, we have learned that becoming a world class business performer is a full-time activity. It is not a task that manufacturing management can work on for the first ten weeks of a quarter and then neglect or put aside for the last three weeks while it gets the product out the door to meet a revenue target. The effort requires a full-court press—unswerving devotion to hard work and attention to detail by all functions and people in a manufacturing company.

Third, there are several fundamental management processes necessary to become a world-class manufacturing performer. Creating a vision comes first. Then an effective planning process must be used to create a long-term improvement program that will substantially bolster the company's competitive position. These steps will be discussed in more detail in the next chapter.

Fourth, management must focus on the right things. As noted before, there is no one "magic wand" to get the job done. Americans especially seem always to be looking for the *one* thing to do above all else in order to find a shortcut to the holy grail. There is no one answer, in general, or even within the confines of one company or strategic business unit. Experience shows that it takes a carefully balanced and prioritized program of several projects to accomplish the goal. In part, this is due to the complexity, magnitude, and scope of the manufacturing business itself.

Finally, the journey to world-class manufacturing business performance has no end. There will be no point where any company can finally relax and say "we're there." Such is the nature of change and competition and of the march of science and technology.

Appreciating the Strategic Big Picture

It is critical for a manufacturer's management team to understand the overall strategic picture before setting out on a major performance improvement program. Exhibit 1-3 represents one useful framework from which to begin.

Few companies, excluding startups, have the luxury of starting from scratch in determining strategy for each of the three left-side boxes in Exhibit 1-3. Indeed, most executives who take over in an established corporation find themselves presented with de facto circumstances concerning where they compete, the way they compete, and the bases of competition they possess. Over time, clearly, the strategies in each of the three boxes are changeable. Strategic planning exercises and market/competitor analysis may uncover great opportunity in new products and markets for the company. Unfortunately, usually little can be done to change a company's established direction toward these two subjects in the short term.

No matter what a company's current circumstances are with the top two strategic boxes, a great deal can be done with re-

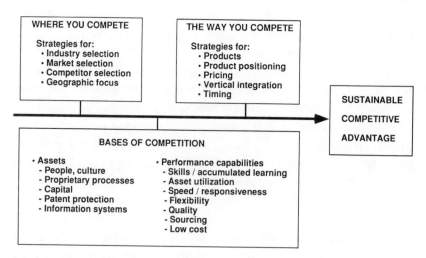

Exhibit 1-3   A strategic picture for a manufacturing business.

gard to the bottom strategic box—the company's bases of competition. Here is where the major opportunity for improvement lies in most manufacturing companies, despite their strategies covering the top two boxes. Huge errors in dealing with where a company competes and the way it competes can seriously cripple a company's business success, but in most cases, companies can make huge performance gains in all respects—financially, strategically, and customer-wise—by focusing their improvement efforts in the bottom strategic box. The ideal combination, of course, is to excel in all three areas, but this is rare, and even if achievable, it takes time to carry out. Getting a company to perform better with its current products in its current markets will generally buy it the time and customer goodwill it needs to improve and modify its choices in the top two strategic boxes. This book is dedicated to that performance improvement goal.

Defining Today's Product and the Business of Manufacturing

Many of today's manufacturers miss major marketplace opportunities as well as opportunities to differentiate themselves by the way they define a product. Traditionally, *product* means the tangible physical product the company manufactures—a hammer, a dress, or a lawn mower, for example. But today, world-class competitors use a broader definition of product to add more value for their customers and differentiate themselves from their competitors. They define a "product" as the tangible physical product along with the *services* they can offer either included with or independent of the traditional product. It is these value-added services that can dramatically improve customer satisfaction.

Think ahead a decade or two. How will your company differentiate itself against its competition then? By that time, the manufacturing cost and quality of each company's physical products will be roughly the same as its competitors' since each company will use the same technology to design and produce their products. In addition to design features and aesthetics, it will be the *service* aspects of the company's offerings that will differentiate it from its competitors' offerings. From this point forth, *product* thus means the physical product *plus* value-added services.

In a similar manner, many manufacturers use a narrow definition of *manufacturing* that undermines their efforts to be a world-class manufacturer. To them, manufacturing is the production activity on the shop floor. World-class aspirants and performers view manufacturing in a more holistic manner. Their integrated definition of manufacturing includes the complete spectrum of activities starting with product and process design, then moving through manufacturing planning and control, production, and distribution, and ending with after-sale service and support of the product in the field. It is this definition that we will utilize throughout this book.

Today's Critical Competitive Factors

When all is said and done in today's competitive arena, the three primary measures that most significantly influence any manufacturing company's success are those having to do with cost, quality, and time. Obviously, cost must be the lowest, quality the highest possible, and time the least in all aspects of a company's business practices. The value of an enterprise's information is another measure, equally valuable, whose importance we are just beginning to realize and which we are just learning to measure on a subjective basis. By *information value,* I mean not only the value of an enterprise's data (all types), but the value of the information system infrastructure it has in place to manage and communicate the data inside the enterprise as well as to its external business contacts. Thus, the primary task of any manufacturer is to have a firm and total understanding of where it stands with regard to each of these four measures.

This implies that (1) a manufacturing company's management understands the complete cost buildup for each of its products from its global suppliers through its value-added enterprise to its global customers; (2) a manufacturing company's management understands its complete quality or yield picture for every step in each of its product's complete process described above; (3) a manufacturing company's management completely understands the total lead time (elapsed time) for every step in each of its product's complete process described above; and (4) a manufacturing company understand its information value and where it stands against other companies in all industries who have state-of-the-art information systems (we'll explore this assessment further in Chapter 9).

Only with an understanding of these four vital activity chains and competitive factors, illustrated for the first three in Exhibit 1-4, will the company's management be armed with

	Source	Fabricate	Sub assemble	Assy & test	Package	
100% — QUALITY	98%	96%	93%		90%	Perfect product
COST						— 100%
						— 0%
TIME (days)	8 - 10	10 - 15	2	1	0.1	

Exhibit 1-4 Documenting a manufacturing company's three vital activity chains.

the knowledge it needs to start a world-class performance improvement program.

Obviously, activites or points that occupy a high percentage of the three activity chains are leverage points that may determine the *priority* of selecting opportunities for performance gains in a company. However, these leverage points may have been "known" for years in a particular company or industry such as the distribution activity for a food manufacturer. Significant improvement potential may thus lie elsewhere in a series of small but cumulatively powerful gains in the cost, quality, and time activity chains. We will discuss this further in Chapter 3.

Addressing the Hierarchy of Corporate Business Needs

Just as Abraham Maslow identified a hierarchy of human needs,[13] I suggest that there is a hierarchy or chain of corporate or enterprise needs that must be fulfilled (an enterprise can be defined as any business unit within or including the corporation). The first and most obvious need for the enterprise is success, as represented by the need for survival first, then growth, followed by prosperity, and most favorably represented by "market presence"—a recognition by the buying public that a company is a world leader as a producer of goods and services that customers value.[14] Companies that have market presence readily come to mind—Coca-Cola, Caterpillar, Boeing, Sony, Levi Strauss, Canon, Apple, Mercedes Benz, and many more.

At the second level, enterprises seek a group of high-level generic business benefits that I will label "meta-benefits." I believe that there are only six of these that really count:

- Greater customer satisfaction
- Higher profitability

- Increased sales
- Greater return on assets
- Higher productivity
- An employee environment of continuous learning and improvement

Just as these meta-benefits can be mapped to their higher-level success factors (some or most to more than one success factor), all other more specific enterprise benefits that we will discuss soon can be mapped to these six meta-benefits.

The third level of the benefit hierarchy or chain comprises specific enterprise benefits:

- More and more timely information to manage an increasingly complex business more effectively
- Higher product quality
  - Less risk of performance disappointment, degradation, or failure
  - More value-added in product
- Greater flexibility
- Lower inventories
- Lower costs
- Better customer service
  - More reliable delivery performance to date/time needed
  - Reduced order-to-delivery lead times
- Quicker time to market

As before, these specific benefits map to the enterprise's meta-benefits. For instance, lower inventories will result in a higher return on assets. Higher product quality will mean greater customer satisfaction, higher productivity, and perhaps increased sales and higher profitability as well.

Finally, for any manufacturer in any industry, we can look to specific world-class business performance concepts and competitive advantage enablers that can be applied to specific leverage points within the enterprise regarding cost, quality, and time that in turn produce the specific benefits cited earlier. In most cases, the implementation of these concepts and enablers will produce specific benefits in multiple areas, just as in our earlier example.

The enterprise benefit chain can thus map both ways—from success factors to the specific concepts and enablers that indirectly produce them, or from concepts and enablers to the chain of enterprise benefits and success factors that they produce, as illustrated in Exhibit 1-5. This benefit chain mapping represents a powerful way to understand and help justify the application of world-class performance concepts and enablers to a manufacturing company from a strategic and financial view.

Getting started on the road to world-class manufacturing performance first requires the *will* to take action—to do something different today than you did yesterday. Given that, the first thing needed is a vision of what it takes to become a world-class performer in manufacturing.

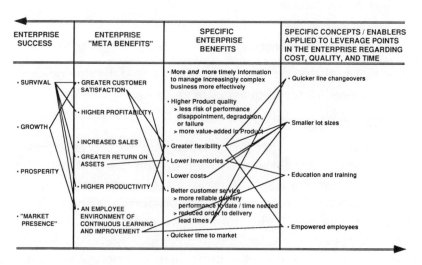

Exhibit 1-5 A partial benefit chain map.

Chapter 1

1. "DOD Urged To Upgrade Existing Weapons Systems," *Metalworking News*, 16 April 1990, p. 15.

2. "Mexican Maquiladora Plants Present a Catch-22," *Electronic Business*, 27 November 1989, pp. 17–18.

3. See "Some Firms Resume Manufacturing in U.S. After Foreign Fiascos," *Wall Street Journal*, 14 October 1986, and "U.S. Manufacturing on Whose Turf," *Industry Week*, 5 September 1988, pp. 53–62.

4. A. Taylor III, "Why Toyota Keeps Getting Better," *Fortune*, 19 November 1990, pp. 66–79.

5. Theodore Leavitt, "The Globalization Of Markets," *Harvard Business Review*, May–June, 1983 pp. 92–102.

6. Robert Reich, "Who Is Us?" *Harvard Business Review*, January–February, 1990 pp. 53–64. (Sidebar by T. Hixon and R. Kimball, pp. 56–57).

7. Kenichi Ohmae, *The Borderless World* (New York: Harper Business, 1990).

8. *1990 Statistical Abstract Of The United States*, Table 872, p. 528.

9. J. Jasinowski, "Manufacturing's Renaissance," *Industry Week*, 15 April 1991, p. 63.

10. R. E. Kutscher, *Monthly Labor Review*, September 1987, pp. 3–9.

11. *1990 Statistical Abstract of the United States*, Table 1387, p. 790.

12. Kay R. Whitmore, National Machine Tool Builders Association, Special Advertising Supplement to *Industry Week*, p. A35.

13. A. H. Maslow, *Motivation and Personality* (New York: Harper & Row, 1970).

14. The Japanese showed Western businesspeople that growth and market share came before prosperity. Typically, U.S. and European manufacturers put prosperity before growth and thus paid out a lot of their profits to shareholders instead of investing in greater market share and renewed competitive vitality.

2

Establishing the Fundamental Management Processes

Establishing a Vision of the Future

I have found, in my experience, that there is a core set of management processes that a manufacturing company must have to get started on the road to becoming a world class business performer.

The first of these deals with the creation of a vision of the future for both the science and business of manufacturing and for the company as an industry participant. I addressed the former part in my most recent book, *Manufacturing for Competitive Advantage: Becoming a World Class Manufacturer.*[1] I traced the development of the manufacturing vision though three examples, starting from the early 1980s and ending with Arthur Young's manufacturing for competitive advantage framework shown in Exhibit 2-1.

The benefits of this framework are many. It provides a holistic overview of manufacturing and shows that everything proceeds from the top down in a strategic picture that encompasses global markets and global competitors. It notes

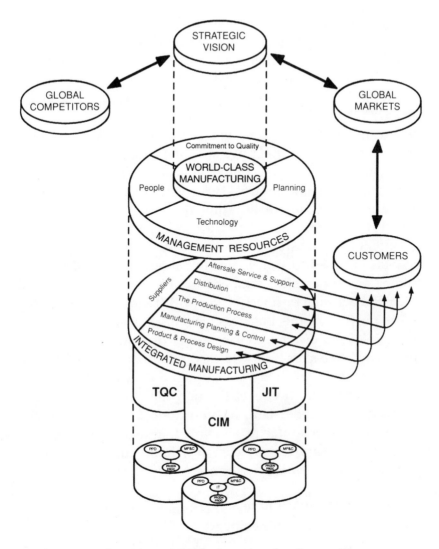

Exhibit 2-1 Arthur Young's Manufacturing for Competitive
Advantage Framework.

that management resources are needed before any technical
tools or philosophies can be implemented, and it defines integrated manufacturing from two points of view: first, across
the manufacturing spectrum of activity, thus defining manufac-

turing in a much broader sense than simply production; and second, by integrating manufacturing forward to the customer and back to the supplier. This integration must take place along both axes—in a business relationship sense as well as electronically—so that both alphanumeric (business) and geometric (engineering) data could be transmitted along either axis seamlessly. Perhaps its greatest power is its recognition of the three major competitive advantage tools and the definition at lower levels of the components of and interrelationships between total quality control (TQC), computer integrated manufacturing (CIM), and just in time (JIT).

With increased learning and the passage of time, and with the intent of establishing an even broader manufacturing business (as opposed to a more functional one) vision, EDS (Electronic Data Systems corporation) and I have jointly developed the manufacturing business vision (MBV) shown in Exhibit 2-2.

The purpose of this business vision is to show in one holistic high-level view the core concepts of management thinking needed to become a world class manufacturing performer. Starting with the obvious global theme built into the model, I will proceed level by level through the model so that you, the reader, can understand it as an up-to-date way to look at the business of manufacturing. Note that there are seven core concepts necessary for any company to become a world class manufacturing business performer:

- A global approach to business
- A balanced business strategy
- Leadership
- A responsive enterprise
- Competitive advantage enablers
- The value-added pipeline
- The company's core culture and values

Proceeding from the top down through the model, I will start by referring to the business strategy level in Exhibit 2-3.

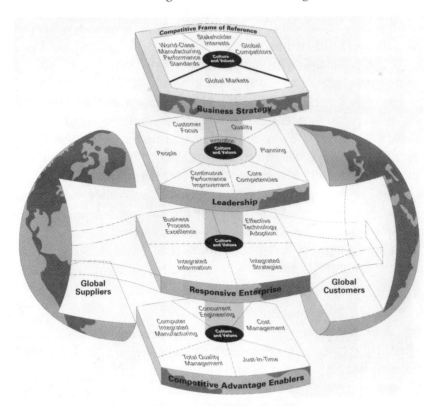

Exhibit 2-2 EDS's manufacturing business vision.

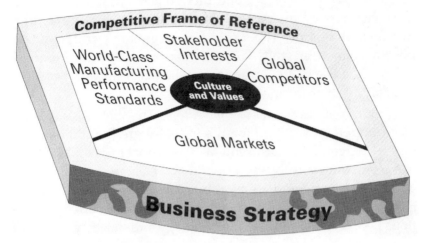

Exhibit 2-3 EDS's MBV: business strategy level.

Observe that all events proceed from the company's or strategic business unit's business strategy. Note that this strategy must be balanced within the competitive frame of reference, which comprises the following elements.

The *global markets* element highlights the fact that business today is global in nature. There are few to no protected market niches left for any competitor in any industry, given the fierce nature of today's global competition. In addition, given the global nature of business but the need for products adapted to cultural or regional differences, world class competitors need global brand or product "platforms" that can be quickly and easily tailored to local customers' tastes.

Balanced against the global markets in which modern companies compete is the need to base desired company performance against three elements:

• *World class manufacturing performance standards.* Representing dramatic changes from today's practices for most manufacturing companies, particularly with regard to increased asset utilization, higher quality, lower costs, greater productivity, and shorter lead times, world class performers use these performance measures to "pull" their company toward increasingly higher performance. Part of this challenge is to first understand *what* to measure, and then to learn what other global manufacturers on a cross-industry basis are achieving as performance standards. The world's leading manufacturers never miss a chance to study another manufacturer's techniques, technologies, and organizations to elicit best-in-class practices to apply to their business.

• (Your company's) *global competitors.* The global companies that compete in your company's industry are the ultimate basis for competitive measurement. The global marketplace tests each company daily. New competitors are emerging from many parts of the world and are becoming increasingly sophisticated in all aspects of business. They too can read, hire bright, ambitious people, and implement technology and new management practices be they from India, the Philippines, Thailand, Korea, eastern Europe, Latin America, or elsewhere.

Note that the two preceding segments provide an external benchmark against which to measure a company's progress toward world class manufacturing business performance. This is in contrast to the usual company practice of focusing on internal year-to-year improvements with traditional metrics. As an example, the management of a company might be quite proud that it has improved its WIP inventory turns from five to eight in one year. Strategically, with all other things being equal, this won't even keep them in the ballpark if at least one of their global competitors is getting forty WIP turns and working on doubling that!

- (Your company's) *stakeholder interests,* namely

• Shareholders	• Customers
• Suppliers	• Community
• Environmentalists	• Employees
• Pensioners	• Your country

These stakeholder interests represent an often conflicting set of requirements that any company's top management must be responsive to. However, all of them have an interest in the company's continued growth and prosperity.

Refer to Exhibit 2-4 on leadership.

Note that the first goal is for a company to have earned a global reputation as a leader and innovator in its industry. Names such as Honda, Toyota, Sony, Apple, Merck, and IBM carry with them an aura as exciting and progressive companies in which to work or with whom to do business. This simplifies their job of attracting top talent and gives them added clout in the marketplace.

Innovation is not only being creative and brainstorming ideas that might either have appeal to customers or improve the business. Innovation is all that combined with the ability to implement those good ideas. Innovative companies seek out

Exhibit 2-4 EDS's MBV: leadership level.

ideas from any source and provide a culture that supports their exposure and development into viable business programs. Responsive companies such as 3M are widely known for their ability to nurture innovation. An additional benefit of an innovative culture is that it creates an environment in which change is expected, and even welcomed.

As we noted earlier, companies need leadership before all else. But leadership must come from within the general workforce as well as from top management if a company is going to achieve world class manufacturing business performance. Naturally, labor unions have an opportunity and an obligation to demonstrate such leadership if they exist in a company.

Leadership encompasses the following subjects:

• *A customer focus.* Peter Drucker stated that "the purpose of business is to create a [lasting] customer."[2] Part of the cultural change that must take place in most companies is a shift away from an internal (and often functional) approach to management to one that intently and cross-functionally focuses on the customer.

This demands two initiatives. The first is to *seek out* customers for advice and product- or service-related input. The second is to listen, listen, and listen again to them and make sure their input is communicated throughout your entire organization, not just to the sales or R and D people. Eric Von Hippel has shown in his research at MIT that 80 percent or more of product development ideas come from listening carefully to and working closely with customers, instead of leaving new product development ideas to an isolated R and D lab.[3]

World class performers aim to *exceed* their customers' expectations for two reasons: to especially please them, and to allow for the time lag between understanding today's customer expectations and their customers' continued learning before a manufacturer is able to fulfill them.

• *Quality.* The highest possible quality is but the price of entry for manufacturers in tomorrow's business world. To accomplish this, companies will have to adopt the broadest possible view of quality—at a minimum the eight attributes of quality David Garvin enunciates in his book *Managing Quality.*[4] The Japanese concept of total customer satisfaction has to be the goal, and zealous pursuit of this goal the overriding concern of the company's entire management team. Quality must become an integral part of the fiber of the organization. This quality attitude must be applied not only to the tangible physical products the organization creates, but to the intangible services that accompany or could accompany the physical product. Manufactuers must strive to make it as easy as possible—even a pleasant experience—for a customer to deal with them.

• *People.* Ultimately, people differentiate successful global competitors from the also-rans. People create strategy, people implement strategy, and people design and make information systems work. For people to be the differentiators, however, they must be educated and trained in an environment of continuous learning. But educating people is only a part of the answer. They also must be motivated by the right performance ideas and metrics and then empowered to get the job accomplished.

One of many things to note about managing people effectively is that changing workforce demographics are creating a much more diverse work environment—diverse in employee race, gender, and age. The work environment itself is changing with the use of flex-time, job sharing, telecommuting, and part-time jobs. Furthermore, the expectations and attitudes of today's workers are different and more demanding. Managing this new workforce in this new environment is considerably more difficult than managing the traditional workforce was, and it demands entirely new approaches to working with people from most manufacturing managers.

• *Planning.* Planning lies at the heart of a company's competitive effectiveness but sometimes for reasons not directly attributed to the plans created. The first thing needed in a company is a culture that encourages and provides ongoing support for planning. This is a tough atmosphere to inculcate in the macho world of manufacturing, where traditionally the emphasis has been on action instead of shared thinking and learning. A company, then, needs an integrated and fairly standardized planning process so that ideas and numbers can come together in a consistent format and a regular timetable. The real value of planning lies in its ability to facilitate learning and teamwork, especially among high-level executives, who often have a parochial concern and business understanding limited to their own function. A superior planning process does lead to improved implementation of improvement programs, but this is the secondary benefit in the long run, according to executives who have gone through such a planning experience for the first time.

• *Core Competencies.* Distinctive companies stand for something. In an age when billion-dollar corporations are just a collection of disparate stand-alone divisions or larger business groupings, the opportunity to gain the synergy of the large corporation on an operating basis (as opposed to a purely financial basis) is lost. Regardless of organizational structure, there is great duplication of effort and fragmented direction in such organizations. Core competencies represent unique corporate capabilities—the "collective learning" of the enterprise.[5] A corporation usually has no more than two or three core competencies.

For instance, Honda has focused its core competencies on two areas. First, it has established itself as the world's leading designer and manufacturer of small engines. Second, it has developed one of the world's most sophisticated manufacturing and systems engineering capabilities to perform all of its plant automation activities. The latter competency gives Honda a decided competitive edge in manufacturing operations and allows it to preserve its proprietary technological superiority for a longer period of time than if these capabilities were also available to its competitors from outside suppliers.

Manufacturing managers must allocate core competency expertise just as they allocate financial funds to corporate business units. In addition, they should use their company's core competencies as a basis for strategic alliances, as well as for sourcing and vertical integration strategies.

• *Continuous performance improvement.* As I have shown, the basis for world class business performance must be cross-industry world class performance standards, and it must include a customer focus. These are needed to stay on top or at least keep up in our constantly changing and more sophisticated world. In addition to having the right performance measurements and standards, the theme of continuous improvement is a must. There are powerful advantages to this philosophy that will be discussed in a later chapter. For now, the theme to remember is "a little bit better every day."

Proceeding to the responsive enterprise level shown in Exhibit 2-5, the key elements of responsiveness are based on a proactive search for feedback from customers and suppliers, and a reactive ability to be a "fast cycle" company that is inherently flexible not only in its thinking but in its ability to do things quickly with short lead times. This responsiveness

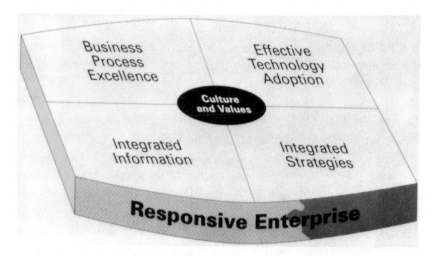

Exhibit 2-5 EDS's MBV: responsive enterprise level.

obviously must apply to the entire company, not just to one division or function.

Reviewing each segment contributing to the concept of the responsive enterprise, note the following:

• *Business process excellence.* The main idea is that the responsive company will focus on excelling at each key manufacturing business process, namely

Product and process design
Production
Logistics
Sales and marketing
Accounting and finance

The goal is to flowchart each total major business process, understand where the company adds value, and eliminate the non-value-added operations that occur in the current process. Multifunctional teams can be used to simplify and speed each cross-functional process. Information systems can provide great leverage for improving the speed and accuracy of each business cycle.

• *Effective technology adoption.* Effective global competitors aggressively seek proven technology for all aspects of innovation and business improvement. Implementing such technology quickly and in a standard manner will bring 80 percent of the benefits with 25 percent of the time, cost, and effort compared to the company developing its own technology solutions. Then the company can go on to fine-tune this technology for even more benefits, or it can implement solutions in other applications where it needs similar benefits quickly. It is true that some companies achieve competitive excellence by developing their own proprietary technology, but often this takes too long, costs too much, and may lock a manufacturer out of technological advances that are being developed in today's fast-moving technology marketplace. The key is to avoid pioneering with all its costs and pitfalls, but to be early adopters once the technology has proven effective. Although it is important to competitive success, I will verify later what many have already learned from bitter experience: technology alone is not the way to world class business performance.

• *Integrated information.* The concept of integrated information, when understood and applied in its totality, is one of the most powerful in business today. It has several aspects. I have already discussed briefly the idea of integrating forward to customers and backward to suppliers. In addition, there are three kinds of data to integrate in the computer integrated enterprise: business (alphanumeric) data, design engineering (geometric) data, and process control (real-time) data. The idea here is not just blind automation of the entire company but to use information systems as a major tool for business process innovation and optimization.

Furthermore, we do not necessarily want to use information systems to automate and eliminate people from skill-intensive work or critical business decision-making processes. Instead, Shoshana Zuboff, in her excellent book *In the Age of the Smart Machine,* suggests that information technology be used to *informate* as well as automate, defining informate thus: information translating and making visible activities, events, and objects. She observes,

> As long as the technology is treated narrowly in its automating function, it perpetuates the logic of the industrial machine that, over the course of this century, has made it possible to rationalize work while decreasing the dependence on human skills. However, when the technology also informates the processes to which it is applied, it increases the explicit information content of the tasks and sets into motion a series of dynamics that will ultimately reconfigure the nature of work and the social relationships that organize productive activity.[6]

Finally, integrated information systems allow companies to create a "virtual" organization unaffected by geographical location or distance.

• *Integrated strategies.* It's common knowledge that for a company's business strategy to be successfully implemented, it must be supported vertically by the company's (or strategic business unit's) internal functional strategies. That is, the marketing strategy should be closely linked to the overall company strategy. What seems to be less obvious to companies is that in a similar manner, the internal functional strategies of the company must be horizontally integrated with each other so that they act in concert to support the company's business strategy. Thus, the marketing strategy should be integrated with the company's manufacturing strategy, as well as with the rest of the company's internal functions. The idea here is to create an organization with a common purpose. While examples of vertical strategy integration can often be found within many companies (for at least one or two of its functional strategies), it is much more rare for functional strategies to be horizontally integrated with each other.

The discussion has now arrived at the competitive advantage enablers level shown in Exhibit 2-6.

Exhibit 2-6 EDS's MBV: competitive advantage enablers level.

Enablers can stand for any combination of concepts, philosophies, technologies, systems, techniques, tools, and methodologies that can be applied to make a manufacturing business more effective and efficient. At this level, no one or two enablers are powerful enough to make a company a world class manufacturer. In addition, no company can implement these enablers in a sequential fashion—there is insufficient time for this given today's global competitive pressure. Instead, companies must be well versed in implementing enablers from all five areas simultaneously. To do otherwise would be equivalent to a football team practicing running one year, blocking and tackling the next year, and passing the third year. It would play football, but not world-class football.

Companies today require a carefully prioritized program using parts of each competitive advantage enabler in support of the company's business strategy. Given the limited resources of any company, the key is to know which enablers to implement and in what order to implement them to gain the most competitive leverage.

Note each segment in this level:

- *Computer-integrated manufacturing* (CIM) represents the integration of all information involved in manufacturing from product and process design through manufacturing planning and control, production, distribution, and after-sales service and support. CIM is absolutely vital to achieve world class quality, speed, flexibility, and productivity.
- *Concurrent engineering* primarily involves the use of a cross-functional team (including representatives from key suppliers and even customers) to work jointly on product and process design. Concurrent engineering is necessary to achieve the kind of customer focus, high quality, low cost, and quick time to market that constitute world class performance today.
- *Cost management* involves the use of activity-based costing principles to more accurately cost product and services. Accurate costs are vital for accurate product strategy decisions and for understanding where the value is added in a company's business operations.
- *Total quality management* (TQM)—formerly total quality control, or TQC, as we noted earlier, is first an attitude about quality, in addition to the application of proven quality enablers to design products, processes, and services. TQM is necessary to achieve today's world class quality standards of less than 50 defective parts per million.
- The central theme of *just in time* (JIT) is the elimination of waste in all business activities. As such, JIT is a key to fast-cycle manufacturing, customer responsiveness, high productivity, and high return on assets.

It is vital that a manufacturer adopt some "mapping" that proceeds from these high-level enablers to the dozens of lower-level enablers that are available for implementation. This will aid in understanding these lower-level enablers and their relationship with each other, as well as reinforce the idea of a common vision, vocabulary, and understanding within a company. I show in Appendix 1 an example of this mapping that is highly suitable for this purpose.

Consider next the value-added pipeline in EDS' manufacturing business vision shown in Exhibit 2-7.

This view shows the manufacturing enterprise as a value-added pump. It takes in materials and components from global sources, adds value to them, and ships them to global customers. Thus materials and products flow through the pipeline.

But there is another perhaps even more important flow of *information* through the value-added pipeline, shown in Exhibit 2-8.

In this view we acknowledge the flow of all three kinds of data and information discussed earlier. Moreover, we see that there are three loops of information flow: from the enterprise's customers to the manufacturing enterprise and back, within the manufacturing enterprise, and from the manufacturing enterprise to its suppliers and back. It's important to note that this flow of information may be even more important to a company's business success than the flow of materials.

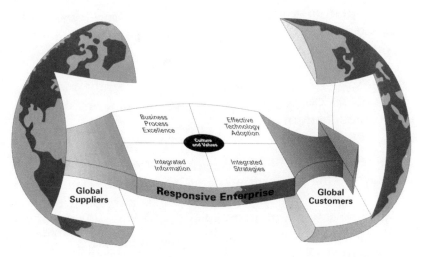

Exhibit 2-7 EDS's MBV: the value-added pipeline, material flow.

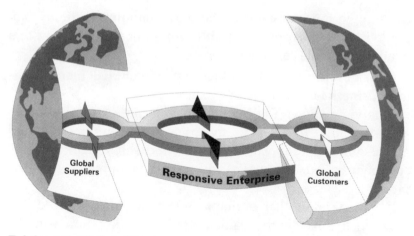

Exhibit 2-8 EDS's MBV: the value-added pipeline, information flow.

The last feature of EDS' manufacturing business vision is that of the culture and value core that permeates the entire organization and connects the four levels discussed previously. It is the glue that holds the company together. The tone for the company's culture and value set is established right at the top of the organization—by the CEO. The vision's core also facilitates the flow of information between levels in this conceptual diagram as well as in the organization.

There are numerous benefits of the EDS' conceptual model or manufacturing business vision. These are some of the most important:

- It provides a holistic top-level vision of all the major elements necessary for a manufacturer to achieve world class business performance.
- It acknowledges the central role of a company's culture and values in achieving world class performance.
- It allows the viewer to understand how each element and level is related to others in the model, and how activity in any one area might affect other areas.
- It looks beyond the four walls of the enterprise to integrate forward to customers and backward to suppliers, thus fos-

tering a faster and more complete exchange of more types of information with them.

- Its hierarchical top-down approach stresses strategy, leadership and responsiveness before the use of competitive advantage enablers.
- It emphasizes a cross-functional approach to improving an enterprise's basic business cycles.
- It bases a manufacturing enterprise's performance measures against external competitors' as well as against current world class performance standards.
- It considers the total constituency of stakeholder interests in its competitive frame of reference.
- It places the enterprise in the context of global markets and competitors.
- It emphasizes vertical and horizontal strategies so that employees work together toward a united vision and common goals.
- It emphasizes the value of planning and the learning and teamwork it facilitates in an industry where planning is neither sufficiently valued nor utilized regularly and consistently.
- It highlights the need to manage and integrate all three forms of data to effectively turn data into information and then into knowledge for all employees.
- It stresses the need to utilize all five major competitive advantage enablers in a carefully prioritized long-term program that supports the enterprise's business strategy.

The EDS manufacturing business vision forms an invaluable conceptual tool for presenting new ideas and stimulating discussion at a strategic level about the business of manufacturing. Readers can use it to create a more specific version that more closely suits their industry or company if they find it to be a valuable overall vision for their own world class business performance efforts.

The vision for the company or manufacturing enterprise as an industry participant is really the company's or strategic business unit's (SBU's) business strategy. One is always there whether explicit or implicit, and whether well done or riddled with flaws. My purpose in this book is not to explain how to develop and communicate this business strategy; I suggest several good books on that subject in the bibliography.

Implementing an Effective Planning Process

Having established a vision of manufacturing as a business and of the company as an industry participant, the company's management must now adopt a planning process to develop the improvement program that will take the company from wherever it may currently be in terms of performance to the goal of world class business performance. One such process was thoroughly explained in my last book, *Manufacturing for Competitive Advantage: Becoming a World Class Manufacturer.* The world class manufacturing planning framework discussed therein is shown in Exhibit 2-9. Since that time, I have enhanced this framework in the area of human resources by adding the three top right elements shown in Exhibit 2-10.

For those readers who have not read my previous book, I will devote the next few pages to a brief review of the world class manufacturing planning framework shown in Exhibit 2-10. This planning process is generic for developing any internal functional strategy, but here I will use the example of manufacturing only. As usual, we start with the strategic picture and with the fact that people create and implement strategies. The business strategy has implications for what the enterprise must do well in manufacturing. These implications will help us create the manufacturing strategy objectives in the planning box.

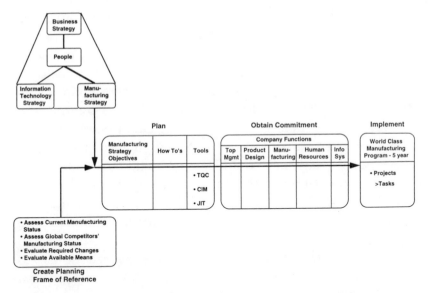

Exhibit 2-9 The world class manufacturing planning framework.

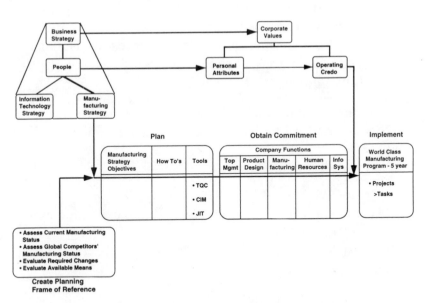

Exhibit 2-10 The people-enhanced world class manufacturing planning framework.

Early in the planning process, it is essential to obtain an objective view of the current operating performance level of your manufacturing company. This should, of course, be measured against general industry standards, world class manufacturing standards, and best-in-class cross-industry performance standards. Because it is so difficult for a company's internal staff and operating people to give an objective and politically unbiased view of a company's operating performance, and because these people may lack a sufficiently broad, up-to-date, and cross-functional perspective to competently assess the operation, I recommend the use of qualified outside consultants to perform this critical analysis and basis for the company's improvement program.

Given the frames of reference of the operations assessment and the implications of the company's business strategy, we then proceed to create the company's manufacturing strategy objectives. These should be strategic in nature and performance-oriented, with certain structural factors (for example, facilities and capacity) either implicit in them or used as "how to's" or "tools" later in the planning process. The manufacturing strategy objectives should deal with such competitive issues as the following:

- Minimizing all lead times, especially new product and process design lead time and customer order-to-delivery lead time
- Maximizing quality
- Maximizing flexibility
- Maximizing return on assets, including maximizing inventory turns
- Maximizing productivity
- Minimizing waste

These objectives should also specify what is to be done, how much, and when. An example of a manufacturing strategy objective might thus be to reduce new product and process design lead time by 50 percent in two years. There are several ways to do that from a broad policy perspective (the how to's). Then there will be even more—and more specific—ways to accomplish the objective by implementing various competitive advantage enablers from the worlds of CIM, JIT, TQM, concurrent engineering, and cost management (the "tools" in the planning box).

After completion of the planning box, the tools are allocated to each major company function in the obtaining commitment box according to two criteria: which functions will play a primary role in the implementation, and which functions will be most affected by the implementation. These tools are then grouped and sorted into a long-term improvement program with both short- and long-term elements that usually consists of about 20 to 30 projects, each having three to six tasks.

The obtaining commitment activity is unique to this planning process and has a great deal in common with the principles of quality function deployment. Its major benefit is that it facilitates the learning and team building process that is so essential to achieving world class business performance. Companies that do not go through this obtaining commitment process in the course of their planning will inevitably find themselves going through it with great pain during their implementation, while at the same time ending up with a plan that woefully understates the tasks that have to be accomplished and the resources required to accomplish them.

This planning process is very much a top-down process because a customer-focused business strategy must drive all subsequent business activity. The choice and prioritization of the enablers to be implemented will thus be driven by the business and manufacturing strategy objectives. This is quite in contrast to the implementation programs at many companies, where enablers are being implemented in helter-skelter fashion without much, if any, regard to what has to be accomplished strategically and in what priority.

I reiterate here that bottom-up planning, no matter how well-intended, almost always fails, for two reasons. The prioritization of projects in bottom-up planning is not likely to be correct because it is seldom performed with regard to the company's business strategy. Instead, projects will be prioritized with a view to which person on the planning committee has the loudest voice, biggest budget, the most political power, or whose division is doing the best this or last year, not the one that needs to be doing significantly better in the years to come.

The second reason bottom-up planning fails is that such efforts are usually too narrow (or functional) in scope, and that the cost justification is not done for the program as a whole, but for each project individually. Projects are typically ranked by return on investment (ROI) and "cherrypicked" starting from the top of the ROI list. The projects (and there will always be some) that are difficult to financially justify on an individual basis get left on the back burner and the synergy of the total program is never achieved. In my experience, the world class manufacturing performance program is always easy to justify when done once for the total program. Thus considering the program from the top down ensures a much more strategically effective improvement program that can be cost justified with little effort.

Creating such a world class manufacturing performance improvement program is only the first step in a long program of implementation and cultural change. One key to success is top management's support to its world class performance improvement program on a sustained basis, despite other "flash fires" and "business opportunities" that arise. As important, executives who are recruited after the program is created must support and even enhance the program, not dismiss it as the previous administration's work and lobby to replace it with their own program once on board.

Good strategic planning, at either a corporate or SBU level, delivers a great many benefits:

- It stimulates people to think strategically about the bases of competition in their business, and how competitive advantage can be obtained.

- It allows strategic prioritization of scarce resources—money, staff, and time.
- It facilitates learning.
- It facilitates cross-functional business process improvements.
- It promotes first strategic, then financial, justification.
- It integrates strategies vertically and horizontally.
- It promotes development of contingency scenarios.
- It unites people behind a common vision and fosters teamwork toward united goals.

As Dwight Eisenhower once said: "The plan is nothing. Planning is everything."

As with the manufacturing business vision earlier, the reader is free to modify or enhance this planning process. The point is that a company must have some standardized planning process that is tested and proven, user friendly, not too complex, and effective. The one above has proven to be all that.

We now have a vision of what it will take to become a world class manufacturing company. We have a planning process that can get us from where we are to where we have to go as a company to survive, prosper, and grow. The company's top management knows that to continue with its current performance is death—perhaps a long, slow one, but death nonetheless. These people finally are suitably driven by competitive pressure and perhaps even personally inspired to put together a major long-term improvement program to move them substantially toward world class business performance. The fundamental management processes are in place. What's next?

Management must develop an appreciation for the scope and magnitude of such a program, for all the things that must be done, and for the ways in which each contributes to world class manufacturing business performance. In addition, they must focus on the right things with an intensity of effort and purpose that shunts aside almost all other considerations until everyone in the company acknowledges and supports the program and the company is performing much more competitively.

We will devote the rest of the chapters in the book to the things that management must focus on to become a world class manufacturing business performer.

Chapter 2

1. Thomas G. Gunn, *Manufacturing for Competitive Advantage: Becoming a World Class Manufacturer* (New York: Ballinger Publishing Company, 1987).

2. Peter F. Drucker, *Managing for Results* (New York: Harper & Row, 1964), p. 91.

3. Eric A. Von Hippel, "Users As Innovators," *Technology Review,* January 1978, pp. 31–39.

4. David A. Garvin, *Managing Quality* (New York: The Free Press, 1988).

5. C. K. Prahalad and Gary Hamel, "The Core Competence Of The Corporation," *Harvard Business Review,* May–June 1990, pp. 79–91.

6. Shoshana Zuboff, *In the Age of the Smart Machine* (New York: Basic Books, Inc., 1988), p. 1.

3

Attaining Business Process Excellence

Recall that in Chapter 1 we introduced the concept of using the four fundamental attributes of cost, quality, time, and information value to characterize any business or product's production process in a manufacturing company and to serve as a basis for the company's performance improvement efforts. In this chapter I shall build on that theme.

Understanding Key Business Processes

In order for manufacturers to understand the essential business processes in which they must excel, a good approach is to start with Michael Porter's generic value chain, shown in Exhibit 3-1.

We see that his generic value chain classifies primary business activities thus:

- Inbound logistics
- Operations
- Outbound logistics
- Marketing and sales
- Service

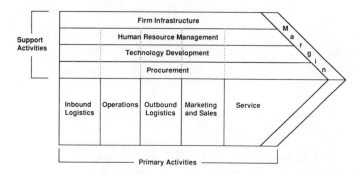

Exhibit 3-1 Porter's generic value chain. Source: Reprinted with permission of The Free Press, a Division of Macmillan, Inc. from COMPETITIVE ADVANTAGE: Creating and Sustaining Superior Performance by Michael E. Porter. Copyright ©1985 by Michael E. Porter.

Porter classifies the following as support activities:

- The firm's infrastructure
- Human resource management
- Technology development
- Procurement

For a manufacturing business, we might adopt a slightly more detailed classification of activities divided into primary activities and infrastructure support activities, as shown in Exhibit 3-2.

I classify the primary activities of a manufacturing business as the following:

- Performing research and development (R&D)
- Marketing products and services
- Designing products, processes, and services
- Managing logistics
- Producing products and services
- Selling products and services
- Servicing sold products

Some readers might consider R&D to be a secondary activity, but in my experience, even if a company wants to

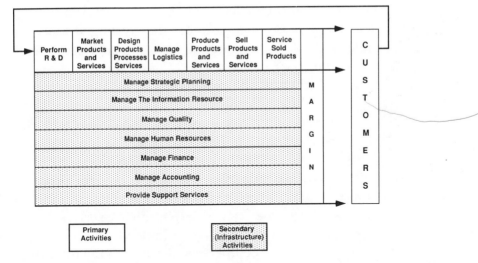

Exhibit 3-2 Manufacturing business activity classification.

be a follower copying other manufacturers' products, process R&D will be essential to its competitive success. In fact, figures reported in MIT's *Made In America* show the focus of R&D in Japan to be quite different from R&D here in the United States, as Exhibit 3-3 demonstrates.

Japanese manufacturers have come to realize that who invents a product idea is no longer very important. It is the company that can capitalize on the product idea and that has the highest quality, lowest cost, and quickest time to market with some form of legal copying (e.g., licensing) or legal patent "workaround" that often wins. Knowing this, they have traditionally put the bulk of their R&D effort into process improvement.

	Product	Process
United States	70%	30%
West Germany	50%	50%
Japan	30%	70%

Exhibit 3-3 Manufacturing R & D spending.[1]

There are also some people—most notably JIT zealots—that might tend to place production under the heading of logistics, since under a strict JIT demand pull environment nothing gets produced without a customer order. I think the two activities are sufficiently different and demanding of different expertise that I have kept them separate.

Some companies never have to service sold products. But for those that do—companies like Caterpillar, Boeing, and auto producers—the sale of spare parts often offers much more lucrative profit margins than the sale of the original product. Furthermore, the opportunity for these companies to competitively distinguish themselves with extraordinary service can be a major source of their competitive advantage.

The company's infrastructure activities include the following:

- Managing strategic planning
- Managing the information resource
- Managing quality
- Managing human resources
- Managing finance
- Managing accounting
- Providing support services (for example, legal services or building maintenance)

Almost by definition, these infrastructure activities are cross-functional, particularly when they are defined and supported in the broadest possible manner by the company's senior management.

There is no universal right or wrong way of classifying these activities. The proper management of all of them is essential if a manufacturing company is to achieve world-class business performance.

The Four Essential Manufacturing Business Processes

What is particularly interesting is how these business activities with all their subactivities or tasks get combined into fundamental business processes that are critical to world-class performance. Clearly, there are at least four of these essential business processes to excel at in a manufacturing company— three for any manufacturing company, and the fourth for certain manufacturers:

- New product and process design
- Customer order to delivery
- Materials management
- Estimating or contracting

It can be valuable to view both the customer order-to-delivery process and the materials management process as part of a company's overall logistics activity, but I separate them here so that the process of dealing with each is simplified.

With respect to the fourth business process listed, estimating is an especially important business process at which to excel in make-to-order manufacturing environments, where several producers generally bid on the fabrication and assembly of large complex machines and systems such as transfer lines, steel rolling mills, and large hydroelectric pumps. Contracting is a vital function to perform effectively and efficiently in the defense industry, where special knowledge is needed to deal with the complexities of doing business with U.S. government agencies and their maze of regulations. Exhibit 3-4 illustrates the first three essential business processes in which all manufacturing companies must excel.

Product and process design lies at the heart of any manufacturing business for here lies the greatest opportunity to control the quality and cost of the final product. Studies at Ford Motor Company and elsewhere have shown that about 75 percent of a product's costs are controlled by decisions made and fixed in the design process.[2] Moreover, effective product and process design is essential to reducing a new product's time to market—a key basis of competition in many industries. This has always been so in the toy and fashion industries. Now it is of paramount importance in industries such as those produc-

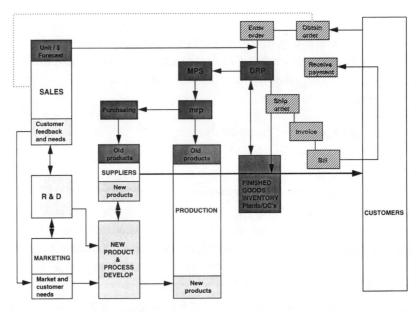

Exhibit 3-4 Three fundamental manufacturing business processes.

ing application-specific integrated circuits (ASICs), computers, automobiles, motorcycles, and an increasing number of other industries.

The customer order-to-delivery business process is a key element in promoting customer satisfaction. In fact, given that the customer is satisfied with the fundamental product itself, it is this business process that will make or break a manufacturer's day-to-day customer satisfaction. The essential attitude necessary in evaluating this business process is to measure everything with the customer's eyes—not with only the manufacturer's. Some companies measure their performance in the customer order-to-delivery process by starting when a customer order enters their order entry system. On the other end of the process, they stop measuring when the products leave their shipping docks. The customer-focused organization sees two flaws in this thinking.

On the front end, the order-to-delivery cycle must be measured from the time the customer initiates the order, whether by mail, fax, a phone call, or by giving it to a salesperson. In several companies I have worked with, it has taken them from 3 to 20 days to get a customer order entered in their order entry "system," whether manual or computerized. This time, if measured correctly, might represent 25 percent of the entire order-to-delivery process—it must not be ignored if the entire process is to be improved.

On the back end, the correct point to measure order delivery is the time at which the customer receives the completed order as requested (100 percent quantity and line item fill) and with customer-defined perfect quality. The customer-focused company knows that it is not a valid excuse to say, "We've done our job. It's in the hands of the shippers now and you know we have no control over them and things like the weather." World-class performers take total responsibility for the complete and timely fulfillment of every customer's order.

Some manufacturers wonder why I place so much emphasis on the materials management function when materials may currently only be 20 percent to 30 percent of their total manufacturing cost structure. They can understand why this might be important for an electronics assembly operation, where materials might account for 80 percent of its manufacturing cost, but not for them. Traditionally, manufacturers with low materials cost have not paid much attention to materials management and often have weak materials management information systems and a company culture in which materials management is hardly visible, much less sufficiently strong and effective. The main idea to realize here is that by the time a manufacturing company becomes a world-class performer, materials almost assuredly will be the dominant portion of its manufacturing cost structure (this will be discussed in Chapter 5). Excelling in the materials management business process really does matter.

Note that all four major business processes are cross-functional. Product and process designers should be practicing concurrent engineering and working with people from

R&D, marketing, sales, quality control, accounting, purchasing, materials management, distribution, and perhaps even human resources. Customer order-to-delivery flows through the sales, credit approval, distribution, and accounting organizations at a minimum. Materials management (including purchasing) has to work with R&D, product and process engineering, production, distribution, and marketing, sales, and service operations. Estimating and contracting involves engineering, production, sales, accounting, and contributions from many other functions in the organization.

Identifying Business Processes Opportunities

Cross-functionality in these major business processes has been the biggest problem, but it presents the best opportunity in terms of improving each process. It usually is at the functional organization boundaries that each process slows or decays. Data is lost or has to be reentered in another computer system, which results in lost time and great potential for data entry error. Different terms are often used by different functions, and thus communication is often misunderstood or incomplete. Data or information on paper generally takes an inordinate amount of time to flow from one department to another. Different functions have different priorities, owing to differences in incentives or company politics. Functionally oriented performance incentives cause people to look only at their small part of the overall problem. No one seems to care about the customer or the total of any of the company's business processes.

Unfortunately, companies are organized functionally for the convenience of their management, rather than around the fundamental business processes that serve the customer. Thus there are a vice-president of sales and often a vice-president of distribution, but no vice-president for customer order-to-delivery. Because this kind of reorganization is not likely to happen in most companies for a variety of reasons, how can manufacturing executives remedy their business process problems described above?

Given the cross-functionality of these essential business processes, the first thing to do in fixing them is to assemble a multifunctional team to get on with the improvement of each process. Second, it is essential that each total business process be clearly understood by all parties concerned. The best way to accomplish this is to flowchart each process in its entirety. However, this task is not as easy as it may initially seem. In most companies there is not a single employee who can accurately describe how any one business process is supposed to work, much less how it actually works. Even with a multifunctional improvement team assembled in one room for this purpose, its first attempt to accurately flowchart the process usually fails quickly. The process starts easily enough; then, however, the real fun begins. Half a dozen activities are drawn on the flowchart, and people start adding feedback loops, or worse yet, open loops, to the diagram to reflect what they think actually happens. After about two hours of this, the "flowchart" looks like a plate of spaghetti that someone dropped on the floor, and people dissolve into helpless laughter at the thought that any company's business process could be so convoluted. (One doesn't know whether to laugh or cry at this stage.) Finally, everyone realizes that no one knows what is really happening. At that point, everyone is assigned to go get the facts. Several meetings later, consensus is finally achieved that the actual business process being utilized is well understood and accurately portrayed in flowchart form.

The finished flowchart of the process should show several things. First, it should include all activities, branches, and feedback loops in the total process as seen from the eyes of the customer. Second, it should show elapsed times for all activities and the cumulative time from the start of the process. Weeks or days are generally good time scales for the first round of process improvement. The goal is to move to days or minutes in subsequent improvement iterations. Third, it should show the buildup of cost and value added (sales minus purchases) in the business cycle. In strategic terms, value added represents how each activity has increased the value of the product or service by its action. Finally, the flow chart should show the quality underlying the process—how yield varies with the activities throughout the process. This can be summarized by showing the process starting at 100 percent and the yield drop at each major activity.

Many companies' experience has shown that, for any of these business processes, the first time this exercise is accomplished one will discover that value is being added to the product only about 5 percent to 10 percent of the total process time. In other words, 90 percent to 95 percent of the time in the process is being wasted! But the first goal is achieved—an understanding of the business process and an analysis of where the waste lies with regard to cost, quality, and time.

Consider the findings of such business process analysis in several companies and industries.

• *An auto company* analyzed the lead time required to produce a fan cover and found that of the 361 hours in the total process from receiving steel to having the part available on the assembly line, value was added only 3.6 hours, or 1 percent of the time! [3]

• *Havelock Europa, a U.K. manufacturer* of retail store equipment such as counters and shelves, analyzed its process to build a sloping front counter for drugstores. Of the 116 steps in its manufacturing process, only 22 (19 percent) added any value. During the seven-week manufacturing lead time, the counter traveled almost a mile around Havelock's Nottingham production facility. Worse yet, Havelock found it was adding value to its product during these seven weeks only 4.15 hours, or 1.5 percent of the total 280-hour time period. They went on to design a new process in which the product would have a one-week lead time, have only 68 process steps, and travel 18 percent of the distance it did before.[4]

• *A Fortune 20 U.S. company* looked at the processes needed to build two components for one of its products. It reduced the number of steps needed for the first product from 101 to 61, and for the second product from 63 to 56. Every little bit counts! [5]

• *Don't think such business process improvements are limited to discrete part manufacturers.* Extensive business and JIT-based analysis has enabled Exxon Chemical's Butyl Polymers Americas unit to reduce its cycle time by 65 percent in its Baytown, Texas, plant, and by 39 percent in its Baton Rouge, Louisiana, plant. They define *cycle time* as the amount of time needed to cycle through an entire flight of products. In one case they reduced a line changeover from about 30 hours to somewhere between 2 and 6 hours. They've also reduced their total inventory by 50 percent, decreased energy consumption 18 percent, and experienced a 37 percent reduction in materials that have to be reprocessed a second time. Incidentally, with all these improvements, they also were one of four winners of the 1991 Shingo Prize for excellence in manufacturing.[6]

Improving Business Processes

In many of a company's business processes, entire activities can be eliminated—one may find that no one knows why they're being performed in the first place. They're liable to be leftovers from some procedures manual written years ago. This kind of wasteful activity is easy to recognize. But others aren't so visible to the untrained eye—especially to those who are not up to speed with world-class manufacturing concepts.

Now the improvement team can go on to eliminate the waste in each business process: anything that adds cost but not value to the product, that negatively affects product quality, or that adds time to the process. This is the essence of the JIT philosophy: to eliminate waste, simplify the entire process, and speed up its execution. Remember, one of the criteria of world class performance is to be a fast cycle company. Increased speed not only pleases customers, but allows a manufacturing company faster progress down the organizational learning curve because its people will go through more iterations of a business cycle in a given amount of time.

Driving Out Cost and Complexity in Manufacturing

One of the goals of business process redesign and world class manufacturing performance is to drive out complexity and cost from a manufacturing organization. Exhibit 3-5 shows some of the items that contribute to complexity and cost in the average manufacturing operation:

• *The number of part numbers* (and therefore parts) obviously influences complexity. Companies that have to deal with only 20,000 parts are a lot better off than those that deal with 300,000. Design for manufacture and assembly techniques go

• # PART NUMBERS	• # DATA ENTRY TIMES FOR SAME DATA
• # ENGINEERING CHANGES	
• # LEVELS IN BOMS	• # DISPARATE DATA BASES AND APPLICATION SYSTEMS
• # TRANSACTIONS	• # DEPARTMENTS / ORGANIZATION UNITS
• # PROCESS STEPS	
• INVENTORY	• # TIMES A PART IS HANDLED
• MFG PROCESS TRAVEL DISTANCE	• # TIMES A PART "INSPECTED"
• # WORK ORDERS	• # SUPPLIERS -- PER PART AND TOTAL
• # PEOPLE INVOLVED IN A PROCESS	• # APPROVALS NEEDED
• # PLANTS / FACILITIES	

Exhibit 3-5 Manufacturing complexity indicators and cost drivers.

a long way toward reducing the parts count in products. But there are other aspects of this subject.

There may be many part numbering systems. Often companies end up with too many different systems as a reflection of their growth by acquisition. Different part numbering systems cause confusion for customers and employees alike, and they increase the cost of the company's information systems and their operation.

The number of characters in each part number also affects the overall manufacturing operation. Many companies have 12 to 25 characters in their part numbers, making the numbers difficult to remember, increasing the time and probable error rate in writing one down, complicating report formats, and increasing the probability that application software systems will have to have their part number fields expanded. The reason for the long part numbers is often that the company is trying to embed intelligence in each part number. Over the years, their length keeps growing as the demand for more product or process information to be embedded in the part number grows. Describing each product or its process with numerical codes or natural language descriptors is a task for group technology, not part numbers. Randomly assigned unintelligent part numbers are all it takes to identify products or parts or materials uniquely and succinctly. Six digits will create 1,000,000 part numbers, so most companies should not need more than six- or perhaps at most eight-digit part numbers.

• *The number of engineering changes* tells a good deal about the quality of the company's product and process engineering function, as well as something about the communication process with its customers. I have seen companies with over 250 engineering changes per month—3000 per year! Informed estimates of the cost of an average engineering change range from about $3000 per change for the electrical and electronics industry to $10,000 per change for mechanical products to $20,000 per change for the aerospace and defense industry. Engineering changes are thus expensive in a financial sense, but even more expensive from a time and quality viewpoint.

• Vollman and Miller showed that *overhead* is strongly related to the number of transactions that take place in a business process.[7] In part, this is why parts count reduction programs have such a powerful effect on cost reduction. If there are fewer parts to begin with, there are fewer to be designed or selected, made or bought, counted and stored and moved, assembled and serviced, and so forth. Obviously, fewer activities mean that fewer people are required to originate, make or purchase, assemble, and service them. Simpler processes also mean fewer transactions. Fewer transactions require less complex and expensive information systems. And so it goes. . . .

• *Manufacturing process travel distance* is often an indicator of poor physical layout and space utilization. In one manufacturer's simple manufacturing environment, for instance, the average part traveled 1200 feet and was handled 44 times before it got to assembly! A U-shaped cell and new shop floor layout (now being implemented) could reduce this travel by 80 percent and cut the number of times the part was handled by 90 percent.

• Manufacturers often have *an excessive number of plants* because of poor product rationalization, poor plant layout, poor space utilization, and poor inventory management. Alternatively, their excessive number of plants may be deliberately created by the company's senior management, who want to keep separate operations small and entrepreneurial. This leads to the "small is beautiful trap," discussed in Chapter 5.

• The number of disparate information system data bases and application systems greatly influences the number of times the same data must be manually re-entered, which, in turn, decreases productivity and increases the chance of errors. Data in information systems is like a part in manufacturing—once you get a hold of it, never let it go.

• The number of times a part is "inspected" increases cost dramatically. One $100 million company with which I'm familiar had 145 quality inspectors out of a total staff of 1500 people. These employees, at a burdened total cost of about $5 million, added no value to the product, complicated the material handling flow, and still allowed faulty products to be shipped to customers. No company can afford this kind of lost productivity and time. Quality has to be designed into the product and the process—it can't be inspected in.

• A good indicator of organizational inefficiency and high cost/slow speed is the number of approvals needed to get things through the organization. From a white-collar productivity viewpoint, the simplest place to look for this is on the company's travel expense report. Often there are two or three approval signature lines in addition to the submitter's. Consider what this says about how some people spend their time, not to mention the level of trust the company shows in its employees!

The job in business process redesign is to eliminate these complexity factors and cost drivers. Once a team of people has been sensitized by JIT thinking and knows where to look for such items, progress in improving the process usually comes swiftly. It's important to realize that business process redesign can also be applied to the white collar or office environment. No company business activity should be neglected as an opportunity for achieving greater competitive advantage.

Improving the Value-Added Portion of Business Processes

All too often, business process improvement teams are content to focus only on eliminating the waste from each business process. This is all to the good, primarily because waste is such a dominant portion of the total process, as we've seen. Besides, it's relatively easy pickings. But on the second or third iteration of each improvement, it's time to start looking at how the value-added portions of the business process can be improved. It's at this point that new technology can become a powerful tool to accomplish this goal. New product or process technology can be implemented, or new information technology can be used to better control and speed the flow of information surrounding the value-added process step. Some solutions combine two or all three of these technologies.

For instance, a new automated machining cell was implemented at EG&G's Rocky Flats, Colorado, nuclear weapons production plant to machine stainless steel forgings for a very complex part design. Throughput time for the part has been reduced from 10 to 14 days to a few hours, owing to the cell concept, and the actual value-added run time for the part has been reduced by about 33 percent by the new process technology, to as little as 2.75 hours. Quality has been significantly improved as well.[8]

Thus, in striving for business process excellence, once management knows that only the right things are included in each business process, its goal should be to perform those tasks as quickly and accurately as possible. In Chapters 7 and 8 I shall explore the great power that modern information systems have to transform the manufacturing business and integrate previously disparate organizations, functions, business process activities, and geographical locations.

There are a tremendous number of improvements that can be made to most companies' business processes without any increased computerization. In fact, I've seen cases where such improvements could be made by eliminating some elements of a company's computer systems. It is these fundamental improvements that should be accomplished before seeking improvements through the application of information technology. There is no question, however, that to be a world-class competitor a company will eventually have to utilize well-designed information systems as the basis for their business processes. This, of course, includes using such systems to communicate with their global suppliers and customers, as well as with financial markets and information utility data bases. No other ways exist to obtain the speed and accuracy offered by information systems. It was once thought that no one needed a computer, but once one company had a computer, every company needed one. Such is the nature of progress and competition.

The performance improvement process has been started with this chapter on business process excellence because it represents the very essence of attaining world-class business performance. In most companies business process reengineering represents potential for order-of-magnitude improvements without vast expenditures on new production equipment or information systems. All it takes to get started is a focus on the customer, some education and training in JIT and process reengineering principles, and some multifunctional task forces who are willing to look at process improvement from a fresh and integrated viewpoint that includes its company and its process links to its suppliers and customers. The focus of business process excellence is to first be sure that one does the right thing, and then that one does it right.

Chapter 3

1. Michael Dertouzos et al., *Made in America* (Cambridge, MA: The MIT Press, 1989), p. 72.
2. "The Billion Dollar Potential of DFA," *Assembly Automation*, 1989, pp. 192–194.
3. Gunn Associates, Inc. files.
4. James Buxton, "Havelock: Running Counter To Tradition," *Financial Times*, 26 June 1991.
5. Gunn Associates, Inc. files.
6. John Sheridan, "JIT Spells Good Chemistry at Exxon," *Industry Week*, 1 July 1991, pp. 26–28.
7. J. G. Miller & T. E. Vollman, "The Hidden Factory," *Harvard Business Review*, September–October 1985, pp. 142–150.
8. Frederick Mason, "This Part Now Takes a Few Hours," *American Machinist*, August 1991, pp. 43–46.

4

Becoming a High-Quality Manufacturer

In the six years since my previous book was published, despite a great deal of talk and publicity, I have seen very few real changes in the world of quality for the average manufacturer. The following situation is all too typical.

A $350 million high-tech manufacturing company surveyed 24 of its plants in 1990 to find out where they stood before embarking on a world class performance program. With regard to quality, questions were asked about how many dollars were spent on scrap, rework, and customer returns. Out of the 24 plants, 10 didn't even track scrap, 14 didn't track rework, and 8 didn't track customer returns. Of the plants that did track these figures, the money spent on only these three categories of waste (40 of 72 possible data elements) amounted to 3.5 percent of sales.

Then, in the early part of 1991, a major consulting firm evaluated the total costs of poor quality in one of the 24 plants above and estimated it to be 25.7 percent of the plant's cost of goods sold, or in the neighborhood of 18 percent of sales, given the company's typical margins. (These are 1991 illustrations, not 1961!) Unfortunately, this company is not alone in its quality standing, and is to be commended for starting, however late, to come to grips with its quality problems.

The only thing that has changed in the world of quality is that the demand for even higher quality levels by consumers and industrial customers continues unabated. Customers are becoming much more educated and sophisticated about the products they buy, and this translates into higher quality expectations. In addition, the pace of life for most people is so fast that they have little free time and thus resent having to fix a problem associated with a product they purchased, or even to get the product routinely delivered or serviced.

We all have experienced this when it comes to the cars we buy. Ten years ago we insisted on a warranty when we purchased a new car because we thought it highly likely that it would break down at some point in our ownership of it. Today, we don't even want to have to take the car in for service! To do this means arranging for an appointment, then arranging for someone to pick us up at the car dealer and drive us to work (or renting another car), then doing the reverse of all that to pick up the car after several phone calls to find out whether the work is finished and what the bill is. Then, it's not uncommon to get the car back with some of its problems unfixed, or with even more or different problems than it had when we took it in! In short, getting any product serviced in today's hectic life is a hassle people want to avoid—especially when the quality of the service is so unpredictable.

Quality: First an Attitude

In the discussion of EDS' manufacturing business vision in Chapter 2, I spoke of quality as first being an attitude that must permeate the entire organization. Quality has to do with how clean the facilities are, how quickly and in what manner people answer the phone, the way people conduct themselves in meetings, and how people focus on the customer whether that customer is the next person in the process (the internal customer) or the all-important external customer.

For employees, the first task is to know personally who their customer is—who is the next person and department in each employee's business process. Once the customer is known, employees should establish a regular dialogue with him or her to learn what is expected and how well he or she is currently being served.

It's essential that customer-supplier relationships be established within each company business process. "Suppliers" must treat the next person in the process as a "customer." "Customers" must treat the previous person in the business process as a "supplier." At a minimum, this treatment involves using concepts such as fact-based dialogue, empathy, respect, and partnership.

Every employee must know and view his company's products from the eye of the external customer. I know of no better example of how to accomplish this than describing the practices of Chaparral Steel: each of its 900 employees must visit a customer on a sales call at least once a year.[1] I did say *visit*, not just shake hands or chat briefly when the customer comes to the plant, not just a phone conversation, not just a get-acquainted letter.

Adopting a Broader View of Quality

When speaking more narrowly of product quality, one still should adopt as wide a view of quality as possible. Knowing no better place to start with this broad definition of product quality than David Garvin's,[2] I list his eight attributes of quality below:

- Performance—the primary functionality or operating characteristics of the product
- Features—secondary characteristics that supplement the product's basic functionality; the "bells and whistles"

- Reliability—a reflection of the probability of a product failing within a specific period of time, measured by mean time to first failure (MTFF), mean time between failures (MTBF), or failure rate per unit of time
- Conformance—the degree to which a product's design and operating characteristics match preestablished standards as the product is produced in the factory and as it is used in the field
- Durability—a measure of product life; the use one gets from a product before it breaks down or physically deteriorates to the point that replacement is preferable to continued repair
- Serviceability—the ease of repair, which includes such factors as the speed of obtaining repair and courtesy and competence of the repair persons
- Aesthetics—how a product looks, feels, sounds, tastes, or smells; impressions an individual customer perceives concerning these aspects of a product
- Perceived quality—the overall impression of a product, often influenced more by subjective rather than objective factors

These eight quality attributes should be recognized as a starting point for any individual company's efforts to define product quality. Even more important factors may be found, depending on the customers' concerns and the unique nature of the product in a given manufacturing sector.

But What Is the Product?

Being a world-class performer in today's business environment means going even further than Garvin's quality view. We need a new way of thinking about what is the "product" in today's and tomorrow's intensely competitive global marketplace. To understand that, I know of no better definition of quality for to-day's business environment than the one coined by Tito Conti, Olivetti's director of corporate quality.[3]

> Today, quality is no longer just meeting customer require-ments. It is a competitive search for value-added—for cus-tomer requirements that have not yet been expressed.

There are a number of ideas implicit in this superb definition. The first is that we already understand the customer's require-ments, which they have communicated to us in response to our questions. Second, we must change our application of the term *quality* from one applying only to the tangible physical product sold to one that applies not only to the physical prod-uct but to the set of services offered or that could be offered with it. The world-class quality company defines product in a new way—products *and* services. Third, we want to know our customers so well that we can anticipate their needs and de-light them with value-added before they even have to discover they want it or ask for it. World-class business performers place a high priority on continuously searching for any way to add value to their products and services for their customers.

A good example of such a new attitude about quality and adding value for customers comes from a manufacturer of iron pipe in the southern United States. No more commodity prod-uct exists than this pipe, which is used for building and ground drains, among other things. The owner of the building usually doesn't care whose pipe goes into the building. The contractor selects the pipe supplier, perhaps initially steered by an archi-tect. This innovative pipe manufacturer found a new way to differentiate its commodity physical product by the addition of a value-added service. When the pipe company prepares the contractor's order for shipping, it separates the total order into floors and bundles the pipe accordingly. Thus, all the pipe for the basement is in one bundle or group, for the first floor in another group, and so on. This means that the contractor does not have to have his people sort out the total shipment and repackage it. It also allows for sequential delivery as the building is erected. So the pipe manufacturer's value-added service saves the contractor time, labor, and storage space for building supplies. The contractor rewards the pipe manufacturer by giving it more of his business. This is the essence of Conti's quality definition, for the pipe company initiated this value-added idea.

Where Is Your Company on Quality?

Exhibit 4-1 shows an interesting framework from which to view a company's current quality status. The first grid aligns status along a company culture and systems viewpoint. The second grid aligns status along effectiveness—a key element of performance.

Interestingly, when I use this exhibit before an audience to survey where they think their company stands, most people

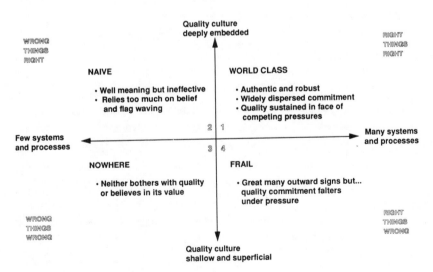

Exhibit 4-1 Quality status grid.[4]

inevitably place their company squarely in quadrant two where the company's quality effort is characterized as naive and, from a world-class performance viewpoint, totally ineffective. In addition, although a company's desired path to world-class quality is from quadrant two to one, from my observations, it seems to end up going from two to four to one. However your company proceeds, and wherever it starts, it must end up at world-class quality to survive, prosper, and grow.

Quality's Relationship to Cost

Quality and low cost used to be viewed as being at the opposite ends of the same spectrum. In other words, a manufacturer could be low-cost, or pay more to be high-quality. But now there is a growing recognition that the only way a company can be a low-cost manufacturer is for it to be a high-quality manufacturer. Companies cannot be cost-effective when they have to carry extra capacity and people to perform engineering changes after the product is released, to inspect products, to rework defective products, to handle customer complaints and returns, to count scrap, and to count and dispose of products rejected from suppliers.

Even after the few years during which companies have pursued the Malcolm Baldrige National Quality Award, it is clear that quality pays and that lower costs are one of the results of higher quality. In a recent survey of the 20 U.S. companies that were among the highest-scoring applicants for the 1988 and 1989 Baldrige Awards, the U.S. General Accounting Office found that companies that seriously pursued higher quality have lower quality costs—by 9 percent on an average annual basis—and greater savings from suggestions to improve products and services to satisfy customers; average annual cost savings from employee suggestions ranged from $1.3 million to $116 million.[5] These are just two of the many benefits that accrued to companies actively seeking improved quality that the GAO documented in its study.

Why Top Management Isn't More Aware of Poor Quality

One of the great problems about quality—the reason it has received so little attention from top management in the past— is that current accounting systems are not designed to capture all the costs of poor quality when a broad definition of quality is used. (I shall discuss this more extensively in Chapter 5.)

Many companies (but not all, even today) routinely capture scrap, rework, and customer warranty costs. For those that do, it is not uncommon for the total of these costs to run between 8 percent and 12 percent of sales. Very few companies utilize the complete Feigenbaum model[6] for collecting their total costs of quality, where quality costs are broken into four categories:

- Prevention
- Appraisal
- Internal (for example, scrap and rework)
- External (for example, warranty claims)

Even companies that try to use this model are hampered by cost accounting and overhead allocation schemes that make it difficult to get accurate costs of poor quality. Notwithstanding this, numerous studies, including the earlier example from the GAO, have shown that, for the average manufacturing company, the total cost of poor quality is at least 20 percent to 25 percent of sales and may run as high as 40 percent of sales in the worst companies or plants.[7]

The reaction of top management when exposed to these figures is first one of amazement and disbelief that any company's quality costs could be so high. This doubt then turns to defensiveness—"That couldn't be so in *my* company!"

Finally, after being confronted by scrap, rework, and warranty costs (usually known) and some reasonable estimates of other costs associated with poor quality (excess inventory, extra manufacturing floor space, equipment, and people), they become concerned, even alarmed, about their company's poor quality performance, especially when they realize that all those wasted dollars could move directly to their bottom line.

But then a curious thing happens. Typically, management then wants to carry out an exhaustive study to find out what really is the true cost of poor quality. Is it 18 percent of sales, 26 percent of sales, or 35 percent of sales? Many companies have gone down this road, spending several hundred thousand dollars and up to a year to try to nail the cost of poor quality figure down more exactly. Sure enough, these studies—if done from a broad enough perspective—almost always show figures in the range cited. When this happens, it is not unusual that the company's top quality executive is replaced, and another great quality "program" begins anew.

Why bother with this time-consuming search for the exact cost of poor quality—wasting many labor-months and, even worse, much time? The point is that everyone already knew the cost of poor quality was too high. The time, money, and effort devoted to the study should have been spent starting the education and training and changes needed to bring the cost of poor quality down. The money spent for the study could have bought new gaging or tooling, a new machine tool, a process capability study, or statistical quality control (SQC) training for management and shop floor employees. Every day and every dollar counts in the quest for world-class performance.

The key to whether this money is being spent effectively and the improvement program is focused properly is to regularly poll your company's customers. Is your company's product and service quality improving (and fast enough)? What are their top three complaints? What else could your company be doing for them?

By How Much Must Quality Improve?

The sad fact of the matter is that most non-Japanese manufacturing companies must increase their quality by a factor of 100 to 1000 times—yes, one hundred to one thousand times—to meet today's world-class quality standards of less than 50 defective parts per million (ppm).

Where's the average manufacturer? Most U.S. production lines operate with a 5 percent to 10 percent reject rate at the end of their final assembly line, or 50,000 to 100,000 defective ppm. This is a low figure for many plants I have seen. Thus, companies aspiring to world-class quality must improve in the quality area alone by 2 to 3 orders of magnitude.

Around 1980 both Motorola and Hewlett-Packard set out on programs to improve their quality by one order of magnitude, or a factor of ten. They both accomplished this with all the resulting benefits by the late 1980s, only to realize how much farther they had to go to be world-class producers and how many more benefits were achievable. It was at the end of this first quality drive that both companies set out on a renewed quest for world-class quality. Many companies today such as Motorola, IBM, and DEC are striving to achieve "six sigma" quality levels, which translates to 3.4 defective ppm with a 1.5 standard deviation process shift allowed, or 2.2 defective ppm with no process shift.[8]

This is the usual pattern for most manufacturers. Thinking they know all about quality (and that it's not much of a problem in their company), they start a quality drive with some education and training and just a few of the many competitive advantage enablers that can help bring better quality to the organization. But along the way they discover how much they don't know about quality and how difficult world-class quality standards really are to achieve. In the meantime, these manufacturers have seen enough evidence from their programs about the vast potential of lower costs, shorter lead times, and more satisfied customers that they totally commit themselves to a real long-term quality drive.

The Road to World Class Quality

The road to world class quality is a journey of many steps, illustrated dramatically in Exhibit 4-2. There are several points to observe in this exhibit. First, note where the typical manufacturer is starting—5 percent rejects, or 50,000 defective ppm. Manufacturers having this reject rate or worse typically inspect during and after production and are performing audits of incoming and finished products. Furthermore, their problem solving activities are product focused rather than process focused. These manufacturers still haven't learned that quality cannot be inspected into a product and, of course, are paying an unbearable competitive penalty for their ignorance.

The next thing to note in Exhibit 4-2 is that SQC is only the very first step toward world-class quality attainment. (I will use the broader SQC, rather than SPC for statistical process

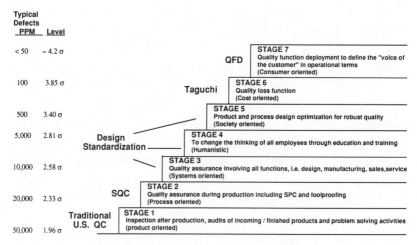

Exhibit 4-2 The journey to world-class quality.[9] (Source: Lawrence P. Sullivan)

control, throughout this book.) I have been in many U.S. and European manufacturing companies where the senior management shows off their SQC effort as the only answer to attaining better quality. SQC alone, even when used properly—and not all companies do that—just won't get the job done.

Problems With Using Only SQC

What's wrong with the way many companies are using SQC? First, in many companies, SQC control charts abound as display items. Either they are out of date, or people are just going through the motions in filling them out without really understanding what the charts mean and taking the proper corrective action for each process. Second, many SQC programs are started without first considering the capability of current gaging and other measurement devices. In many cases, the manufacturing process and equipment in place is not even capable of meeting the specifications called for on the part's drawing. This may be due to the fact that the engineers, not knowing which dimensions are critical to the part's quality performance, have made all the specifications too tight, thus increasing the cost of manufacture unnecessarily.

The limiting power of SQC is unwittingly told time and again in numerous SQC "success" stories. Executives or quality heads will boast about reducing quality defects in their plant by 50 percent with their SQC program. But, for world-class aspirants, the question remains, "What about the *other* 50 percent of the defects that need to be eradicated?" SQC won't tell you that you're measuring a parameter that has little effect on quality, or what are the critical manufacturing parameters to control. There's one more trap that users often fall into with SQC. Many users of SQC spend most of their time chasing a shifting process mean instead of concentrating on reducing variability about the mean so that the process can shift somewhat without resulting in parts that are out of specification.

The fundamental goal of world-class quality is to reduce variation around the target value of either the product or the business process. In statistical terms, the goal is a distribution of results that have a smaller standard deviation, illustrated in Exhibit 4-3.

A distribution of quality measurement points is statistically characterized with a mean and standard deviation. When the mean changes, the process is said to have shifted to either a higher or lower (mean) value. Process shifts are always likely to occur because of random events or noise factors (such as temperature, humidity, machine wear, building vibration, or dust) over which one has little control, or over which control is expensive. Reduced variability about the target value is a pow-

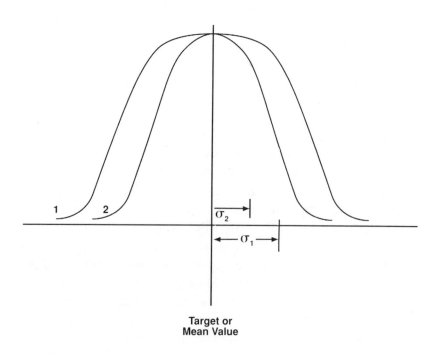

**Target or
Mean Value**

**Standard deviation σ_2 is less than standard deviation σ_1
(Normal distribution shown.)**

Exhibit 4-3 Reducing variation about the target value.

erful way to cost-effectively accommodate such noise factors. This is demonstrated in Exhibit 4-4. Note that with a "tighter" distribution (a smaller standard deviation), the mean can shift more without resulting in a faulty part.

It's interesting that some of Japan's highest quality manufacturing plants use few, if any, SQC charts for two reasons. Many of their production machines are designed to shut off if they produce a part out of tolerance. Thus, they may have a record of shutoffs for one part of the machining process, but no record of quality readings of one dimension from a "run" of the same products, as SQC charts provide. Furthermore, many Japanese companies have done such a good job of designing robust quality into the product and process with their quality engineering that there is little or no need to constantly check the process with SQC. (Statistically, they have achieved Cpk ratios of 1.33 or higher, more often 2 to 6.[10]) SQC is akin to driving through the rear view mirror, but when used correctly it remains a vital and necessary first step on the long journey toward quality manufacturing.

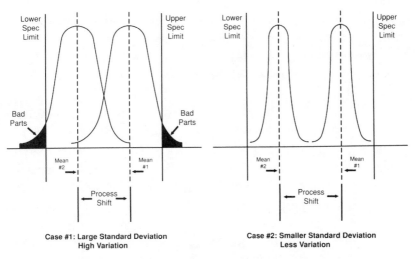

(Normal distribution shown, equal amount of process shift in both cases)

Exhibit 4-4 Process shift vis-à-vis reducing variability.

The Value of SQC

SQC's value can be demonstrated by the following results obtained by General Electric at their aerospace facility in Pittsfield, Massachusetts, where U.S. Army weapons are assembled. During the period from 1986 to 1987, they were spending $2 million a year on scrap in their machine shop, in spite of having 32 quality inspectors and 10 process and quality control engineers on the job. Their SQC program has had the following results so far:[11]

- Defects reduced by 66 percent
- Scrap reduced by 51 percent ($1.1 million)
- Number of inspectors reduced by 17 (53 percent)
- Number of process and quality control engineers reduced by 7 (70 percent)

These results are typical for a well-executed SQC program. But now, GE has to do even better to eliminate the other much more difficult 34 percent of their defects to be a world-class producer.

Stages 3 through 5 in Exhibit 4-2 all involve design standardization, education and training of all employees in the attitude and principles of world-class quality, and the product and process design aspect of Taguchi methods. Two very powerful and important quality enablers shown in this exhibit are still being ignored by the vast majority of U.S. manufacturers—Taguchi methods and quality function deployment (QFD). Both are relatively new techniques, with the former being developed in Japan by Genichi Taguchi and applied by some progressive Japanese companies first in the late 1960s and 1970s, and the latter being developed primarily by Professor Yoji Akao and used first in Mitsubishi's Kobe shipyards during the mid-1970s. Using QFD ensures that quality is built in from the eyes of the customer. Using Taguchi methods allows quality to be engineered into each specific component of product design.

The exhibit shows the progression toward world-class quality sequentially, with QFD last—this is the order of historical development. This order need not be followed in your company's implementation. If your company has the management support and learning capability, it can pursue Taguchi methods and QFD simultaneously.

A Powerful Quality Tool: Taguchi Methods

Taguchi methods were first brought to this country around 1980 by Ford, Xerox, and ITT. (The American Supplier Institute in Dearborn, Michigan, is still the only organization licensed by Taguchi to teach Taguchi methods in the United States, but there are now many more sources of this knowledge in the country.) Incidentally, the term *Taguchi methods* is an American term, which is not used in Japan. There, Taguchi methods are an integral part of quality engineering. I believe that in the short term, given the woeful state of quality in most non-Japanese manufacturing companies, that Taguchi methods are the most powerful quality enabler available. Why is this so? Consider Exhibit 4-5.

Taguchi methods utilize a rigorous yet practical method to ensure that robust quality is designed into the product and process. Their design methodology utilizes a step largely ignored in traditional American practice called *parameter design*. Parameter design is a way to make a product or process design as robust as possible in spite of noise factors in the manufacturing process; that is, as insensitive as possible to uncontrolled variation in the factory or in use before having to go to tolerance design.

Traditional U.S. design practice is to ignore this step and go right to tolerance design, where material or process changes and tolerance tightening unnecessarily add cost and complexity to the product.

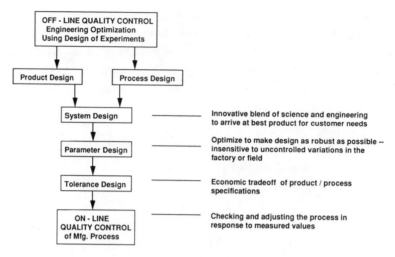

Exhibit 4-5 Quality engineering with Taguchi methods.[12]

Taguchi has also created special sets of orthogonal arrays that minimize factor test time. For instance, if a product or process has seven design factors, each one of which could have two settings, a full factorial experiment would require 128 tests to cover all possible conditions. Using Taguchi's L8 orthogonal array, only eight tests have to be conducted to identify the significant factors or parameters to control. This represents to any manufacturer a considerable savings in money and, more importantly, time. The interested reader will find references to many Taguchi method texts and articles in the bibliography.

There has been an ongoing debate akin to that of how many angels can dance on the head of a pin for several years between a group of U.S. statisticians led by George Box and followers of Taguchi about the validity of Taguchi methods as opposed to traditional design of experiments (based on more "pure" statistics) in quality engineering. My advice to the reader is to not get dragged into this dispute, which is being carried out on a rather lofty level. Taguchi methods are much more than design of experiments—they are an entire proven philosophy of design for the practicing design and manufacturing engineer. The fact of the matter is that Taguchi methods work, and they are powerful. I don't know of a manufacturer anywhere that couldn't benefit from their implementation in its company's product and process design function.

Consider the benefits of one Taguchi exercise at Xerox to optimize a light sensor system. There were 21 independent variables that were either controllable factors or noise factors. An L27 orthogonal array was used for parameter design. After parameter design, tolerance design was used to change three specific resistor tolerances from 5 percent to 1 percent. As a result of this exercise, no change had to be made to the power source, and two critical components' specifications were kept within the limits of their supplier to supply them with no modifications, price increases, or further sorting needed. The benefits for Xerox were as follows:

> Taguchi methods ... systematically identified those variables that significantly contribute to variation, identified the magnitude and direction of changes that led to an optimized system, decreased the potential defect rate from 70 percent to less than 1 percent, while eliminating costly process steps.[13]

As powerful as the design aspect of Taguchi Methods is, I believe that Taguchi's quality loss function is even more important to making top management understand and convincing them to empower employees to do something about quality. The quality loss function allows a discussion about quality in financial terms, not statistical terms. Before Taguchi, quality managers always had to resort to statistics to talk about quality with top management. Unfortunately, the vast majority of CEOs do not speak or understand statistics, and they probably never will. What they always understand, though, is money. So Taguchi's quality loss function finally enables communication with CEOs and boards of directors about quality in financial terms.

Taguchi's quality loss function states that costs of poor quality rise exponentially as we move away from the target value, according to the formula and curve shown in Exhibit 4-6. Using the formula given therewith, you can evaluate possible quality improvements for their economic effect.

For example, we can calculate the cost in dollars of poor quality for a part, caused by its current process. Let us say this cost of poor quality in our example is $50,000. We do the analysis and come up with the fact that a new piece of machinery, for instance, will cost $30,000 and reduce the variation by 50 percent. This 50 percent reduction in variation will, according to Taguchi's loss function, reduce our cost of poor quality to $10,000. Should we buy the equipment? Surely, for we get $40,000 of immediate benefit for only $30,000. (We're assuming here that there are no competing products and processes where a larger payback may exist.) Any CEO can understand this example. We didn't have to discuss the quality problem in terms of means and standard deviations and sigma limits. Any CEO will vote for quality when the problem is as straightforward as this. This is the real power of the Taguchi loss function.

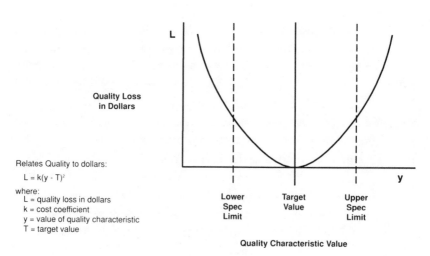

Relates Quality to dollars:

$L = k(y - T)^2$

where:
L = quality loss in dollars
k = cost coefficient
y = value of quality characteristic
T = target value

Exhibit 4-6 Taguchi's quality loss function.

Understanding the Implications of the Voice of the Customer with Quality Function Deployment

QFD deploys the voice of the customer throughout the manufacturing organization. In the words of Professor Akao,

> ...this is a method for developing a design quality aimed at satisfying the consumer and then translating the consumers' demands into design targets and major quality assurance points to be used throughout the production stage.[14]

Thus, after rigorous study of the customer's needs and desires and analysis of competing products, design requirements are specifically linked to manufacturing process steps. What benefits result from the application of QFD? According to Professor Akao,

> In many of the published cases, the use of quality function deployment has cut in half the problems previously encountered at the beginning stages of product development and has reduced development time by one-half to one-third, while also helping to ensure customer satisfaction and increasing sales.[15]

Eaton Corporation Controls Division used QFD to design a blend door actuator for an automotive air conditioner. In addition to getting closer to its customer, it obtained the following more quantifiable benefits from its first application of QFD:

- Size reduced by 30 percent
- Selling price reduced by 50 percent
- Engineering costs reduced by 50 percent
- Drafting costs reduced by 20 percent
- Noise specifications reduced from 50 decibels to 38 decibels
- Mounting flexibility expanded to three car lines[16]

In most of the companies that are now actively using QFD, the entire process is done manually by laying out large matrices on huge sheets of paper. Ford Motor Company and a handful of other manufacturing companies or software companies are computerizing the QFD process (Ford is now on its third generation of QFD software). Once this is accomplished, and some simulation capability included, a manufacturer will in effect have a large, expert system that is able to translate customers' needs for its product or changes in those needs into new requirements for design, production processes, and quality. Such automated QFD systems will be powerful aids in the quest for totally automated product and process design tools during the next 10 to 15 years.

The Effects of Time and Lot Size on Quality

JIT and TQM have a mutually reinforcing effect on each other with regard to quality. JIT in this instance means eliminating the waste of time—the foundation of time-based competition. Reducing set-up time also means that a plant can operate with smaller lot sizes—perhaps as small as one. Note the influence of JIT on improving overall quality in the following example.

Assume, for instance, that the lot size of a part being machined is reduced from 300 to 30 (not an uncommon need), that each part takes 20 minutes to produce, and that each costs $10. In pre-JIT practice, we'd have produced 300 parts in a lot over a period of at least 100 hours, or about 13.3 work days assuming one 7.5 hour shift per day. Assuming that a defective process or engineering change went unnoticed until the part was going to be assembled, the quality problem would remain unknown until we went to use the part at least 13.3 work days later. In the meantime, we've made 300 defective parts at a cost of $3000, which may be all wasted if the parts are not reworkable—at further cost!

Assuming the same problem with a lot size of 30, we would realize the problem the next day (10 hours later) and would have risked only $300 in bad part quality. If we had a lot size of 3, we'd recognize the quality problem in one hour and could fix the production process, saving 2.5 to 3 weeks of wasted lead time and production. Note that the quality and lead time reduction benefits described here don't show up in any economic order quantity lot size calculation.

The point is clear. Smaller lot sizes of internally produced or purchased goods mean a much quicker reaction to problems and a great savings in dollars. There are clearly other ways to ensure perfect quality, but these are not yet in use in most U.S. companies, so this example represents today's real-world manufacturing environment.

Standardization: A Key to Obtaining Quality

I have commented before on the mutually reinforcing central themes of TQM and JIT. Nowhere are these issues more important than with the subject of standardization. Commented the late Professor Kaoru Ishikawa, developer of the Ishikawa cause and effect (or "fishbone") diagram, and a leading Japanese quality guru:

> None of the Japanese success in quality would have been possible if we had not linked progress in quality control with advances in standardization. . . . We must establish two kinds of standards: standards for materials such as products, parts, and raw materials; and standards for systems such as operation, engineering, and new product development.[17]

Many people think standardization means bureaucracy, stacks of policy manuals, and long lead times to change anything, but this need not be the case. More than anything, standardization means discipline. Part of this discipline is working to the rule that "we do things the same standard way each day until we find a better way". This is a great saying, for it not only promotes standardization, but also implies a continual search for that better way. The Japanese emphasis on standardization allows them to be more flexible, for their production workers are a well-rehearsed team accustomed to a stable production environment and the idea of making continual improvements in all aspects of their work. When changes come along, they are quickly adopted. Whether standardization promotes teamwork or vice versa, it remains an important part of any company's consistent approach to world-class quality.

Will the Baldrige Award
Actually Improve Quality?

There's been much hoopla lately about the Malcolm Baldrige Award and how good it is for U.S. industry. I'm not so sure. It's sad to see that management in this country requires a contest to get interested in quality. It seems as though they aren't aware of the business contest they fight every day that has quality as one of its most significant components.

More than 180,000 copies of the Malcolm Baldrige Award application were mailed out in 1990 alone, but the National Institute of Standards and Technology (NIST) received only 106 applications for the 1991 Baldrige Award, of which 38 were manufacturing firms, 21 were service companies, and 47 were small businesses. In the four years from 1988 to 1991 that applications have been received, only a total of 151 manufacturing companies have sent applications, some more than once.[18]

In 1986 there were approximately 125,000 manufacturing establishments (single physical locations) employing 20 or more workers, with approximately 38,000 employing 100 or more workers.[19] If one assumes an average of ten plants per company that employ more than 100 people, then only about 1 percent of all U.S. manufacturing companies applied for the Baldrige Award in 1991. Counting small businesses, many of whom are manufacturers, might boost the applicant number to 2 percent or 3 percent. Where are the rest?

It does take time for companies to "get in shape" to apply, but by now one might expect at least ten times the current number of applicants. The small number of past applicants either reflects manufacturers' apathy or their poor state of preparation—either of which is damning. Furthermore, the Baldrige Award has been criticized for focusing too much on the management process for quality and too little on a company's actual product and service quality.[20] It has also drawn criticism because manufacturers can nominate themselves for the award. Perhaps only customers should do the nominating.

One may well wonder whether the criteria for the Baldrige Award will be improved, thereby making it a major tool to focus U.S. manufacturers on the real issues of quality. Or will it remain another American fad? What about the considerable cost for a company to apply that could be better spent on improving product quality? What if 10,000 manufacturing companies ever apply? How will the program be administered fairly and on a timely basis, and who will bear its cost?

One could argue that anything that improves the public's and management's awareness of quality must be good. Moreover, if enough companies will go through the process of entering the competition, that is bound to be good for them, although they may not win the award and they may not achieve world-class quality performance. This is all true. But the numbers above do not show significant effort in this regard yet.

Some U.S. companies, keeping an eye on the 1992 European Community event, have instead focused their quality efforts on meeting the International Standards Organization (ISO) 9000 quality certification. This effort, too, is all to the good, but product and service quality isn't defined by awards and certification. It is continually tested and redefined by an industry's customers. Unlike awards and certifications, customers get smarter and more demanding every year.

Which Quality Guru Do We Listen To?

Over the years I've had many executives ask me which of the quality gurus they should use to attain world-class quality in their company, for example, Deming, Juran, Crosby, Fiegenbaum, Shewart, Shainin, or maybe Taguchi or Akao if the client has heard of them. The answer, of course, is all of the above, for each person and his philosophy appeals to a certain group of people.

Top management usually likes Crosby, for his teachings are "soft," people-oriented, and not very mathematical. (As I said before, no statistics for top management!) Deming also appeals to top management, but eventually he gets more rigorous and more disciplined than Crosby. Juran, Fiegenbaum, and Shaman appeal more to middle management because of the more mathematical approach they take to SQC.

Taguchi appeals to engineers, who respect the results his method produces. Talk to any group of product and process engineers who have performed their first few Taguchi case studies. Their common reaction is something like this: "We've been making that product with that process for 40 years and thought we knew all about it. Taguchi methods showed us that we knew little or nothing, but quickly demonstrated what parameters were critical to control at the lowest cost to achieve lasting world-class product quality." Some people are intimidated by the mathematics used in Taguchi methods, but there are several good software packages available today that eliminate this concern. Top management also likes Taguchi, once they've become acquainted with his quality loss function, for his method's ability to allow people to discuss quality in dollars. All of the quality gurus' teachings are valuable, and a company will be wise to expose employees at various levels to the work of each of these great management consultants.

Why Real Quality Improvement Is Such a Tough Sell

I have mentioned one reason quality is such a tough sell—the fact that senior managers don't realize what the absence of it is costing their company in its business performance. The other reason that quality is such a tough sell is that it is just plain hard work, requiring a rigorous engineering approach if world-class quality is the goal. Obtaining the first 50 percent of quality improvement is generally easy; it's getting the last 50 percent that's the tough part. Doing so requires a sustained, detailed, relentless campaign on the part of all employees. This goes against the American management's grain of looking for simple, quick, one-shot improvements with a minimum of investment in equipment and people.

There is no question that poor quality in products, services, and business processes is the toughest problem that manufacturers have to solve. Poor quality is the major basis for high costs, poor schedules, high inventories, poor productivity, and many other indicators of poor manufacturing effectiveness and efficiency. In addition, poor quality is not a very good selling feature with which to attract and retain customers. Superb quality and a good preventive maintenance system are prerequisites for effectively implementing JIT. Even with the right quality approach, it will take the average company 5 to 10 years to reach today's world-class quality standards. Any quality improvement is a win-win situation for everyone—suppliers, the company, and most of all, the company's customers. So don't wait any longer. Get on with it!

Chapter 4

1. Terence P. Paré, "The Big Threat to Big Steel's Fortune," *Fortune*, 15 July 1991, p. 107.

2. David Garvin, *Managing Quality* (New York: The Free Press), 1988.

3. Tito Conti, "Process Management and Quality Function Deployment," *Quality Progress*, December 1989, p. 45–48.

4. Gunn Associates Inc., composite of several inputs.

5. U.S. General Accounting Office, *Management Practices: U.S. Companies Improve Performance Through Quality Efforts*, May 1991, GAO/NISAD-91-190.

6. Arnold V. Feigenbaum, *Total Quality Control* (New York: McGraw Hill Book Company) 1983.

7. Two such studies are: KPMG Peat Marwick, Illinois Manufacturers Association, *American Machinist*, January 1991, p. 17; and The Willimantic Division of Rogers Corporation, *Quality Progress*, July 1986, pp. 21–24.

8. Sigma is the Greek symbol used to represent standard deviation in statistics. For a normal distribution, plus and minus one standard deviation (one sigma) represents 68.27 percent of the total data points in the distribution. Three sigma represents 99.73 percent of all the data points being within "good" limits, or 2700 defective parts per million (1,000,000 minus 997,300).

9. Adapted from L. P. Sullivan, "The Seven Stages of Company-Wide Quality Control," *Quality Progress*, May 1986, pp. 77–83.

10. For an excellent discussion of Cp and Cpk ratios, see the following: SPC Made Easier, Simpler, More Statistically Powerful, K. R. Bhote, *Target*, Association For Manufacturing Excellence, Fall, 1987, pp. 12–20; and the "Statistics Corner" columns in *Quality Progress*, written by Bert Gunter, that appeared in January, March, May, and July 1989, entitled "The Use and Abuse of Cpk."

11. Tom Inglesby, "Time Waits For No Man(ufacturer)," *HP/Manufacturing Systems*, June 1991, p. 9.

12. Adapted from American Supplier Institute, Inc.

13. R. B. Dingwall and M. J. Duell, "Taguchi Method Optimization of a Sensor System," ASQC Quality Congress Transactions, 1989, pp. 710–718.

14. Yoji Akao, *Quality Function Deployment* (Cambridge, MA: Productivity Press), 1990, p. 3.

15. Ibid.

16. De Vera, et al., "An Automotive Case Study," *Quality Progress,* June 1988, pp. 35–38.

17. Kaoru Ishikawa, "Quality and Standardization: Program For Economic Success," *Quality Progress,* January 1984, pp. 16–20.

18. "106 U.S. Companies Vie For Baldridge Award," *Quality Progress,* June 1991, p. 16.

19. Statistical Abstract of the United States, 1990, Table 872, p. 528.

20. Jeremy Main, "Is the Baldridge Overblown?" *Fortune,* 1 July 1991, pp. 62–65.

5

Becoming a Low-Cost Manufacturer

Many companies fail to realize the importance of becoming, at a minimum, a low-cost manufacturer, if not the lowest-cost manufacturer in their industry. Note that *low cost* in this context describes costs 30 percent to 50 percent lower than today's total product cost. This means that a company must have the lowest manufacturing cost—traditionally made up of material, labor, and overhead—as well as the lowest combination of selling, general, administrative, and R and D costs—to achieve this low total cost target. Thus, management's skills and attention must be continually devoted to decreasing its total costs over time. But the way most companies go about this today is ineffective in the long run and not supportive of any effort to become a world-class business performer.

The Perils of Conventional Management Efforts to Achieve Low Cost

Conventional cost reduction efforts that directly (rather than indirectly) pursue low cost in a manufacturing company have a number of pernicious effects. These conventional methods used to reduce costs include the following techniques and consequences. Direct labor cost—the most readily identifiable portion of total labor costs—is reduced, which usually depletes capacity and always affects the remaining workforce negatively. Capital investment in new plants is also reduced or curtailed at the expense of operating efficiency or effectiveness or both. Existing assets are milked and cash cows are decapitalized. Accounting policies are changed to bill early and pay late, thus maximizing the float at the expense of customers and suppliers.

Preventive maintenance on plant and equipment is often reduced or curtailed, leading to reduced product quality and reduced capability to meet shipping schedules with minimum inventories. Basic R and D funding is cut or postponed for both product and process design, mortgaging the company's future with its customers. The investment in new product development is reduced or curtailed; existing products are 'stretched' with superficial, if any, changes. This, in addition to the fact that existing product designs are often cheapened with the use of lower-quality (and lower-cost) components, opens the way for competitor inroads. Capital investment in new product and process or information systems technology is reduced or curtailed, crippling the company's future competitiveness. Inventory levels are reduced in finished goods and service parts at the expense of customer service.

The company's suppliers are squeezed for lower prices, which encourages them to reduce the quality of their products and to batch their shipments in even larger lot sizes to gain the benefits of long product runs. In turn, suppliers often deemphasize their design function to further reduce their overhead, relying on their customers to more fully design or specify their products. Purchasing buyers are rewarded for buying the lowest-cost products with little or no regard for quality or delivery (lead time or schedule compliance) considerations.

Company salaries and wages are held below market rates, thus lowering the motivation of existing workers. The best and brightest people leave. Good employees become harder to attract. In many cases, operations are moved offshore in pursuit of lower labor costs, but the hidden costs of doing so end up raising total costs and increasing business process lead times. Corporate staff is reduced or eliminated entirely. Planning and other important management functions often cease.

Production rates are usually kept high, regardless of demand, in an effort to keep factory and machine utilization up and absorb existing overhead. Overhead is absorbed, but who will absorb all the production no one currently wants, and at what eventual price? Education and training spending is reduced or curtailed, thus depleting the company's intellectual capital and discouraging the retention of employees who desire professional growth. A focus on short-term low-cost objectives is often accomplished at the expense of developing, communicating, and implementing a vision of the future.

The result of this misguided approach to low-cost manufacturing is that, for the majority of U.S. manufacturers, their annual cost of poor quality exceeds their return on sales by a factor of two to four. In addition, they are easy prey for effectively managed manufacturers, based either domestically or internationally. Sometimes companies whose management has tried most of the preceding approaches are restructured in a vain attempt to buy (the current management, perhaps) time. Sadly, this painful approach seldom gets at the underlying reasons for the company's manufacturing impotence.

These are the very actions that have driven U.S. manufacturing capability and global competitiveness to its current nadir over the past 25 years. They directly counteract measures that are critical to supporting the company's business strategy, all because the basics about cost have been forgotten. They are a result of a control-oriented "cut, cut, cut" mentality that leads to significant erosion in competitive advantage.

The approaches above are wrong because executives have lost sight of the fact that in manufacturing as well as most other activities, low cost is the result of doing other things well, or effectively. In mathematical terms, low cost is a dependent variable, not an independent variable. Managers thus need to shift their emphasis toward becoming more effective and efficient at executing their company's fundamental business processes, and lower cost will follow. Clearly, long-term, low-cost, world-class competitiveness cannot be achieved by budget cutting.

Traditionally, companies have focused on reducing direct labor cost as a way to lower overall costs. Indeed, many companies have large groups of industrial engineers solely devoted to this purpose. Yet direct labor today is a small percentage of many companies' manufacturing cost—from 15 percent or 25 percent to as little as 1 percent to 3 percent, depending on the industry and how much the company has invested in modern production processes and equipment. Today, cost reduction efforts must focus on total labor reduction—white-collar as well as traditional blue-collar—in order to achieve world-class productivity levels of greater than $375,000 in sales per worker per year.

The Trend in Manufacturing Costs

I include here a manufacturing cost reduction curve (which also appeared in my last book) because few companies seem to understand its implications or take sufficient action to achieve what it shows. Referring to Exhibit 5-1, the left side of the illustration shows a typical cost structure for an average discrete part manufacturer today. Materials might be as high as 85 percent and direct labor might be as little as 2 percent of manufacturing cost in an electronics assembly operation. In other industries, such as furniture making, materials might constitute only 30 percent of cost and direct labor might be as high as 30 percent of cost. But look at the results demonstrated by today's world-class performers. Direct labor will continue to be

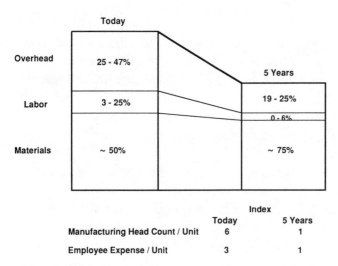

	Index	
	Today	5 Years
Manufacturing Head Count / Unit	6	1
Employee Expense / Unit	3	1

Exhibit 5-1 The Trend In Manufacturing Costs.

reduced by more (and more flexible) factory automation, parts count reduction efforts brought about by design for manufacture or assembly, and by companies becoming less vertically integrated. Overhead will continue to decrease as a result of supplier reduction programs, business process reengineering, better information systems, and the outsourcing of current inside service functions.

For instance, in the 1980s Xerox reduced its number of global suppliers from 5000 to about 300. Imagine the hundreds of clerks, accountants, and lawyers they no longer needed to deal with the 4700 suppliers they dropped, not to mention the significant reduction in information systems size and other gains that Xerox discovered.[1]

Ford Motor Company, after studying Mazda's accounts payable operation, took advantage of business process reengineering and better information systems to create "invoiceless processing" and reduce their 500-person North American accounts payable group by 75 percent. In addition, they gained simpler material control and more accurate and real-time material and financial information.[2]

The result of these and other efforts is not only a dramatic reduction of today's manufacturing cost, but a change in its composition as well. Note that, despite some reduction in material cost, materials automatically become a much more significant portion—more often than not, a dominant portion—of a world-class company's manufacturing cost. This places an increasing emphasis on selecting the best material, optimizing the product design through computer-aided engineering analysis, and tightly controlling the entire logistics chain from global suppliers through the manufacturing company to its global customers.

Note the dramatic reduction in overhead in Exhibit 5-1. I've seen several companies recently where overhead represented 45 percent to 55 percent of their manufacturing cost structure! No company can survive, much less prosper and grow, with this kind of albatross around its neck.

Four Steps to Becoming a Low-Cost Manufacturer

Becoming the low cost manufacturer today requires four significant steps:

- Market-based costing as a basis for product and process design efforts
- Understanding the relationship between cost and quality
- Possessing accurate cost systems that promote world-class performance
- Understanding the relationship of transactions to overhead

Market-Based Costing

The cost strategy for any product must be driven by market conditions that set the acceptable price for a product. That price then dictates a current product cost target that must be met by the company if it is to achieve the profit margins required by its business strategy and shareholders. Moreover, given global competitive forces, the march of technology, the learning curve effect, and other factors, the company must be able to meet a significantly lower cost target for the same product in the future years of its life cycle.

Note that I said "able to meet a significantly lower cost." It may not be necessary to meet a lower cost target in future years if there is no pressure from competitors to do so. The extra profit margin generated by having the lowest total cost might well be invested in more R and D, advertising, sales and marketing efforts, or better manufacturing and information systems technology.

The Japanese have used market-based or target costing for many years. They deliberately set the target cost low for two reasons. The first is to ensure adequate market share growth as compared to their global competitors. Second, in the words of a recent *Fortune* article:

> The critical feature of the Japanese [target cost] system is its focus on getting costs out of the product during the planning and design stage. That's the point at which virtually all subsequent costs are determined, from manufacturing to what customers will have to spend on maintenance.[3]

Setting target costs low forces product and process designers to be innovative in their work and seek new low-cost ways of doing things. The American "design it, then cost it" method tends to perpetuate old ways of doing things, from the use of old business processes to old product and process technology.

The Relationship Between Cost and Quality

Despite all the publicity about quality recently—different companies' six-sigma programs, the Malcolm Baldrige Award in the United States, or ISO 9000 in Europe—executives find it difficult to break old habits of thinking about cost and quality. The traditional view of these two topics is that they lie at the opposite ends of the same spectrum. In other words, high quality costs more. World-class performing manufacturers from all parts of the world have shown us that not only is this not true, but the opposite is true. The only way to be a low-cost manufacturer is to be a high-quality manufacturer. Quality is the major independent variable that influences the cost outcome for most manufacturers.

Accurate Product Cost Systems

According to a mid-1989 survey conducted by the National Association of Accountants of 3200 corporate controllers (1344 of whom responded):

> 50 percent of corporate controllers say their company's cost accounting systems are out of date and 78 percent say existing cost systems frequently understate profits on high-volume products and overstate profits on specialty items. . . . [4]

So we see that by the admission of their own financial people, a great many manufacturing companies are saddled with product costing systems that are relatively useless for making pricing decisions and for performing accurate financial modeling based on anticipated product profit margins. Why is this so?

First, recognize that most current cost accounting systems were primarily established to value inventory for financial and tax purposes according to SEC and FASB regulations. They were not designed as product costing systems, and, as a result, our efforts to make them into accurate product costing systems are at best compromises.

The major place where these conventional product costing systems fall down relates to their method of overhead allocation. This allocation is usually based upon volume-related direct-labor hours—which as we know are the least significant part of product cost in most industries. In this process, all overhead is spread "peanut butter" style over the total direct-labor-hours planned to be worked during the year to arrive at a rate that each direct labor hour is burdened. These overhead rates are already 800 percent to 1500 percent in many companies. Obviously, as direct labor continues to be reduced in each plant, these rates will rise even higher and assume more ridiculous proportions.

Product cost distortions are introduced as a result of allocating overhead in this manner. Typically, standard high volume products are overcosted and low volume special products are greatly undercosted. A company therefore has a very poor basis for understanding which products are really contributing to the bottom line and which aren't. It may raise or lower prices based on erroneous information about margins. Even more important, the company's management may make decisions about including products or dropping them out of the company's product portfolio based on this erroneous cost information. Another criticism of today's product costing methods is that they do not sufficiently emphasize the process thinking and value-added analysis so vital for any manufacturer to become a world-class business performer.

Fortunately, there is a cure for all these shortcomings in a concept called activity-based costing, or ABC, cost systems. In actuality an old cost accounting methodology that has been dressed up and acronymed, ABC cost methods recognize that activities consumed by or associated with certain products cause costs. The goal is to identify cost drivers that accurately reflect the consumption of cost by each activity and the resulting consumption of activities with each product. Examples of such cost drivers include, but are certainly not limited to the following:

- Engineering changes
- Number of setups

- Lead time
- Number of circuit board insertions
- Number of purchase orders
- Number of parts in a product
- Number of molds or dies
- Number of material moves
- Number of phone calls to obtain a fully specified customer order

ABC cost systems allocate overhead in proportion to the activities associated with a product or product family. For instance, if one product by its nature has a lot of engineering changes associated with it, it will bear a significantly higher engineering burden than another product that is more stable in design. In companies that have tried using ABC methods, it has not been uncommon to see some low-volume special products rise in cost some 200 percent to 500 percent, but also to see other high-volume standard products decrease 50 percent or more in cost compared to their costs under conventional product costing techniques. You can imagine the significance this can have to a company's financial projections, product portfolio strategies, and profitability.

Although more accurate product costs are a big plus with ABC costing methods, the real value of this costing methodology is that it promotes understanding of the total business process associated with each product and of the company's buildup of value added in that product. Therefore, ABC costing methods really form a basis for value-added and business process analyses and redesign that world-class aspirants must perform.

The Relationship of Transactions to Overhead

Tom Vollman and Jeffrey Miller showed in their excellent article "The Hidden Factory"[5] that overhead costs in business are almost a direct function of the number of transactions that occur in the operation of the business. With this in mind, let's see how the application of just a few competitive advantage enablers or tools can help reduce the number of transactions in a manufacturing company.

In product and process design the use of design for manufacture and parts and process standardization reduces the number of new parts as well as total parts in a product. To the extent this is accomplished, there will be less need for engineers or suppliers, less room and equipment to store parts, fewer people in purchasing and production, fewer people to receive, inspect, stock, and pick parts, fewer accountants and clerks and legal people, less complex assembly and service tools, less cluttered and confusing parts and service manuals, and so on. A Japanese study on one product showed that reducing the parts count in the product by 50 percent lowered its cost by 30 percent.[6] Motorola reduced its parts count on a battery charger by 85 percent and reduced its direct material cost alone by 50 percent.[7] NCR, now part of AT&T, reduced the parts count in its model 5223 passbook/general purpose financial printer by 80 percent (from 438 to 87), including a reduction in fasteners from 114 to 7, and saved 40 percent in labor costs with a 63 percent reduction in assembly time and a 55 percent reduction in process steps over their previous model 5023.[8] These are three points on a very powerful cost reduction curve.

Then, on the shop floor, using JIT principles, a cross-functional improvement team can re-design the production line in a closely coupled U-shaped cell with fewer but more flexible workers. Instead of recording labor and material tracking for some 10 to 30 operations in the product's assembly, it is recorded only for the starting and finishing operations—or input to and output from the cell—on each product. For the few operations we do want to track on the shop floor, CIM technology such as bar-code-based information that is fed directly to a real-time shop floor monitoring system can be used instead of one or more people. Alternatively, a voice input system can be used to allow operators or quality inspectors hands-free data input. Elements of all three enablers—TQM, CIM, and JIT—have thus contributed to a reduction in the number of transactions in the work environment.

Note that all the cost drivers and complexity factors discussed in Chapter 3 cause excessive transactions. The TQM, CIM, JIT, and cost management enablers or tools can be used to improve today's business processes and mitigate the effects of these cost drivers and complexity factors. But the real power of these tools comes from using them in conjunction with business process reengineering so that the enablers are applied to the right underlying process.

ABC costing gives a company a wonderful tool to identify and reduce resource consumption by increasing both efficiency (productivity) and effectiveness. But the key is for corporations to take action after these new costing methods have pointed to new and improved ways of doing things. Referring to an example of parts count reduction, Cooper & Kaplan point out the following in a recent *Harvard Business Review* article:

> If it [the company's management] doesn't redeploy the resources or cut spending, the actions to reduce parts count will have merely created excess capacity, not increased profits.[9]

But a flip side of this argument can be found, for instance, in purchasing, where executives often use proportional thinking to estimate headcount and cost reduction potential. This type of thinking says that if it takes a 50-person procurement organization to manage 4000 suppliers, it will only require 5 people to manage 400. This may be true if one plans to manage it the same old way. But world-class procurement excellence dictates that much more time and effort has to be spent with each of the suppliers a company retains if they are to be made into world-class suppliers to your company. Action based upon shortcomings revealed by ABC costing *is* necessary, but intelligent action that is strategically based and oriented toward moving a manufacturing company toward world-class performance is every bit as important!

The message and the experience of progressive manufacturers is clear—fewer transactions mean lower costs. Don't forget the duality of the word *cost;* costs are represented by both dollars and time. Fewer transactions generally mean less time, too. This is the essence of the pursuit of world-class performance: to find a way to eliminate both cost and time.

The "Small Is Beautiful" Trap

My consulting work over the years has brought to light an insidious cost trap that lurks in many companies. I call it the "small is beautiful" trap. Usually these companies are led by top management that devoutly believes in establishing or preserving an entrepreneurial work environment, maintaining a highly decentralized organization structure, and believing, in the words of Joseph Schumacher, that "small is beautiful."[10] I have found $300 to $350 million companies that have from 28 to 35 national or worldwide facilities. Some may be as small as 50,000 to 70,000 square feet in size doing $5 to $15 million in sales with 30 to 100 employees. It would take an extremely rare company to be a world-class competitor, or, I argue, even a moderately successful one with this kind of infrastructure. Why?

First, these companies' asset turns and return on assets (plant and equipment, as well as inventory turns) are typically low and uncompetitive. There are too many separate assets. No company can afford that many janitors, phone operators, facilities to maintain, parking lots to pave or plow, and so forth. In addition, there are too many corners where inventory or obsolete equipment can accumulate.

Second, the number of physical facilities overburdens the job for the company's senior management, who must frequently travel to each (usually remote) location or ask those locations' management to travel to corporate headquarters or some other common meeting ground. Communication and management coaching suffers, and the company pays a much higher than needed travel cost. The remote locations usually mean flying through commuter airlines with huge holes in their schedules; travel to and from these remote locations is therefore time-consuming and physically tiring for all people concerned. As a result, management productivity suffers.

Third, many of the company's facilities are too small to possess critical mass in any skill or manufacturing technology. Such plants are often considered too small to justify an investment in new and more productive manufacturing technology or in educating and training the employees to possess world-class skills. Many of the plants are running at 50 percent to 60 percent of capacity—at or near breakeven. The plants are too small and often too remotely located to be able to attract the top talent needed at all levels—but particularly those in product and process engineering, operations supervision, information systems, and materials management—to operate consistently at an average performance level, much less a world-class performance level. Furthermore, such a plant's small size works against it when it comes to offering a competitive salary to attract or retain top talent, or especially to provide an attractive career path for its more ambitious employees.

Fourth, because of existing financial pressure, many such small plants are running (and have been for years) at a minimum staffing level. To hire one or two people with new or additional skills represents proportionately higher percentage consequences on costs than it would in a larger operation and thus is prohibitive under the company's current budget constraints. Moreover, there are usually several functions where a fraction of a person is needed, but an entire person can't be justified. As a result of this "lean and mean" staffing, the current employees—particularly the plant's management—are worn out, physically and psychologically. They see no hope for budget or talent or capacity relief on the horizon. These plants are run as the equivalent of baseball teams with only 9 players or football teams with only 11 players. There is no depth or backup or relief in them. As such, it's difficult (impossible, really) for the plant manager to financially justify education and training for any of these people or to afford to do without them while they obtain it. In such environments, few, if any employees have the time or energy for absorbing new ideas, much less trying to implement them. Ask the harried and exhausted general manager of these small plants how beautiful things are.

Fifth, there are too many less-than-qualified people having to fulfill identical management and supervisory roles in too many plants. Many small companies are short on talent anyway, and if there were fewer plants, the company could take more advantage of the few talented people it has. Another way to look at this problem is to view it as analogous to the "too many suppliers" problem. No company can afford to train all its people in these many small plants.

Sixth, the generally remote locations of these plants mean increased logistics costs and time, whether shipping by truck, rail, or air. For both incoming supplies and outgoing customer shipments, these remote plants are severely penalized in the new manufacturing environment of short lead times and low costs.

Thus, small is beautiful offers little hope for prosperous growth and for building a world-class performing company. Companies have to quickly rationalize their capacity and physical resources so that they build critical mass in facilities nearer to the mainstream of business, education, and major logistics centers.

How small is beautiful? Specifically, that answer depends on industry, product or process, and volume. In general, experience dictates that plants should be at least $40 to $60 million in size and employ about 250 to 400 people in order to facilitate the parent corporation's attaining world-class performance. The real management challenge is to preserve an entrepreneurial environment in organizations of this size while making genuine progress toward world-class performance.

Chapter 5

1. L. Connorton and P. Landry, "JIT Purchasing at Xerox," *Target,* Winter 1987, pp. 4–10.

2. Michael Hammer, "Reengineering Work: Don't Automate, Obliterate," *Harvard Business Review,* July–August 1990, pp. 104–112.

3. Ford S. Worthy, "Japan's Smart Secret Weapon," *Fortune,* 12 August 1991, pp. 72–75.

4. "Accounting," *MIS Week,* 28 August 1989, p. 16.

5. J. G. Miller and T. E. Vollman, "The Hidden Factory," *Harvard Business Review,* September–October, 1985 pp. 142–150.

6. Toshio Suzue, "Integrated Management," *The International QC Forum,* No. 16, November 1986, pp. 50–63.

7. Therese R. Welter, "Motorola Gets a Charge Out of DFMA," *Industry Week,* 3 September 1990, p. 75.

8. Miles Parker, "A New Manufacturing Mind Set," *Manufacturing Systems,* June 1991, pp. 42–44.

9. R. Cooper and R. S. Kaplan, "Profit Priorities from Activity-Based Costing," *Harvard Business Review,* May–June 1991, pp. 130–135.

10. E. F. Schumacher, *Small Is Beautiful* (New York: Harper and Row, 1973.)

6

Improving Performance with People and Culture

General Electric, currently one of the world's largest and most successful business corporations, after an already wrenching decade under chairman Jack Welch, is on a renewed quest for corporate change and enhanced competitiveness with three people-oriented management techniques they label work-out, best practices, and process mapping. Why is such a successful company spending so much time and money on educating and changing its people? Welch explains.

> The only ideas that count are the A ideas.... That means we have to get everybody in the organization involved. If you do that right, the best ideas will rise to the top.

These techniques focus on getting people involved so that, according to Welch,

> [General Electric] can sustain the rapid growth in productivity that ... is the key to *any* corporation's survival in the competitive environment of the Nineties.[1]

As I noted in the discussion of EDS' manufacturing business vision and of the world-class manufacturing planning framework, and as the General Electric illustration above reinforces, *people* will ultimately distinguish one manufacturing company's performance from another. Note that I say *people,* not a *person.* One person can make an extraordinary difference, particularly if he or she is the CEO. The CEO can set the tone for the organization and provide a vision and leadership to inculcate positive and lasting change in the organization. But world-class business requires the active cooperation and participation of all the company's employees—to attain it and especially to sustain it. Achieving world-class performance requires developing the right people and creating the right corporate culture in which they can work and grow.

Three Techniques to Improve Performance

A major aspect of attaining world-class business performance comes down to how a company selects, guides, and motivates its people. In my experience, successful companies use three major techniques to achieve these objectives.

Using Corporate Values to Establish the Right Corporate Culture

First, a company must establish a set of overall corporate values that either capture the historical values that have made the company a great performer or that portray what culture the corporation aspires to create in order to become a world-class performer. By corporate culture I mean the shared values and beliefs that provide employees with an organizational context for their behavior and performance.

The process of reaching agreement on corporate value statements is extremely valuable for developing a close-knit management team if done as a thoughtful exercise by a representative cross section of executive and lower-level employees. Often, the use of an experienced outside facilitator is useful for this task. Such a group exercise will then reflect the corporate vision and management style of the people involved in the company's future success.

Typically corporate value statements contain ideas such as the following:

- Customer satisfaction comes first.
- Teamwork is our style.
- Innovation is our way of life.
- The highest ethical standards are our guides.
- We put quality into everything we do.

Canon, a world-class Japanese company, has the following corporate values:[2]

- We respect cultural differences among ourselves, our customers, and our communities.
- We believe that self-awareness, enthusiasm, and responsible behavior are three keys to good results.
- We respect dignity, value initiative, and recognize the merit of each individual. As members of the Canon family of companies, we trust and respect each other and work together in a harmonious atmosphere.
- Above all, we sustain our physical and emotional health in order to lead full and happy lives.

Although statements of corporate values are valuable in establishing an overall atmosphere for people, they can often (depending on how they are presented and on the credibility of the company's senior management) come across sounding like "apple pie and motherhood" and as a symbol of more corporate flag waving. In addition, every corporation's values seem to end up being nearly identical to every other corporation's (there seems to be a certain universalism to "goodness"). However, if presented correctly, I believe they serve a very useful purpose in establishing a corporate umbrella of values for all employees to follow and in which to take pride. The difficult task is not the articulation of the values, but finding a way to encourage employee behavior and performance that supports those values.

Developing Employees with the Right Personal Attributes

Second, successful world-class business performers aggressively seek people with the right personal attributes as a basis for employee retention and retraining, and/or as a basis for their initial hiring. It's easy to create a list of the attributes that anyone would like an employee to have. Traits such as the following come to mind:

- Ambition and drive
- Leadership
- Vision
- Responsiveness
- Perseverance
- Problem-solving skills

- Excellent character
- Integrity
- Efficiency
- Effectiveness
- Teamwork skills
- Interpersonal skills

What's harder for many of today's manufacturing companies is to refine over time its total workforce so that it includes people with only these attributes. For companies establishing plants in new geographic areas, selecting the right people is still hard work but usually can be accomplished much more quickly. The Japanese have proven adept at this in staffing their U.S. auto transplant operations, focusing their effort on picking only the best possible potential employees from huge applicant lists. After all, why not retain or hire the best?

When Nissan was initially staffing its new Smyrna, Tennessee, operation it received 70,000 applications. It carefully reviewed these, and then interviewed and tested about 7000 people—most of whom had never worked in an automotive assembly plant before—before picking 3000 (less than 5 percent) from the applicant pool to start further unpaid training and eventually work for the company.[3] What Nissan was looking for in these job applicants was mainly excellent character, a base level of education, good problem-solving skills, good interpersonal skills, and the ability to work effectively in a team environment. Their new workers didn't have to know a thing about the design and production of automobiles.

Guiding Employees' Thinking and Performance with an Operating Credo

Given that a company has established a statement of corporate values and has created a workforce of people with the right personal attributes, it has still not created any specific guidelines for how it expects its employees to think and perform on their jobs. In my experience, creating a corporate operating credo will go a long way toward accomplishing this and encouraging the transformation to a world-class business environment.

In the following pages, I'll illustrate one such operating credo that was implemented in order to galvanize an organization's action toward lasting positive change. After I discuss its elements, I'll outline a way to successfully implement it so that it does not end up being just another set of slogans on the wall.

Establishing a Credo.   Experience has shown that incremental daily improvement by individuals on their jobs, when aggregated and compounded daily over time, provides far greater and faster positive change in a company than searching for an elusive magic wand, silver bullet, or big bang fix. Improving people's daily job performance can have a powerful impact on improving the effectiveness and efficiency of a company's operations. Nine important principles of the following operating credo have proven themselves to be powerful change drivers when promulgated throughout an organization.

1. **Satisfying our customers—external as well as internal— must always come first. We can only do so by being totally committed to quality in its broadest sense in everything we do.**

Customer satisfaction and the creation of new satisfied customers is the essence of competitive success in business. This requires that the broadest possible view of quality be delivered in every way every day. This also means measuring company performance from the customer's perspective, not by myopic internal company standards. Furthermore, important attitudinal changes so necessary to foster process improvement can be promoted by encouraging each employee to regard the next person in any process as an internal customer who also must be satisfied completely.

2. **Anything that adds cost but not value to our products is waste. The nature of competition will not tolerate waste— and neither must we.**

Given today's intense global competition in all industries, there simply is no room for wasted effort or resources— people, money, or time. Experience tells us that the value-added time as a percentage of total cycle time in most companies' business processes today is less than 10 percent. Survival and growth cannot happen with this handicap. Today's companies are usually organized by function for the convenience of internal management. But customers care only about results, not about their suppliers' internal functions or their organizational structure. Corporations must find ways for cross-functional product- and process-related teams to work in parallel—not serially, by function—as a way to reduce waste.

3. Low cost is a dependent variable, the result of doing other things well. Our superordinate goal is always to be the lowest-cost manufacturer in our marketplace.

Whether a company is a low-cost manufacturer depends on the excellence of their product and process quality, how few assets (inventory, plant, space, people, and so on) it requires to produce a given quantity of product in a given time, how little overhead is required, and other factors. Long-term, competitively successful low cost cannot be achieved by budget cutting—treating cost as an independent variable. Lowest total manufacturing cost also allows more investment in marketing, sales, and R and D relative to higher-cost manufacturers, thus promoting growth without necessarily sacrificing profitability.

4. Systems that permit shared access to timely and accurate information must be the basis of our decision making.

Having the right information to communicate—and the capability to communicate it quickly—is of key importance in today's fast-paced global markets. This demands consistent corporate-wide data definition and management, as well as global telecommunication networks to transmit alphanumeric and geometric data. It also demands on-line access to real-time information and state-of-the-art applications systems that turn data into useful information at a variety of management levels. The most successful companies are run with one set of numbers available to the people who need them for planning and decision making. Information systems must be viewed and utilized as an indispensable competitive asset, not a cost.

The Phillips Petroleum Company, under president Robert Wallace, successfully used more effective information systems to change its corporate culture. The goal of improving its information systems was to streamline operations, promote teamwork, and to empower employees with better information to manage the company. Did these new information systems work? Here are a few quotes from Wallace:

People throughout the organization started to work...
more as a team.

There was a total change in how they [employees]
thought—first of themselves, and more importantly of
their role with respect to others.

I could spin through [review] all of our global operations
in a matter of minutes. . . . I could actually see what was
going on in all the operations.

You just can't believe it. It became an overnight success
story. Unbelievable. It was beyond my wildest expectations. I have seen our system increase the profitability of
Phillips Petroleum Company by $25 million to $40 million
a year in a matter of weeks![4]

**5. Time is our most precious competitive asset. A sense of
urgency must permeate all our activities.**

Time, unlike other assets, cannot be replaced. Companies
that can maximize the output per unit of time of any process
will inherently boost its competitive advantage. Executives in
most companies today are too complacent. They woefully un-
derestimate the degree, scope, and intensity of their global
competition, as well as the time it will take for their company
to gain sufficient competitive advantage to ensure itself a place
in tomorrow's global business world. "Faster" inadequately describes the effort needed. "Urgently faster in every business
process" better states the goal.

One of the key areas where urgency is needed is in today's
executive suite. Yet today's executives often remain trapped in
yesteryear's processes and timetables for decision making.

Kathleen Eisenhardt, an associate professor at Stanford University at summed up her research on how managers can
accelerate decision making:

Overall, fast decision makers use simple, yet powerful tactics to accelerate choices. . . . They maintain constant watch
over real time operating information and rely on fast, comparative analysis of multiple alternatives to speed cogni-

tive processing. They favor approaches to conflict resolution which are quick and yet maintain a cohesive group process. Lastly, their use of advice and integration of decisions and tactics creates the self-confidence needed to make a fast choice, even when the information is limited and stakes are high.

At the other end of the spectrum, slow decision makers become bogged down by the fruitless search for information, excessive development of alternatives, and paralysis in the face of conflict and uncertainty.[5]

6. **We will promote a work environment where each employee acts with integrity and is treated with respect, trust, and compassion. Mistakes, while undesirable, are viewed as learning experiences, not failures.**

Integrity of the individual is the essence of people relationships, both horizontally and vertically. Integrity allows and promotes trust—which then engenders respect (at least for others' views) and compassion for others' human failings. People must be encouraged to dream, to question, to try new ideas, and to contribute new ideas or critique others' by speaking freely. The factors in this principle are fundamental to continuous learning and continuous improvement.

7. **Integrated strategies must be the bedrock of our approach to business. To compete effectively in our global marketplace, we must act with one corporate voice to our markets and customers.**

The term *integrated strategies* means integration vertically as well as horizontally. Vertically, internal functional strategies must support the overall corporate or business unit strategies. Horizontally, all functional or business unit strategies must be consistent with each other—united in support of the corporate or business unit strategies. The intensity of today's global competition leaves no room for maverick functions or business units that either eschew the value of planning or create plans that are not in concert with the plans of other functions or business units. Companies must obtain the greatest possible leverage or effect for their size. To do less is to exist as a collection of small, autonomous business units that, in most cases, are competitively impotent. Integrated strategies ensure one consistent corporate approach to customer satisfaction and market leadership.

8. **Excess complexity in our products, procedures, or organization adds cost—measured in dollars and time—exponentially. We will pursue simplicity as a key to our competitive effectiveness.**

Excess complexity of parts in products, of steps in processes, or of levels (barriers or filters) in communication processes adds cost, both direct and indirect, as well as time to the operation of a business. Simplicity in the pursuit of overall effectiveness and efficiency is the goal. This approach should be differentiated from many current managers' overly simplistic approach to the complex problems inherent in today's business environment.

9. **Our activities must be driven by a theme of continuous improvement wherein our goal each day is to do better than the day before.**

We must expect to achieve quantum leaps in improvement as rapidly as possible. As noted earlier, however, we achieve these quantum leaps through incremental and continuous small victories that are won and compounded daily. Furthermore, goals expressed as future accomplishments often become limits. For a variety of reasons, people often only aspire to the stated goal, never dreaming that far more could be achieved, or purposely saving some progress toward the goal until the next measurement period. Focusing on improving yesterday's performance every day unfetters people and organizations to achieve targets they never dreamed possible. Inherent in the concept of continuous improvement is the theme of continuous learning—continuous improvement of the company's most precious physical asset—its people.

Making The Credo Work.   Initially, management must be sure every employee has a copy of the credo, that it is prominently featured in corporate newsletters and other publications, and that it is displayed in many areas around the corporation's plants and offices. Furthermore, it's vitally important that top management reinforce the credo by personal example and continual reference to its principles if it is to succeed.

A key to reinforcing the vital competitive ideas expressed in the credo is to incorporate them (however each company might choose to modify them) into employee performance ratings. For instance, when personal performance objectives are being established for the year (or, more appropriately for a company aspiring to be a world-class performer, for each of the next four quarters as well as for the year), each employee in the organization should be asked to state how he or she will embody in his or her job each of the nine credo principles. How, specifically, will he eliminate waste in his function? How, specifically, will she personally show a sense of urgency and inculcate a sense of urgency in her organization? Establishing this procedure on a level-by-level basis with personnel throughout the organization really helps to focus their actions and attitudes on living the credo principles daily.

When a credo is first established, it pays to reinforce the credo principles by starting any organization meeting with a question to the employees, asking them to state what any of the credo principles is about. A few weeks later, an employee in a meeting can be randomly picked and asked what he or she is doing on the job to implement any of the credo principles. With such reinforcement, these principles soon become ingrained in the corporation, helping it gain a lasting competitive advantage.

The three human resource factors discussed—using corporate values to establish the right corporate culture, developing employees with the right personal attributes, and guiding employees' thinking and performance with an operating credo—go a long way toward harnessing the power of people in effecting change in an organization. They reflect the fact that it is people who devise and implement strategy and who are the foundation for successful competitors—from business organizations to athletic teams.

Eliminating the Performance Improvement Bottleneck

Experience has shown that the pacing element in organizational change is the human learning process. Throwing money and technology alone at the problem of improving company performance doesn't work, as General Motors amply demonstrated in the 1980s—spending billions on factory automation while losing 11 points in market share. Slogans and flag waving don't work, and neither does a program of the month, quarter, or year.

What does work is establishing the right motivation for a company's workforce and providing it with the knowledge and tools to get the job done. Since people's brains can't be physically injected with information and knowledge, much less wisdom, this demands permanently creating and reinforcing an environment of continual learning and improvement in the business with an ongoing education and training program for all of its people.

Why must companies do this? First, because of changing technology, new materials, and new manufacturing processes, even today's experienced workers need new knowledge to help them become more efficient and effective on the job. Many of these people were never adequately prepared to work in today's manufacturing environment, much less tomorrow's.

Second, it has been amply demonstrated and lamented that our schools certainly are not doing a sufficient job of preparing today's youth to enter business. Many people who graduate from high school today are functionally illiterate and cannot perform simple mathematics, such as calculating a percentage of a number. For many reasons, including consideration of the "raw materials" they get, our universities aren't doing the job either. Many colleges and universities have few, if any, courses at an undergraduate or graduate level in manufacturing and the myriad of subjects needed to completely cover the manufacturing business spectrum—from product and process design to logistics to quality engineering to information management to managing people, to name but a few. The courses that do exist for the most part rest on dated thinking and are taught by professors who have little or no real-world experience in manufacturing or any business. In addition, there is seldom any focus in academia on the integration of these subjects into a comprehensive whole, as there must be in a manufacturing corporation.

Third, much of today's potential workforce may be from other parts of the world and may not speak our language or share our work customs, or they may not have any education at all. Finally, a company might be able to hire people with the right background in a general sense from an applicant pool, but these people must then become acclimatized to the company's specific products, processes, and management style.

Companies can take advantage of courses from local colleges and business and technical schools. But in the end these alone are insufficient as a basis for making the company a world-class performer—most of them are not designed to address the litany of problems noted previously. It is thus inevitable that companies must have their own intensive education and training programs for all their employees.

To eliminate the performance improvement bottleneck, it's no small coincidence that many of the United States' leading manufacturing companies have established their own business or manufacturing "universities" or training centers; examples include Motorola with Motorola University, General Electric with its executive education school at Crotonville, New York, and IBM with its corporate education center at Thornwood, New York.

The design of an effective education and training program must support the company's world-class performance improvement program. This usually means starting by performing a careful analysis of the current educational condition of the workforce. How many can really read English, or can understand what measuring and testing equipment is telling them, or can understand what their supervisor is telling them about what they expect to be done? One electronics company I worked with had elaborate assembly and test instructions written in English and made available at all its shop floor workcenters. They were almost totally useless, though, because the majority of their assembly workers were Vietnamese or Mexican people who could read or speak little or no English.

Once the workforce assessment has been performed, a plan has to be created that starts with the basics and that doesn't get too far ahead of the implementation efforts of the company's performance improvement program. Companies that prematurely educate and train their people only increase the level of frustration with the old way of doing things, raise unrealistic expectations about the timing and impact of new improvements, and end up having to do it all over again if the time between learning and implementation was so great that people forgot a lot of what they learned before they could apply it.

Interestingly, one shouldn't go to Japan asking manufacturing executives there what their companies spend annually on education and training. You—as I did—will get a blank stare. Education and training is such an integral part of the work environment and culture that Japanese manufacturers don't even account for it separately. Maybe some day we won't need to, but for now, the burden of proof for greater education and training—as well as for performance improvement—is upon us. We need the separate accounting to see that the education and training effort is genuinely being made and to serve as a frame of reference for measuring the results. I shall discuss more fully in Chapter 12 what constitutes the appropriate level of education and training effort to move a manufacturing company toward world-class business performance.

Employee Empowerment—A Major Tool for Change in the Right Circumstances

One major key to better performance for manufacturers is an investment in educating and training their people. The other, used after the education and training program is well established, is to empower the company's workers at all levels to make the changes necessary to becoming a world-class performer. This usually means pushing decision making down to a much lower level in the organization. From my experience, it's important to understand a few main points about empowerment.

One, today's workforce cannot be empowered without it first having some education and training about what has to be done and how to do it. Of great benefit in this endeavor is to have established the vision for the company, created the world-class performance improvement program, and to have the company's operating credo in place before the empowerment occurs.

Two, empowerment does not equal permissiveness. It does not mean turning the plant over to the workers. It does not mean the complete freedom for any worker or manager to go off completely alone to solve problems in his or her own way. The establishment and attainment of the corporation's business strategy, its core competencies, and its information systems needed to capture knowledge and communicate effectively, far override that kind of personal freedom in the workplace.

Empowerment works best with clear and well-communicated management goals in place so that all employees will know to what end their efforts are to be expended. Empowerment without this strategic structure is management abdication, and the ensuing leadership vacuum will quickly result in chaos in most aspects of the business.

Peter Senge, who has spent a lifetime teaching and advising corporations about organizational change, says in his book *The Fifth Discipline*,[6]

> To empower people in an unaligned organization can be counterproductive. If people do not share a common vision, and do not share common "mental models" about the business reality within which they operate, empowering people will only increase organizational stress and the burden of management to maintain coherence and direction.

Three, empowerment doesn't require a certain organizational structure. Empowerment is an attitude, and is thus not dependent on physical or organizational location. Its success depends on a free flow of new ideas and new ways of doing things, and on building a real sense of teamwork in the organization.

One guaranteed result of empowering a company's workforce is that this move will place a tremendous burden on foremen and supervisors. In fact, some of them, even with the best support, won't be able to handle their new work environment. Consider the traditional role of the foreman or supervisor—the source of all knowledge and authority within his or her area, thinker or problem solver for the work unit, usually capable of performing any job in the department, and often without much formal education or training in interpersonal skills or in motivating workers. Suddenly, new education and training programs and empowerment shift the responsibility for problem solving and decision making to the shop floor worker below the foreman. The foreman's new job is to be a motivator and coach. In the new environment, the authority to give orders and get things done his or her way-is eroded, if not completely removed. Companies need to pay special attention to working with their supervisors and foremen when pursuing the new work environment needed for the attainment of world class business performance. Educating and training these people in motivational and coaching techniques to replace their ingrained top-down style can have a critical effect on the overall success of the company's empowerment program.

Fostering Employee Support for Change

What do people really want from their employers? At a micro level, the answer is different for each person. Some want money and advancement. Some want political power. Some want independent fame. Many studies have shown that money is not the best motivator of people. What often counts more is personal recognition, the feeling of belonging to a group, and the knowledge that they and their group are making a difference in their company's performance. At a higher level, it's my experience that most people want to be assured that their company will champion their personal growth—no matter how they individually measure that—in exchange for their commitment and hard work.

There are two broad stages of enlisting a company's people in support of its world-class performance program. Stage one is eliminating active or passive resistance to change within the company. Because such resistance to change affects all humans, eliminating it requires an open and honest management style and a great deal of education and training about such fundamental and often overlooked ideas as "Why are we doing this?" "Why do we have to be world-class performers?" "How will this affect me?" and "What will happen if the company doesn't do this?"

The easiest and fastest way to overcome such employee resistance to change (unless a company must immediately downsize for survival) is a guarantee of permanent employment in some job within the corporation. This, however, should not be done without a careful study of the company's workforce demographics and a careful analysis of the overall company's growth potential. Note that I said *some* job—not necessarily the employee's current job. The message is that if the worker has or can acquire the basic educational skills, has the right attitude, and is willing to undergo company sponsored reeducation and training, there will usually be a spot reserved for him or her on the company's payroll.

Whether such a guarantee can be established depends on the company's current performance status. Many companies' productivity is as low as $50,000 to $60,000 sales per worker per year. No matter what their industry, it is clear that this must be improved by a factor of three just to be average—not even world-class—performers. Employment guarantees for every worker are the last thing possible in such situations.

Stage two is to take the now neutral workforce and get it to support the program and actively contribute to its success in as short a time as possible. An effective way to accomplish this is to include workers or their representatives in creating and planning the world-class improvement program. Actually, experience tells me the workforce conversion never quite happens in discrete stages as described above. There will be some people from all levels of the company way out front in leading the changes. Others will resist and be the last to change. Still others won't change and will have to be let go. Nonetheless, even for the chargers, it's useful to think of eliminating the reasons for resistance before adding the reasons for support in moving toward world-class performance goals.

In working with the people side of world-class performance in some companies, I have often heard that a particular individual has to be fired—he or she is "no good anymore." Our initial response to such a statement is, "Wasn't that person good when you hired her (him)?" Inevitably, the answer is yes—when that person first arrived on the job, he or she was full of energy and ideas, was extremely enthusiastic and motivated, and really had the company's best interest at heart. The obvious next question, given that there are no political, personal, or health issues involved, is, "If all this is so, then what have you (the company) done (or not done) to demotivate or destroy this person? What barriers have you put in the way to sap your employees' energy and enthusiasm—bureaucracy, the not-invented-here syndrome, the 'you don't understand our industry or company' attitude? How have you not supported them with education and training and career advancement opportunities?" One company that I have worked with has had the same plant manager in one of its plants for 16 years! What a roadblock to people's growth—including the plant manager's. Before replacing an employee, one should consider who's really at fault and how that employee's initial job energy and willingness to contribute ideas for the company's betterment might be rekindled.

Roger Penske has put a lot of the ideas that we have covered so far in this chapter to work in his revitalization of Detroit Diesel Corporation. He purchased 80 percent of ownership of the company from General Motors and implemented his unique flavor of management in a company that had been on the ropes with a loss of market share for diesel engines from 28 percent to 3 percent in 1987. Penske has been successful with the same senior management and workforce that did so poorly under GM. He started with a TEAM approach, in which

T is for teamwork

E is for effort

A is for attitude

M is for manage your business, manage your job, and manage your personal life

The key to Penske's success has been his ability to change the operating culture of the company and inspire his employees to do better quality work with more discipline and speed. This has resulted in world-class productivity of $400,000 in sales per employee for Detroit Diesel.[7]

Organizational Structure—How Much Does It Matter?

There is considerable debate about the effects of size and organization structure in regard to becoming a world-class performance company. I have already touched on the influence of plant size on a company's cost structure and operating effectiveness in Chapter 5. From a structural point of view, in the last 10 to 15 years a movement from highly centralized organizations such as shown in Exhibit 6-1 to highly decentralized ones as shown in Exhibit 6-2 has taken place. These two exhibits as well as Exhibit 6-3 are, of course, logical views and do not convey any geographical meaning.

But the move to decentralization in many companies has simply spread the overhead horizontally instead of vertically. In fact, there is some hard evidence that decentralization costs

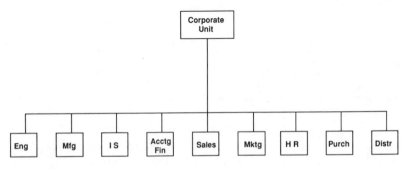

FROM CENTRALIZED.......

Exhibit 6-1 A centralized organization structure.

TO DECENTRALIZED.......

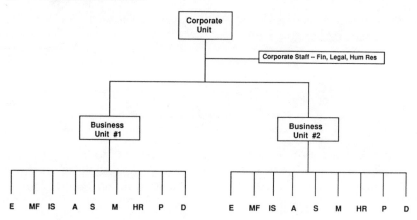

Exhibit 6-2 A decentralized organization structure.

more. An A. T. Kearney study of one company's finance department showed costs of 1.3 percent of sales for the centralized operation versus 2.7 percent of sales for the decentralized business environment.[8] I believe that the pendulum is swinging back toward centralization—but in a unique way, as pic-

TO NEW HYBRID

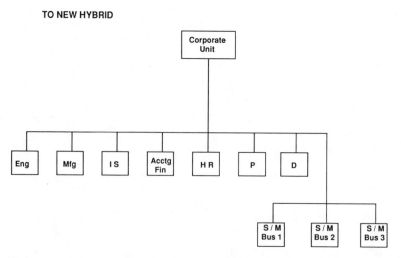

Exhibit 6-3 The future hybrid organization structure.

tured in Exhibit 6-3. In this new hybrid structure, sales and marketing will remain highly decentralized and allied to their brand names and market identity. Their current distribution channels will thus be preserved. These small autonomous sales and marketing units will preserve their entrepreneurial atmosphere and focus on their ability to stay close to the customer and foster innovation in their products and services.

On the other hand, operations will be more centralized. Product and process engineering, production, purchasing, distribution, production control, and materials management need to be highly integrated. The goal is centralized coordination and decentralized execution. The need for centralized coordination places a critical importance on the company possessing state-of-the-art information systems utilizing real-time information available throughout the (global) corporation.

This new hybrid organization will enable far more effective management of flows of both materials and information rather than functions. These flows, of course, refer to the bases of the critical business processes discussed in Chapter 3. In other words, tomorrow's world-class performance organizations will be structured to best serve the customer and attain a superior return on assets—plants; design, production, and distribution technology; space; and people.

One thing that we can predict with certainty is that organizational structure will continue to change. In part, this change will take place in response to new market opportunities and strategic changes in direction within the company. But we also have to recognize the reality that organization structure is often a function of people—personal relationships within the company's senior management team—and politics. These factors are continually in play as people leave the company because of death, retirement, or another job, and as new people enter the company fresh in their careers or recruited into senior management positions.

Thus, despite the fact that many companies are permanently embroiled in a highly emotional, political, and counterproductive debate about whether the company should be centralized or decentralized, it seems useless to make this the issue. In my experience it is a red herring in terms of improving the company's performance. It erroneously sets up organization structure as a major factor affecting a company's performance. The real performance issue is how quickly the company can create a set of superior corporate core capabilities around which any organization structure is possible without degrading the company's operating performance. That is, the real issue should be how quickly the company can build the right skill and information system infrastructure around the superb execution of the company's fundamental business processes relating to serving its customers with distinction.

We know that there will be much less hierarchy in tomorrow's organizations. This is primarily caused by work flow simplification of the company's fundamental business processes, and by the dramatic productivity increases and communication efficiencies brought about by modern information systems. We will also see in Chapter 7 how information technology can be used to overcome geographical separation and integrate disparate company locations into one logical or virtual organization.

Certainly a major influence on organization size and structure is the trend toward outsourcing services traditionally performed within a manufacturing company. The most common of these contracted services probably are those of security, food services, and building cleaning. But in keeping with the exhortations of Professor Brian Quinn and other leading strategists, all other services performed in a manufacturing company are candidates for outsourcing. Quinn and his coauthors point out in his excellent article "Beyond Products: Services-Based Strategy"[9] that a manufacturing company really includes a collection of service organizations—potentially everything from product and process design to purchasing to distribution to customer order entry to operation of the company's information processing centers. Quinn advocates that, to the extent that these services can be performed more effectively and at a lower cost by outside organizations, they ought to be. In other words, no internal business function should be safe from external free market competition.

The key is to recognize which services performed in the organization are or should be a part of the corporation's strategic core competencies, and thus should be performed in-house to keep and further hone proprietary skills and technologies. For instance, some manufacturers have outsourced the operation of their information system data centers because they are essentially giant engines that routinely process data and maintain communication networks. However, some of these manufacturers have preserved their own data definition and management capabilities, as well as their applications programming staffs to the extent they are needed to integrate application software packages or design proprietary information systems that provide competitive advantage to the company.

Perhaps the biggest value of outsourcing is the threat of it to the company's traditional internal functions and service organizations. It's amazing how these traditional company units can find ways to improve their services and become more cost effective when faced with outside competition. I do not mean to deride the substantial improvements many outside service organizations can bring to companies that have little chance of duplicating their results—particularly in the short term, when performance improvement is so vital to the company's survival.

People remain at the center of any company's efforts to become a world-class performer. Their contribution to the company's competitive success will only gain importance as technology and better use of information systems provide companies with enormous productivity increases relative to today's average levels. It's simple: with fewer people in a company for a given sales and performance level, each person's importance to the company's success rises commensurately. Smart companies recognize this by making a real investment in their people's future—for people *are* the company's future.

Chapter 6

1. Thomas A. Stewart, "GE Keeps Those Ideas Coming," *Fortune*, 12 August 1991, pp. 41–49.

2. "Canon and Technology," *Forbes*, 2 September 1991.

3. See *Automotive News*, 14 March 1983, p. E7; *Automotive News*, 13 February 1984, p. 16; and *Automotive News*, 7 October 1985, p. D8.

4. Mary E. Boone, "Computers Reshape Phillips 66," *Industry Week*, 1 July 1991, pp. 12–18.

5. Kathleen M. Eisenhardt, "Speed and Strategic Choice: How Managers Accelerate Decision Making," *California Management Review*, Vol. 32, No. 3, pp. 1–16.

6. Peter Senge, *The Fifth Dimension* (New York: Doubleday Currency), 1990, p. 146.

7. Joseph B. White, "How Detroit Diesel Out from Under GM Turned Around Fast," *Wall Street Journal*, 16 August 1991, p. 1.

8. "Odds & Ends," *Wall Street Journal*, 25 January 1990, p. B1.

9. J. B. Quinn et al., "Beyond Products: Services-Based Strategy," *Harvard Business Review*, March–April 1990, pp. 58–67.

7

Using Information Systems as a Competitive Weapon

The world has witnessed an unparalleled rate of change in information technology in the last four decades, since the invention of the transistor and solid-state electronics. This rate of change has left even information systems cognoscenti and advocates gasping for breath. It's no wonder that it has left the average manufacturing executive completely in the dark—bewildered, apprehensive, and unappreciative of how (and how much) information technology can benefit his or her business both financially and strategically.

Given this state of affairs, the biggest challenge for vendors and informed advocates of information systems within a manufacturing company is to change executives' attitudes about information systems so that they view information systems as a competitive asset and strategic tool, not just another business cost. I know of no way to do this other than to continually educate top management about all aspects of information systems in general terms while emphasizing their business benefits, not their underlying hardware and software technology.

Luckily, many of today's top executives are more computer-literate than those of a decade ago. Many of them use a personal computer today (sometimes at home but not at work), or at least had to at one time while in college or graduate school. In addition, many have children who routinely use computers for schoolwork and entertainment and eagerly share some of their experiences with their parents. However, today's executive's computing experience is a two-edged sword. On the positive side, it causes the experienced user to ask, "Why can't our business systems be this user-friendly?" (This concern arises especially if he or she uses an Apple Macintosh, a PC, or a PC clone with Microsoft Windows 3.0.) In addition, it teaches management something about the need for consistent data definition and security, and about the power of using the same applications software across a group of people or business units. It might also prompt the user to ask, "Why can't we just instantly access the data we need from anywhere in the world?" But on the negative side, such computer use does little to give him or her an appreciation of the business and technical issues involved in applying information systems to an entire manufacturing enterprise in a structured, consistent, and failsafe manner that is modular and upwardly scalable to accommodate changing business conditions and company growth.

A few JIT zealots are urging their readers or clients to throw out their computers and run their plants with kanban signs, colored golf balls, and the like. Although simplification of a business process before computerization is a must (as discussed in Chapter 3), there is simply no way for a modern manufacturing company to be a world-class performer without the extensive utilization of information systems in all aspects of its business. Why is this so?

Properly programmed, computers are well known for their ability to quickly analyze huge amounts of data and to communicate the results of the analytical algorithm in the form of information at practically the speed of light to the user. Originally, no one really needed a computer, just like no one really needed an automobile. But once one person had an automobile and enjoyed its benefits of speed, quality of ride, comfort, flexibility, and productivity, everyone "needed" an automobile. And then everyone needed the latest automobile with even better performance. In addition, we needed better roads to provide ready access to more places.

The cycle is the same with computers. Once one business enjoys their benefits of speed, quality, flexibility, productivity, and convenience, all businesses must utilize computers or they will quickly become uncompetitive. However, we also need access through electronic networks to more data from more places to most effectively utilize these new tools. And thus, the great computerization race is on, propelled by a quest for user benefits and competitive advantage on the one hand, and fed by the greatest rate of change of any technology invented to date on the other.

In 1991 information system managers predict their need for mainframe MIPS (millions of instructions per second) will grow by 23 percent per year, and their disk storage needs will grow by 27 percent per year over the next three to five years to handle new applications and the implementation of newer technologies such as document and image processing, voice mail, and electronic mail.[1] There seem to be no limits to user's demands for greater processing speed and more data storage.

Many have argued that computers aren't that flexible or productive or don't provide that many quality benefits. But those opinions have more to do with many people's and companies' learning experience with utilizing them effectively, not necessarily the nature of the product itself. It is true that computers have become more economical and user-friendly in recent years, and they can and will become even more cost-effective and user-friendly—indeed, someday they will be almost totally transparent to the user.

We often take for granted the information systems in place today and the management information they provide—no matter how far from ideal they are. But consider the alternatives. One would involve hiring back masses of people to manipulate all that data and provide accurate and timely information to run the business of today. The second alternative would involve doing without much of the information that managers of manufacturing companies have at their fingertips today. Although some managers and companies could do without some of the information they receive today, this idea is just out of the question for any company that wishes to remain competitive across the market, organizational, and geographic span its business occupies.

Riding the Wave of Information Technology Change

On virtually every front, change of information systems technology is still occurring with few limits in sight. Consider these examples.

In the mid-1950s it took 800 cubic feet of space to store two megabytes of data.[2] (Two megabytes of data would represent about 1600 pages of double-spaced typewritten text. By convention, a character—the letter a, for instance—is represented by one byte, which, in turn, is made up of eight bits.) Eight hundred cubic feet is a cube about 111 inches on each side. Today, with the advent of the 2-megabyte (16-megabit) chip made possible by 0.5 micron line width technology (a micron is a millionth of a meter, or about 9.8 millionths of an inch), we can store this amount of information in 0.000036 cubic feet— 36 millionths of a cubic foot! And four to five years from now, with the advent of 0.25 micron line width technology in DRAM chips, we'll be able to store 16 times that amount of data— 32 megabytes, or 25,600 double-spaced typewritten pages—in the same-sized chip, which measures about one-third by three-fourths by one-fourth of one inch. In every memory chip generation over the past 20 years, memory has increased by a factor of four while size has been reduced by a factor of 1.5 every three years.[3]

A recent *Scientific American* article describes data storage progress another way:

> From 1950 to 1990, the number of atoms required to store a single bit of information dropped from 100 billion billion to one billion. If progress continues at that rate, magnetic storage systems should pass the 100,000 atoms per bit before the year 2000.[4]

Consider also the advances in microprocessor power since its invention in 1971. The original Intel 4004 microprocessor contained 2300 transistors, in contrast to the i860XP announced in 1991 that has 2,600,000 transistors.[5] Every year for the last 30 years, MIPS per chip has increased by 50 percent, circuit density by 40 percent, and clock speed by 20 percent. During this time, the price performance in MIPS per dollar has improved by 1 million to one.[6]

This kind of progress will allow astonishing advances in products that we assume are fully developed today. For instance, think about today's video camera, already the subject of a wave of miniaturization efforts to a handheld size over the past three years by Japanese electronics companies. Researchers at Edinburgh University in Scotland have invented a computer chip

> . . . that can hold the complete circuitry of a video camera. Lens and all, the chip is the size of a postage stamp. The retail price of the camera—which may be available as early as next spring [1992]—could be as low as $40.[7]

And yet today's technologies pale before the advances of the next 10 to 20 years, when nanoelectronics and quantum transistors will allow switching speeds up to 1000 times faster than anything we now have available.[8]

In telecommunications, the increases in data transmission speed shown in Exhibit 7-1 have been no less impressive. To-

	Megabits per second
ETHERNET	10
usual exchange	1 - 2
T1 LINE	1.544
TOKEN RING	16
T3 LINE	45
NETWORK SYSTEMS HYPERCHANNEL	50
FIBER DISTRIBUTED DATA INTERFACE (FDDI)	100
NWS DATAPIPE/DX	380

Exhibit 7-1 Telecommunication speed performance.

day, fiber optic systems represent the state of the art in being able to handle large amounts of data at very high speeds. Such a rate of technological change in information systems technology has powerful implications for the future role of today's mainframe computers vis-a-vis personal computers and workstations.

There are two business management questions associated with the technological advances discussed previously. First, how can a manufacturing company embed that kind of information technology in its products to provide value-added benefits for its customers? Second, how can manufacturing company managers embed it in their management processes to bring about a more effective, efficient, and competitive company?

Stepping up to the Computer Integrated Enterprise

For maximum competitive performance, it's critical at the start to take the broadest possible view of data and information management in a manufacturing company. I call this "stepping up to the computer-integrated enterprise." Traditionally, in any manufacturing company, the head of information systems usually only has (or thinks he or she has) responsibility for business information systems: alphanumeric data such as that commonly found in sales, accounting, and materials management systems. But there are two more important sets of data to manage.

The first of these is engineering, or geometric, data—used in computer-aided design (CAD) systems to describe the tangible products the company manufactures. Engineering systems have grown somewhat haphazardly in many companies, often with no person formally in charge of them. Because no single CAD system does everything well, for example, both mechanical and electrical design, and because of the several stages of evolution CAD systems have gone through historically, it's not uncommon for manufacturing companies to have several—sometimes 10 to 15—CAD systems in use throughout several divisions. Someone has to be responsible for rationalizing the engineering data and applications found on these many engineering systems and for integrating them to the extent that is both possible and practical with the company's business information systems.

In many manufacturing companies, there's yet another set of data to be managed: process control data, or the real-time process feedback coming from semi- or fully automated production machinery such as plastic injection molders, flexible manufacturing cells or systems, heat-treating ovens, plating operations, and so on. Data from these systems often references or feeds quality, scheduling, safety, and material movement systems used elsewhere in the business.

So the real job of the company's information czar is to step up to the computer-integrated enterprise and manage all three kinds of data as well as their application systems and underlying infrastructure. One approach would be to have one person—the company's chief information officer (CIO), in fact if not in title—be responsible for managing the company's engineering, business, and manufacturing process or automation systems, as well as for managing the data definition and management, telecommunications, and operating hardware and system architecture underlying each general system. Only then will the company make the most integrated and effective use of its data on a corporate and cross-functional basis; only then will the greatest opportunity exist to leverage the power of information systems on a strategic and financial basis.

The Importance of Data Definition and Management

In my experience, most manufacturing companies have a real need to accurately define the data—all three types discussed above—that they utilize in their business. These data will be sorted and analyzed by the company's information systems, turned into the information needed to effectively run the business, and communicated to the employees who need it.

Data must be defined in a standard manner across the corporation in order to obtain the most effective use of them. A bolt in a plant in Iowa should be called a bolt in the company's other plants, not a capscrew, so that common design or purchasing requirements for fasteners can be pooled across the corporation. Part numbering schemes should be standardized: for instance, into two digits, a dash, then six to eight digits, with no intelligence contained therein. Such conventions will have big paybacks for the application of standard computer programs (whether they are commercial packages, or developed in-house) and for the corporate use of data for rationalization efforts or to save other corporate business units from developing something that already exists elsewhere in the corporation.

Once data are consistently defined across the corporation, it must then be managed effectively. This involves organizing data into different data bases—first logically, then physically. In the logical organization, we might establish backorder information in the company's sales information data base, while placing the weight of each part in a product in the product data base in engineering, which can be accessed by the company's bill of materials application software. Then, requirements for physical distribution of the data can be analyzed to decide at which company locations it will be needed—one or many—and on what floppy disk or hard disk drive (or even tape reel) it will exist.

The data definition and flow analysis is an integral part of sound information systems planning that must occur in all manufacturing companies. Today, many of these steps are built into computer-aided software engineering, or CASE, tools available in the information systems marketplace. Such tools are important for achieving a high level of software quality, good documentation, and high software development productivity. CASE tools are growing more integrated and sophisticated every year. One of their primary goals is to someday automatically and quickly generate applications code based on functional requirements. Practically, this remains an elusive goal today.

In companies that used CASE tools from early on, experience shows that their first use is a learning experience that proceeds only somewhat faster than conventional analysis and coding techniques. It is in the succeeding applications of the CASE tool that real productivity improvements of 20 percent to 40 percent show up, as well as substantial improvements in the quality of the code and its documentation.

Of growing importance in today's business environment is the establishment of global telecommunications networks that are able to transmit quickly and cost-effectively both alphanumeric and geometric data between your company's facilities as well as from your company to and from your customers and suppliers. Exhibit 7-2 shows how, in the United States alone, network services will be transmitting far larger amounts of data with far less voice communication. Revenues from data transmission will double by the year 2000 on a percentage basis, but will increase by a factor of 6.6 in absolute terms.

U.S. VENDOR REVENUES FOR NETWORK SERVICES

	% 1989	% FCST 2000
VOICE	72	39
DATA	11	22
PRIVATE NETWORKS	9	18
HOME INFOTAINMENT INCL CABLE TV	7	17
IMAGE (FAX)	1	3
VIDEO (VIDEO CONF / CORP TV)	-	1
TOTAL MARKET REVENUES	$220 B	$725 B

Exhibit 7-2 Telecommunication network usage.[9] (Source: Networking Management magazine, January 1990, pg. 16, "The
networking industry: Reshaping for the millennium," by
John Gantz.)

With the use of these global networks and the right application software, well-managed companies can gain a significant
competitive advantage. For instance, Digital Equipment Corporation (DEC) can close its worldwide financial books in seven
to eight days from the end of any accounting period.[10] Most
global companies anywhere near DEC's size take 15 to 35 days
to accomplish the same thing. Imagine how much more closely
DEC can stay on top of its financial, cost, and asset management tasks with such timely information. They can react two
to five times faster to any negative or positive financial picture.
This is the essence of world-class performance.

Most manufacturers are ensuring their competitive mediocrity by spending a woefully insufficient amount on their information systems. The problem is that no one can say what
the right amount of spending must be as a percentage of
sales or by any other measure. It's my judgment that leading manufacturers around the world are spending between 5
percent and 10 percent of sales for all their information system
needs on all three types of systems: business, engineering, and
process control telecommunications.

Indeed, even though inadequate, the investment level in computers and telecommunications in U.S. companies now runs from one-third to one-half of companies' total capital spending on equipment.[11, 12] As long ago as 1988, Japanese businesses were spending 25.2 percent of total corporate capital investment on information equipment and software.[13] Peter Keen makes an eloquent argument in his latest book, *Shaping The Future*, that the traditional view of managing the information systems function as an expense is shortsighted and impairs the role that modern information systems can play in ensuring a company's competitive success. In his view,

> ... management must develop an asset, instead of a budget, view of these costs. This means funding the corporate infrastructure separately from business applications. The infrastructure is a shared corporate resource that enables a range of foreseeable and unpredictable uses. Telecommunications networks, shared data base management resources, and security and network management utilities are all part of the infrastructure and should be funded by top corporate or divisional management as a long-range capital investment justified by corporate policy requirements.[14]

Yet year after year, the majority of U.S. manufacturers manage to spend for information systems at a rate averaging about 1.5 percent to 2.5 percent of sales. When these levels of spending are multiplied over ten years or more, the low spenders cumulatively fall quickly behind the leaders. This is especially so when today's dollar spent on information systems offers a 200 percent to 1000 percent improvement in performance over what money spent on information systems in 1980 bought, excluding the effects of inflation.

These numbers are the average in the United States, yet I have seen many companies that were spending about 1 percent of sales on information systems. Their only saving grace is that when and if they wake up, they will pay less for to-day's information technology than they would have for yester-day's. But unfortunately, it will take them years and a lot of money to educate and train their people to effectively utilize the new information systems technology they have to acquire. In the end, the cost savings for today's better hardware tech-nology will be relatively negligible to them. These companies are uncompetitive and will have to work long and hard to dig themselves out of their information systems and manage-ment hole.

The information I have given comes from my practical experi-ence according to information system spending as a percentage of sales—a crude measurement figure that has been used in in-dustry for years. I do not mean to imply that spending a lot of money in itself will guarantee a competitive or even effective business organization. There is no proven correlation between information systems spending and a corporation's total busi-ness success.[15] However, all other things being equal—good planning, an integrated approach, sound management of in-formation resources, and so forth—the companies spending more are getting more in competitive benefits from their infor-mation systems. Could they be doing even better? The answer is, in most cases, yes.

Paul Strassman, a noted information systems and strategic planning executive who formerly worked for Xerox, has spent a considerable amount of time attempting to prove that effective spending on information systems has a big competitive payoff. His latest book on the matter, *The Business Value of Computers*, peels away the mystery surrounding this subject and develops a new way to evaluate information system spending and the effective management of information systems.

First, he develops a new return-on-management (R-O-M) measure based on value-added to evaluate the effective use of information technology in making companies more competi-tive. Next, he separates management activities from operations activities according to the following criteria:

- Operations constitutes all activities essential to deliver products and services to today's customers.
- Management constitutes all activities not in operations.

Then he notes that it is not the absolute level of information systems spending that is important, but where money is spent on information systems within the corporation. One of his many valuable findings is that, by his R-O-M measure,

> Only Over-achievers [those with R-O-Ms over 175 percent] spent more of their total information technology on mission critical Operations systems than on Management information systems. This shows that information technology should apply where it has a direct and favorable effect on the generation of revenues.[16]

As one might expect, this confirms the need to understand the manufacturing business from a strategic viewpoint and to understand where financial and strategic leverage lie as a guide to effective spending on information systems that process all three kinds of company data—business, engineering, and process control.

Exploiting the Downsizing Trend

As I noted, the pace of the price performance curve has been electrifying in computing technology over the past 20 years—so much so, in fact, that it has outstripped many companies' capacity to absorb it. Many companies are just now experiencing 30 percent to 40 percent cuts in information systems costs by converting from a mainframe computing environment to a minicomputer-based one on equipment like IBM's AS/400, DEC's VAXs, H-P's HP9000s, and the like. But this is only the beginning!

In some companies, especially large ones, mainframes will still be needed but will exist solely as a repository for the corporation's data, and, as such, a main hub in its telecommunications network. The application software used by each of the corporation's businesses and functions will be distributed to its users' sites, as will much of the data used in the day-to-day running of the business. Distributed data bases will keep themselves updated concurrently, and each will have adequate security and backup and recovery safeguards.

Many functional business applications are today being run on minicomputers. But changing computing technology is way ahead of most companies. What's becoming increasingly possible is putting most applications and even local data base sources (file servers, in today's lingo) on local-area-networked personal computers or workstations working in a DOS, OS/2, or UNIX operating system environment. Experience shows that another 20 percent to 30 percent savings is often possible in this environment. The growing sophistication of local area network (LAN) management software from Novell, Microsoft, and Banyan will make these systems even more effective and cost-effective in the future.

Most companies are not aware of how fast things are moving with regard to this scenario. How much is technology on the side of the microcomputer? A recent study described in *Computerworld*[17] showed that mainframe "horsepower," measured in MIPS per engine, has increased about 20 percent annually since 1981. In the same period microcomputer MIPS—measured comparatively—have been increasing at a 52 percent annual growth rate. Mainframe cost per MIP is currently about $100,000, while today's PC MIPS cost about $2000 to $3000 per MIP. The cost per MIP on a mainframe has thus been decreasing by about 11 percent per year. The comparative number for PCs is 27 percent per year. Because their price performance ratio is so attractive, it is inevitable that microcomputers are going to win this marketplace battle. What are the implications for manufacturers?

The first is that many small manufacturers are already using these computers and networks as a basis for running their integrated manufacturing resource planning (MRP) and financial applications software. One of the most significant findings from their experience is that the implementation of these systems goes much faster (often 3 to 6 months instead of 9 to 18 months) and is much more effective. This is caused by the sense of ownership the users develop for these systems. The system belongs to them, not to the information systems function. The computers are out in the everyday working environment, not in a hermetically sealed room in the company's offices. The users, not the information system people, implement the systems. The key to the successful use of these systems is to use only object code in them so that each corporate user can't uniquely modify the fundamental code. Thus, when upgrades become available, as occurs frequently with any new technology, the entire company can quickly take advantage of the new applications features and benefits.

Many larger manufacturers have wrongly concluded that these "little systems" aren't for them because their plants are too large or their businesses are too complex. But a new way of thinking about their business—or, more properly, *businesses*—can change the picture entirely.

As an example, suppose a manufacturer had one monolithic business in a 500,000-square-foot plant and was using either a mainframe or a powerful minicomputer to run the entire materials management (often MRP) and finance-accounting applications for the factory. By splitting the one business into three or four businesses based on product families, each business could be made more entrepreneurial—even a profit center. In addition, we could give each business a LAN microcomputer-based system with an integrated MRP and finance-accounting package. Kodak is doing this on a large scale, giving each plant or plant-within-a-plant its own PC-based LAN and Fourth Shift's integrated MRP/finance/accounting package. They now have over 50 of these systems implemented and have bought more than 100 for further implementation.[18] Such is the way of the future. With further increases in computing power and network management effectiveness, it will soon be possible to network hundreds of microcomputers together, with each running state-of-the-art application packages on distributed data bases.

Some people are legitimately worried about data security in such an environment of distributed microcomputers. One way some companies are currently getting around this is to have only (or mostly) diskless computers on the network. People access the data they need and download it from a data base on the corporate mainframe or a file server in a local area network, work with it, and, if need be, send it back to its source, modified and ready for further use. This minimizes risk from people stealing company data or information, or from computer viruses, for that matter.

There are two caveats necessary in evaluating the feasibility and attractiveness of downsizing to distributed microcomputer-based networks. The first is that, given today's accounting practices, there may be many hidden or not easily identifiable costs associated with the distributed computing environment compared to the mainframe environment, where all expenses are more easily identified and aggregated in one cost center. So today's apparently large savings promised by downsizing may not materialize to the extent predicted, depending on the application and business environment. Second, the nature of distributed computing mandates *even more* planning and standard setting, operational discipline, and education and training than needed in a mainframe environment if the networked systems are to be operationally effective, secure, and easily changeable or upgradable. These caveats, however, apply to many applications of new and more distributed technology of any kind. Prudent managers will observe these cautions and in doing so may slow—but not stop—the inevitable move to networked distributed microcomputer-based informations systems in most businesses.

Companies should ultimately be using computers to add value to their products and services for their customers and to gain competitive advantage by changing the basis of competition in their industry. This is shown in Exhibit 7-3, my enhancement of a graph developed by Michael Porter.

Unfortunately, most manufacturers are still mired in stages one and two. Only a few are working strategically and in a corporate manner on stages three and four. Even fewer are working on stages five and six, where the real payoff lies, not that gaining competitive advantage using information systems (or any other technology) is easy or provides very permanent competitive advantage these days. However, world-class companies today are looking for and using every competitive advantage tool possible to maintain their competitive lead.

Nowhere is this more true than in Japan, where many top companies are laboring mightily to design and implement on a global basis integrated sales, logistics, and manufacturing systems as well as to integrate their engineering systems with manufacturing.

Sharp Corporation, a top Japanese electronics company, is establishing a global telecommunications infrastructure to link 52 corporate centers in 30 countries. The system will be used to provide real-time information to all employees about global

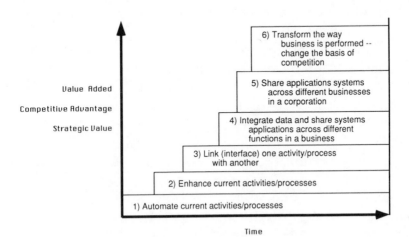

Exhibit 7-3 Six stages of information systems utilization.[19] (Copyright 1989 by CW Publishing, Inc., Framingham, MA 01701– reprinted from *ComputerWorld*.)

logistics and the communication of design data. Two expected benefits, when the system is completed in 1992 (it is nearly 80 percent complete now), are a three-week reduction in inventory and a 30-day reduction in procurement leadtime—"the equivalent of a month's work by 60 office staff."[20]

Sony Corporation has a similar effort underway to link its more than 60 major plants and marketing offices in more than ten countries. In an article describing Sony efforts, two quotes are significant:

> Sony is committed to the Computer Integrated Enterprise. . . . The goal is to speed up our business. . . . That's strategic.[21]

An earlier article describing Sony's efforts states,

> Sony intends to . . . create a new global computer integrated manufacturing system.[22]

These new global telecommunication networks not only are being designed to link offices and facilities within the four walls of their global company, but are being extended to other applications outside the company.

Ford Motor Company, through its direct data link (DDL) program, now lets its suppliers have direct computer access to its Materials System III, a corporate inventory control system in Detroit. In this case, up to 1500 suppliers can get real time information about inventory status and shipments in transit of their parts for each of Ford's 17 North American assembly plants. In providing this system, Ford has made each supplier responsible for identifying shortages of its products and remedying the situation—which gives them an opportunity to eliminate or reassign a substantial number of the 95 expediters that Ford used to perform this function previously. Ford also benefits by having substantially fewer production stoppages because of part shortages. Their suppliers are happier, too, because they have more control over their own success as a Ford supplier.[23]

At Phillips Petroleum, the same information systems mentioned in Chapter 6 also provide links to the company's major customers. Phillips executives can communicate by electronic mail with customer executives, thus promoting more informal and much more frequent contact with them. In addition, Phillip's information systems allow its executives to scan external databases to pick up news from trade associations and the legislative front on matters that may be of importance to the company.[24]

There is little question that many leading global manufacturers are moving quickly to realize the many competitive benefits that a corporate infrastructure of computing and networking applications can bring to their business. The only question that remains is when the rest of the pack will see the light and get on with this critical task, before they are no longer competitive at any level in an industry's rankings. Clearly, if a company is not already thinking about this task and planning for it, it is already way behind. Start catching up, *now.*

Chapter 7

1. J. Moad, "Demand Solid, Budgets Soft," *Datamation*, 1 June 1991, pp. 74–77.
2. Charles P. Lecht, "To Dream, Perhaps of DRAMS," *Computerworld*, 2 February 1987, p. 17.
3. Derek Leebaert, (Ed.), *Technology 2001* (Cambridge, MA: The MIT Press), 1991, pp. 47–48.
4. Russell Ruthen, "Quantum Magnets," *Scientific American*, July 1991, p. 28.
5. S. K. Yoder, "Intel Announces New Rics Chip, Plant Closing," *Wall Street Journal*, 6 June 1991.
6. John Gantz, "Advanced Technology: Where Is It Leading Us?" *Networking Management*, May 1990, pp. 33–48.

7. "The Incredible Shrinking Cam," *ID Systems*, August 1991, p. 10.

8. Otis Port, "Creating Chips One Atom at a Time," *Business Week*, 29 July 1991, pp. 54–55.

9. John Gantz, "The Networking Industry," *Networking Management*, January 1990, pp. 33–48.

10. Digital Equipment Corporation public relations materials and conversations with Peter E. Brown, DEC's corporate telecommunications manager.

11. "Capital Punishment?" *The Economist*, 18 May 1991, p.72; see also Howard Banks, "What's Ahead for Business," *Forbes*, 16 September 1991, p. 35.

12. Peter G. W. Keen, *Shaping the Future* (Cambridge, MA: Harvard Business School Press), 1991, p. 50.

13. Hiroshi Nakajima, "Japan Firms Turn Information into Profit," *The Japan Economic Journal*, February 1989, p. B2.

14. Keen, *Shaping The Future*, p. 154.

15. Paul A. Strassman, *The Business Value of Computers* (New Canaan, CT: The Information Economics Press), 1990.

16. Ibid., p. 138.

17. Mark Ames, "Mainframes Stalled in Wake of Micro Performance Gains," *Computerworld*, 6 May 1991, p. 48.

18. "Dismantling Seen for Centralized MIS," *Information Week*, 22 May 1989, p. 26.

19. Michael Porter, "Building Competitive Advantage by Extending Information Systems" *Computerworld*, 9 October 1989, p. SR/ 19.

20. "Sharp Set To Put All Its Pieces Together," *The Nikkei Industrial Daily*, 17 August 1991, p. 9.

21. Clinton Wilder, "The Japan View," *Computerworld*, 13 August 1990, pp. 10–12.

22. Naoaki Fukuzaki, "Sony Plans Global Net To Streamline Inventory," *The Japan Economic Journal*, 22 April 1989, p. 20.

23. Wayne Eckerson, "Ford Profits by Letting Suppliers Tap into Systems," *Network World*, 1 July 1991, p. 1.

24. Mary E. Boone, "Computers Reshape Phillips 66," *Industry Week*, 1 July 1991, pp. 12–18.

8

The Role of Manufacturing Planning and Control Systems in World-Class Manufacturing

Because this is not a book on manufacturing planning and control systems, we will consider this subject only from a management viewpoint. Readers versed in this subject area may wonder why I cover it at all, for MRP has been around for 20 or more years, and JIT for ten years or more. But the fact remains that, especially at senior management levels, the two subjects still are not well understood—particularly the effective combination of them applied to a highly complex discrete product-manufacturing environment. Other readers may wonder why this chapter is so "technical." Rest assured that we will only scratch the surface of this highly complex subject of manufacturing planning and control systems. Consider this the minimum amount of material on this subject that any senior manager must know.[1]

Manufacturing planning and control systems play a vital role in determining how effectively a manufacturing company performs because they cover the entire logistics spectrum from procurement to manufacturing to distribution and after-sale customer support. They thus play a critical role in a company's performance of the two logistics business processes—the customer order-to-delivery cycle and the materials management cycle. Their traditional roles cover materials management (purchasing, inventory control, and distribution) and production scheduling. Recently, with the advent of the MRP II concept, such software systems also include integrated accounting and finance applications. As such, they represent major business application systems that cut across a majority of any company's activities. In terms of sophistication, manufacturing planning and control systems run the gamut from simple two-bin inventory management systems, neither paper nor computer-based, to computer-based manufacturing and distribution resource planning (MRP and DRP) software packages.

There are total quality management (TQM), computer-integrated manufacturing (CIM), and just in time (JIT) aspects of manufacturing planning and control systems, as shown in Exhibit 8-1.

We will focus first on the CIM-based aspects of manufacturing planning and control systems, and then return to a broader view of this subject that includes integration with the other two elements, especially JIT.

The Functional Growth of MRP

As a first step toward this goal, consider the growth of MRP systems over the last 25 years. Exhibit 8-2 shows the growth in functionality of MRP systems since their inception in the late 1960s and expected growth in the near future. When MRP was first being developed by people such as Ollie Wight and Joe Orlicky and by IBM with its PICS software package, it was called material requirements planning (now called mrp—"little MRP"). In those days, mrp consisted of two primary software

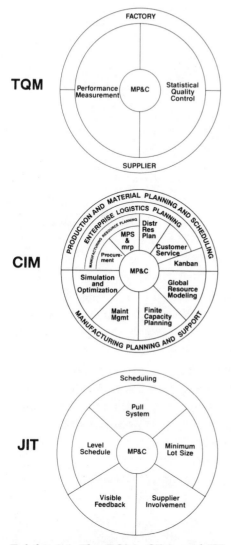

Exhibit 8-1 The TQM, CIM, and JIT aspects of manufacturing planning and control systems.

modules that ran in a batch mode: material requirements planning and (infinite) capacity requirements planning. Over the next 20 years and two to three generations of software, functionality (including more on-line capability) was added in soft-

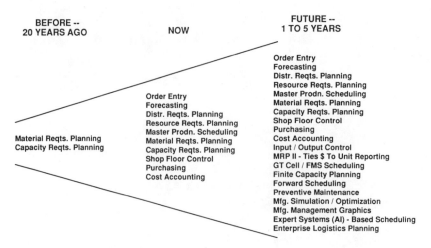

Exhibit 8-2 The growth of MRP systems.

ware modules until the average package sold today generally contains, at a minimum, the functionality for manufacturing shown in the middle column of Exhibit 8-2. (Note that all aspects of procurement systems are included under MRP.)

As more functionality was added, the name changed to a broader term, manufacturing resource planning. When accounting and financial applications were added to the overall package, the name was changed to MRP II to indicate the package's even greater overall capability. (We'll continue to use the term MRP as a descriptor for all MRP II systems.) During these 25 years, software packages were developed to run on all three CPU sizes—mainframes, minis, and micros (personal computers or workstations)—under many different operating systems, and in conjunction with many different data base management systems. More important today, however, is where these systems are going in the future, as indicated in the right column of Exhibit 8-2. Additional capability has and will continue to be added in response to growing user sophistication and needs that gives MRP software the following capabilities:

• *Scheduling group technology–based shop floor cells or flexible manufacturing systems.* The MRP netting algorithm in this case would gather all parts with certain GT codes to schedule through one or more of these cells or systems before proceeding to process lower levels in each part's bill of materials

• *Performing finite capacity planning.* Some manufacturers built very sophisticated finite capacity planners into their MRP systems as early as the late 1970s. Most of these, unfortunately, were disasters when implemented because the rest of the manufacturing environment was not under sufficient control with regard to quality, master production scheduling, quick setups, lot size reduction, work-in-process tracking, data accuracy, and the education and training of employees. As a result, most of these finite capacity planners just pushed work out (on the time horizon) to reflect an overloaded master production schedule, overly long lead times, and priorities within the finite capacity planner that all were in the highest 2 percent to 5 percent of their priority range. Even though the designers of these in-house MRP systems (or finite capacity planning modules) were theoretically correct, the rest of the company wasn't ready for this level of sophistication. (Indeed, few are today!) As a result, most of these finite capacity planners were unplugged and the plant went back to operating with infinite capacity planning or no capacity planning at all without much degradation in performance.

• *Performing forward as well as backward scheduling.* This capability is an important part of building more simulation capability into MRP software. The algorithm for forward scheduling is the same as that for backward scheduling, except that the starting point is different—the current date or any date is used instead of the customer due date.

• *Providing an integrated preventive maintenance (PM) capability.* Most preventive maintenance software sold today is sold separately from MRP software by different vendors. This complicates the communication and coordination between MRP and PM. The goal is to have an integrated PM software module in the MRP package that automatically takes a machine out of consideration for scheduling by MRP when it is due to be down for preventive maintenance, or when it is out of commission for unplanned maintenance.

• *Utilizing true probability-based simulation* based on Monte Carlo sampling from known probability distributions. Net change MRP systems provide either-or simulation—either condition one *or* condition two—depending on a human's input of likely conditions or outcomes. Simulation capability could provide the likely outcome of following a specific course of action based on the laws of probability that more closely mirror the real-world manufacturing environment.

• *Utilizing true optimization capability with linear programming.* This could be used to establish transportation network models that analyze optimal warehouse locations or the best shipping carriers and routes for a given set of criteria.

• *Allowing more graphically based reporting,* thus doing away with pages of difficult-to-read or interpret numbers. MRP output could be summarized in colored easy-to-interpret graphs whose trends and messages could be understood more quickly by managers.

• *Utilizing expert system knowledge* (artificial intelligence). Materials and scheduling experts could build a knowledge base and a set of experience-based rules that could be automatically applied when the MRP system was run for a single part or production facility. In some cases this could eliminate most of the need for human planners to work daily with the system's output and exception messages.

• *Allowing enterprise-level logistics planning.* MRP systems were initially designed for single plants and had no DRP capability. Currently, many MRP systems provide multiplant capability, and a few have integrated DRP capability. Future MRP systems will have both capabilities and will thus be useful at a corporate or group level to provide an overview of that entire business unit's logistics activity, from global suppliers through the business unit to global customers.

The trend in MRP systems is increasing functionality and integration, and I see no let-up in their development for the next decade. The manufacturing press is full of reports of a few so-phisticated manufacturers enhancing their MRP systems' functionality. It usually doesn't take more than five years for these attributes to start showing up as features or options in the software packages of most of the leading MRP vendors.

It is interesting to note that the growth of the MRP software industry has resulted in a diminished *rate* of functionality enhancements in MRP software over the past five years. MRP software vendors have been preoccupied with acquiring other companies in their industry to gain installed base and preempt their competitors. In addition, they have been consumed with porting their systems to new platforms either horizontally— across a given level of mainframes or, especially, minis—or vertically—from mainframes to minis and then to microcomputers. Now that a greater degree of industry consolidation has occurred and a "final" solution platform has been identified (a UNIX workstation or PC), we can expect renewed progress toward more functionality and integration in these powerful software packages. In particular, we can look forward to vastly improved user interfaces with the recent advent of graphical user interfaces, or "GUIs," as they are known.

MRP for Different
Manufacturing Environments

Consider the typical manufacturing environments in which MRP systems must function. Discrete part manufacturing is typified by electromechanical fabrication and assembly such as in the electronics, machine tool, appliance, aircraft, or automobile industries. There are three major manufacturing environments found therein.

A *job shop* manufacturing environment includes variable routings; every product requires a different sequence of operations. Such manufacturers use individual shop orders or job orders and are likely to have relatively low production volumes, often one unit per product.

In a *repetitive* manufacturing environment, routings are generally fixed (the products go down a line), production schedules are reasonably fixed and rate-based, and the production volumes are medium to high per product. Production rates are usually expressed as units or cases per week, day, or shift.

In the *government or defense* manufacturing environment, different management practices and extra regulations complicate matters. Examples of these are 20- to 35-digit part numbers (horrors!) as well as the need for lot control, serial number effectivity for engineering change control, and configuration management. In addition, manufacturers using MRP systems in these industries must comply with the Defense Contract Audit Agency's (DCAA) ten "rules" for MRP systems and with the U.S. government's cost accounting, work breakdown structure, and progress payment regulations.

The process manufacturing environment consists of *batch* and *continuous flow.*

Batch is typified by many food, drug, or consumer product manufacturers producing such items as soups, cosmetics, or pharmaceuticals, where materials are combined in an initial batch and then separated into a variety of initial and final packaging—cans, bottles, tubes, capsules, pills, and so forth.

Continuous flow is best exemplified by large oil refineries and chemical plants that change pressure, temperature, or flow rate conditions to refine raw materials into final products.

As the MRP software industry has matured, there has been increased differentiation of MRP software packages to more closely fit the five manufacturing environments described. There are three different versions of MRP for discrete part manufacturing:

- *Job shop.* This is the oldest and most traditional form of MRP. It uses variable routings and individual shop orders, is material based, usually schedules backward from a customer due date, and, at a minimum, uses infinite capacity planning.

- *Repetitive.* In this MRP package, routings are relatively fixed and schedules are rate based. Production may be scheduled cumulatively against a monthly or yearly schedule. Inventory relief occurs after production is complete (as contrasted to before production, in the case of the job shop) with a "backflush" or post-deduct technique that multiplies only completed units against the bill of material to arrive at inventory to be relieved from raw material and WIP stores balances.
- *Government or defense industry.* This type of MRP system can be similar to either previous package, but it includes features to comply with the environment described earlier.

The last type of MRP system is that used for batch process manufacturers. These systems are more capacity-based than materials based to reflect the fixed-capacity nature of process manufacturing and the variability of the manufacturing process caused by changes in the quality of each batch mix. Lot control is an essential feature required to comply with strict governmental regulations regarding traceability of all products used in food and pharmaceutical manufacturing. These packages often feature forward scheduling capability and must have the ability to handle derivative bills of materials to cover the materials or products that are a by-product of the fundamental manufacturing process.

MRP Software Selection

It's not hard to see that with three levels of potential systems architecture, at least four (and sometimes more) kinds of operating systems, consideration of what data base management software the package works with, and the five different manufacturing environments mentioned, there are scores of MRP systems and computing environments available for a user to select from. However, within any specific computing environment (CPU, operating system, and data base management system), there are always three or four packages at the top that are roughly equal in functional capability and vendor support. The job for manufacturers is to pick one of these quickly and get on with its implementation. In the end, it's how well any of these top packages are implemented that will make the difference, not which one is chosen.

I have seen companies waste months, even years, and untold hundreds of thousands of dollars going through overly elaborate software specification and evaluations. One southern manufacturing company spent 18 months and over $1 million in consulting fees to come up with a functional specification for its MRP requirements (in a very straightforward manufacturing environment) and to select an MRP package. In that time, with a more results-oriented approach, it could have selected a package and had it at least half-implemented, even with its conservative approach to management.

Some companies looking for an MRP package begin in such a state of ignorance about how these systems work that they are unable to write an intelligent user specification for the software. Furthermore, they don't know very much about what systems are available, and who some of the leading vendors are. As a result, they shotgun their request for proposal to up to 20 vendors to start the long learning and selection process. (I pity the poor vendors!) This is why a qualified, results-oriented consultant is so valuable at this stage of an MRP software selection. He or she can quickly size up how "average" a company's requirements are, save the company much time and money, and help it select a much better package or vendor for its needs. With a good consultant's help in an average manufacturing environment, it shouldn't take more than four to eight of a company's people two to three months of part-time effort to define user specifications and select a software package.

Master Production Scheduling: The Achilles Heel of Many Manufacturing Companies

In my consulting work over the years, I have been exposed to hundreds of manufacturing plants. The majority of these plants and companies have in common a glaring lack of capability in the area of master production scheduling—from both a software capability as well as a management point of view. It's not uncommon to go to a company's senior management meeting where a particular product or product line is being discussed and find that no one has all the necessary information or numbers for the product in question in a consistent format on a timely basis.

Here's the usual situation concerning any one product:

- The inventory management people have the figures from last Saturday (Sunday's computer run), but today is Thursday and they are not sure what has transpired since.

- Purchasing has scheduled receipts due in monthly time buckets, and it is not sure how many have been received or shipped from the vendor yet, or even that the vendor will ship them all in time for them to arrive this month. Purchasing also needs accurate requirements from production to place orders in a reasonable lead time with their suppliers.

- The sales forecast for the product in question is for the quarter, and there is a $50 million difference between the unit forecast and dollar forecast for the quarter.

- Production has its schedule in weekly time buckets but is past due on several products and hasn't rescheduled those products in a month. In addition, the production manager has to have a reasonably accurate sales forecast for this product for the next nine months to see if he or she needs to order more tooling and hire more assembly workers.

- Sales demand for the product is arriving daily, but its input into the company's order entry system often occurs days after the customer placed the order.
- There are supposed to be many of these specific units in finished goods inventory, but a lot of the company's customers are not getting their shipments on time. The lack of a finished goods allocation system means that the same units keep getting sold to many customers.
- The company's biggest customer wants 300 of these particular units delivered a month from today. He's been promised he'll get them this time, but no one really knows for sure.
- Finance would like a reasonably accurate projection of sales, inventory, and production over the next six months to see whether the company will meet its financial projections for the year.
- Everyone has his own set of numbers to defend his position and shift the blame to some other department or person, or even to the customer or supplier. Tempers flare. Political considerations abound. Problems are hidden. Arguments abound in increasingly loud and insulting language. Does this sound familiar? Management is flying blind in this environment, and the customers (those that are still there, anyway) are suffering for it. Of course, the company's performance is suffering the most.

Why is an effective master production schedule (MPS) so important? It should contain the most important information any company has and needs to deal quickly and accurately with its customers. It is the major tool needed for good customer service. An effective MPS will solve or alleviate the problems (and many more) described above. Here's how.

The average MPS, shown in Exhibit 8-3, operates with five lines of information—three input from various functions and two calculated by MPS logic that management defines and controls. Incidentally, all this information must be in units, not dollars, for a specific stock keeping unit (SKU) or end item

MPS

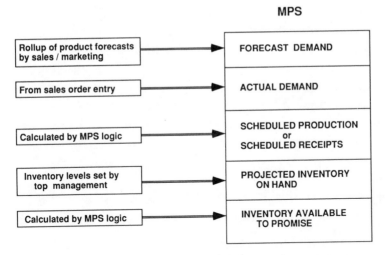

Exhibit 8-3 Master production schedule inputs and outputs.

part number. The time bucket used ultimately must be days, but a company may have to start with months or weeks before getting to days to instill the necessary discipline in its operations and people. For a make-to-stock company, the MPS shows units of specific SKUs. For a make-to-order company, the MPS shows production "slots" for a yet-to-be-specified (by the customer) particular configuration of a general product.

The top line of information in Exhibit 8-3 is the sales forecast in units for a particular SKU. This sales forecast will be wrong, but it will be a start. (There's an old saying that forecasting is easy unless it's about the future.) A forecast from sales, tempered by historical patterns and management judgment updated on a regular basis (perhaps 4 to 12 times a year, as a start), is a good way for a company to minimize forecast error. What's important here is to have the visibility into the future provided by the MPS and the ability to react quickly to increasing forecast error without having huge amounts of inventory as a buffer between the always unpredictable customer and the company, or between the company and its often unreliable suppliers.

Note also that the shorter the lead times a company has, the less it has to forecast into the future. If any customer order could be designed, made from scratch, and shipped to arrive at the customer in a day, there'd be little need for production to see a sales forecast. This short a manufacturing lead time is unlikely in most industries, and still wouldn't eliminate the need to plan by forecasting the overall business and products or product line sales within it. The point remains that forecasts inherently get increasingly inaccurate the further out they go in time. Shorter lead times in order processing, manufacturing, and distribution reduce the need to forecast out as far and thus lead to using the more accurate parts of forecasts—those closer to the present.

Incidentally, it is worthwhile to reduce lead times and assemble to order in less time than today's customers will tolerate as a reasonable order lead time. Hal Mather refers to this as the P:D ratio;[2] P is the production or procurement lead time, and D is the customer demand lead time. For ultimate flexibility and customer service, this ratio should be less than one. But remember, the customers' ultimate goal is for D to be zero (and why not?), so some forecasting of sales will be necessary no matter how low P gets on a practical basis.

The second line of input is actual customer demand, before filtering by anyone to check whether the company can sell it. This information should be filled in at the appropriate customer-requested due date—the *first* date that the customer requests. Note that we must distinguish between *customer demand* and *sales*. Many companies don't because in their order entry process, the order entry people essentially filter out the orders that can't be handled in time and in their initial desired quantity by the company. Sales are therefore often less than demand, the true demand information is lost forever, and the company consistently underestimates its needed manufacturing capacity and sales potential.

The third line of input is scheduled production from the company's plant (or plants) or scheduled receipts from suppliers (the company's outside plants). This line is calculated by MPS logic that the company controls.

The fourth line is the projected on-hand finished goods inventory of the SKU, based, of course, on the amount of goods actually there at any given time. As we will see, this projected on-hand inventory is insufficient to use as a basis for making customer promises, even if it is real-time information. The target levels of finished goods inventory should be set by the company's top management, in aggregate and with regard to each level of SKU (A, B, or C, for example) and each type of customer from a customer service aspect. Examining SKU classification levels and customer service requests points to the desirable practice of separating your company's products and customers into various degrees of value according to an ABC or Pareto analysis.

The fifth line—available to promise—is the most valuable, for it is or should be the basis for making promises to your company's customers. It, too, is calculated by MPS logic controlled by the company.

Exhibit 8-4 shows a sample MPS for an SKU and illustrates the power of a good MPS.

Note that the format includes a past-due time bucket to reflect anything that is late and that the company has no more capacity to produce. Past-due items must be immediately

FOR: SKU # 12345

| | Past Due | \multicolumn{8}{c}{Time Period} | Period Total |
		1	2	3	4	5	6	7	8	
FORECAST DEMAND		120	120	120	120	120	120	120	120	960
CUSTOMER BACKLOG	0	130	280	75	90	360	60	30	20	1045
SCHEDULED RECEIPTS		0	0	0	50	50	50	70	70	

Inventory Position	Begin OH									
PROJECTED ON HAND	800	680	560	440	370	300	230	180	130	
AVAILABLE TO PROMISE	800	670	390	315	275	-35	-45	-5	45	

Exhibit 8-4 A sample master production schedule report.

rescheduled, assuming that the customer still wants them, which often means pushing other scheduled work out into the future, especially if the plant or line is already working at capacity. Also observe that, initially, the sales forecast can simply be a level loading of a certain number per week as it is in the example. In this example, the time horizon only covers eight time periods. Normally, one might go out one quarter in days, one quarter in weeks, one quarter in months, and then one quarter in a quarterly time bucket, for a maximum total of 49 time buckets covering a year—on a rolling daily basis.

Ignore the available-to-promise line when first looking at Exhibit 8-4. Observing only the projected on-hand line, it looks like the company has plenty of inventory to cover the sales forecast, given its starting position and the amount it plans to receive from its suppliers in time periods four through eight. This is because the logic that calculates the projected on-hand inventory works off of the sales forecast line. In effect, it says that if sales come in at the rate we forecast, this will be our projected on-hand inventory. Given this, one can see how easy it would be to tell customers, "Sure, we can handle your order— no problem!" But unfortunately, sales rarely come in as forecast!

In this example, they don't either. Note the lumpiness of the actual sales demand compared with the forecast. The available-to-promise line is calculated from the actual sales demand (customer backlog) line. It says that, given the company's actual demand as of this date, it will run out of product to ship customers in time period five! The situation that looked great using the projected on-hand figure now is a real problem using the available to promise figures. But, the problem is exposed five time periods before it will occur, and the company has time to take corrective action by moving scheduled receipts in, increasing its orders to its suppliers, or asking certain customers if they could accept their orders a bit later. The MPS thus gives a company visibility into the future and is a critical tool with which to manage its customer expectations and its operations more effectively.

The example in Exhibit 8-4 highlights only one benefit of the MPS—the fact that it provides future visibility to problems of over- or undersupply through its available-to-promise calculation, thus allowing the company to react before the problem occurs. However, the MPS provides many more benefits.

- The MPS displays all data needed to effectively manage an SKU on one sheet of paper (or computer screen) in a consistent format. The time bucket sizes for each line of data are consistent, for example, in days, as are the necessary information flow cutoffs so that the five lines of information are consistent and accurate.

- Its weekly (or daily) format allows more timely reaction to increasingly volatile world market conditions and relatively inaccurate forecasts. Using quarterly time buckets, it may take 90 days to find out about a problem and react to it. Monthly time buckets cut this to 30 days, and weekly time buckets reduce it to 5 or 7 days, thereby allowing a company to react 4 to 13 times faster than monthly or quarterly schedules. Obviously, daily time buckets allow next-day reaction—the best possible until real-time MRP systems come along.

- The MPS provides two-level linking capability to link an end-item SKU to its many possible lower level SKUs through a planning bill of materials.[3]

- The MPS can manage thousands of SKUs on an exception basis. Its reschedule or "problem" messages are only triggered when management has determined that planner action (human judgment) is required.

- The MPS's order planning logic is automated using management-selected parameters to control lot size, safety stock, and ordering policies. These parameters should reflect top management's desired results for effective inventory management and customer satisfaction.

- The MPS allows critical time fences to be observed and necessary lead time offsets to be built into the MPS logic, thus preventing the company from being driven by impossible-to-achieve demands, that is, an overloaded MPS.[4]

- The MPS, expressed in units, is easily extendable by each unit's cost to dollars, thus automating and simplifying financial planning. The financial impact of new unit sales forecasts or production plans can readily be evaluated at a corporate, group, divisional, plant, or even line level. The MPS further ensures that the corporation is driven by one set of numbers. Its unit and dollar forecasts finally match.

- The MPS dramatically increases materials management personnel productivity. It frees people from clerical data gathering, data checking, and calculation work so that they can perform essential management-level inventory control and scheduling tasks that ensure maximum customer satisfaction.

- The MPS promotes a "rolling calendar" approach to planning, wherein the schedule is rolled ahead by the smallest time bucket (for instance, a day) at a time. One production day becomes like any other. This moves the company away from a "one-quarter-at-a-time" mentality and helps dampen traditional end of the month, quarter, or year blitzes that wreak havoc on a company's manufacturing operations and its people, as well as its quality reputation with its customers.

I have discussed only the most basic MPS example. More advanced MPSs can include built-in simulation capability to evaluate the implications of schedule changes. Furthermore, expert systems can be integrated into an MPS to help with analysis and to recommend solutions to executives or plant floor personnel. Color computer graphics can be built into computer screens or paper-based reports to convey information at a glance, rather than in pages of alphanumeric computer output.

Even the simple MPS outlined in this section would be a major benefit for most manufacturing companies, whether implemented at a corporate, group, divisional, or plant level. Not only is an MPS the basis for superb customer service, but it also drives the more detailed plant scheduling and procurement parts of the MRP system.

Distribution Resource Planning

Distribution resource planning (DRP) fits on the front end of MRP and recognizes that all forms of inventory are related. DRP extends the MRP logic of lead time offset and applies it to the distribution environment. It anticipates and aggregates distribution needs from many customers and distribution centers as time-phased requirements for input to the MPS. In doing so, the sales forecasting responsibility is transferred to each local (and therefore most knowledgeable) distribution center or sales staff. DRP can be used to improve the planning of all distribution resources—warehouse space, truck scheduling, and so on. It is a powerful tool to help reduce the average finished goods inventory level (U.S. manufacturers and wholesalers are currently at 6.5 percent of sales) while improving customer service and satisfaction.

Enterprise Logistics Planning

As noted earlier in this chapter, most manufacturers have attempted to gain control of their total logistics activity from the bottom up in a sequence that started with MRP in one plant, then multiplant MRP, then DRP (assuming a distribution-intensive environment). Now, to maximize customer satisfaction with a minimum of resources in a global business environment, sophisticated companies are realizing that enterprise or corporate-wide logistics planning and control systems are both feasible and necessary.

One reason for this need is the increased customer focus at an enterprise level that customers are demanding and that world class manufacturers are finding beneficial. Many large manufacturing companies with dozens of manufacturing plants and many divisions and groups are finding that they can't answer the simple question, "How much and what specifically did we sell to Ford Motor Company (for example) last year? More important, what are Ford's corporate requirements for the next two years, how are we going to satisfy them, and how can we find a better (more effective, lower-cost, quicker, higher-quality) way for us as a total corporation to give Ford even better customer service in the future?"

A second reason for enterprise logistics planning is that it saves money and promotes better use of corporate resources. Digital Equipment Corporation uses such a system to more closely couple sales forecasts and manufacturing schedules. In the two-year period after implementing this system, DEC reduced its inventories by $700 million.[5] Above the one-time decrease in working capital required, that represents a saving of a minimum of $140 million a year just on inventory carrying charges!

With enterprise logistics planning, the logistics system environment will change markedly, as shown in Exhibit 8-5.

Two features of enterprise logistics planning are centralized coordination (to maximize customer service with a minimum of corporate resources) and distributed execution of the corporate-wide plan. At a minimum, the benefits of such planning are greater customer satisfaction, lower costs, and better use of the corporation's manufacturing and distribution capacity.

The farthest extension of enterprise logistics planning is the development and use of global resource modelers for optimizing production options, capacity utilization, and other manufacturing policies or activities. Many large corporations have spent dozens, if not hundreds, of labor-years developing these models, and they have now reached a state of great

EACH PLANT AUTONOMOUS	WITH ENTERPRISE LOGISTICS PLANNING
MRP Each plant has its own	All plants' materials management/logistics systems integrated in one common system
DRP Optional, seldom used	DRP part of integrated system for distribution-intensive products
Information to/from corporation P & L summary only to corporation from plants	All plant, supplier, and customer information flow is available electronically to corporation. All order entry and scheduling information flows from corporation to plants.
Logistics staff Full complement needed at each plant, including purchasing—each plant does its own staffing and training with little regard for corporate welfare	Minimal staffing at plants, main strength at corporate level—all staffing and training done with a consistent approach and to maximize corporate strength
Suppliers Each supplier supplies each plant separately, and thus must deal with n customers in the corporation	Suppliers deal with corporation on aggregated major product purchases; lesser buying done locally; suppliers have to deal with fewer customers and can be more effective for the corporation
Material tracking throughout the logistics pipeline Each plant does its own in different ways to a different extent	All material movement tracked fully on a common computer system, including use of EDI throughout the logistics pipeline
Capacity management Each plant does its own with little regard for corporate performance	Performed centrally (first) with regard to maximizing corporate performance, then plant performance
Inventory Management Each plant does its own with little regard for corporate performance	Performed centrally (first) with regard to maximizing corporate performance, then plant performance

(continued)

Exhibit 8-5 Old-think logistics versus enterprise logistics planning.

Customers	
Managed by each plant separately and to various degrees of customer satisfaction, with little regard for overall corporate customer priorities	Managed with regard to overall corporate priorities—strategic and operational
Information systems	
Each plant has its own—electronic communication between plants difficult, costly, and usually nonexistent; plant to corporate telecommunication usually primitive. Even aggregation of data from separate plant systems difficult, owing to different definitions, MRP system use, and timing cutoffs	Corporate systems uses standard data dictionary, data base management systems, operating system, application system (ELP), and telecommunication system to create and effectively use management information
Ability to exchange design (geometric) data between plants	
Limited to none; each plant may have its own CAD system; plant to plant telecommunications usually nonexistent or primitive	Full corporate engineering network with sufficient graphics capacity running standard CAD/CAE applications available at all plants

Exhibit 8-5 (continued)

sophistication. With the advent of more powerful personal computers and workstations, as well as more sophisticated computer graphics, some of these models have even become user friendly and more inviting to use by senior managers and their staffs. But the use of these models requires great enterprise-wide discipline in planning and forecasting. The entire enterprise must run with one set of numbers if the greatest possible benefits are expected from these global resource modelers.

General Motors has spent over a decade working on its PLANETS and CASM global resource modelers. Westinghouse has built similar models to evaluate the tradeoffs between offshore and U.S. production of circuit boards. Professors and researchers at universities such as M.I.T., Wharton, and Stanford have also created such global resource modelers. Typically these modelers combine several forms of analysis and modeling, in some cases including linear programming techniques to optimize—not merely simulate—an outcome (such as corporate after-tax profit) around some set of boundary conditions. Most such modelers contain data about the following:

- Market demand by product and geographic area
- Facility (current or proposed location) and its production capacities
- Tariffs, duties, and local labor content laws for each country considered in the model
- Material flows from suppliers through plants and distribution to customers
- Material costs from different suppliers in various parts of the world
- International governments' trade offset requirements
- Variable and fixed costs for all manufacturing-related activities
- Corporate transfer pricing rules
- Corporate tax rates by country
- Access to current and projected currency exchange rates
- Tooling requirements for each product family
- Allowable combinations of products; for example, whether an engine gets produced near the production of a transmission

Cohen and Lee describe the use of such a model to analyze global manufacturing strategies for a personal computer manufacturer.[6] These global resources modelers can save companies millions—perhaps billions—of dollars, and, even more importantly, years of time, especially time lost doing the wrong thing.

Many small companies are sometimes discouraged (perhaps from a third-party source) from creating or using these models because they know how incomplete or erroneous much of their data are. Indeed, some companies don't seem to have a hard number in the place; trying to find one is like trying to nail jelly to a tree. However, people who have had extensive experience with these models know that they can be surprisingly accurate with estimates obtained from the experienced senior members of a company's management team. Occasionally, the modelers may find in their sensitivity tests that more accurate data are needed in one particular area. If this is the case, these data generally take no more than a few days or weeks to ascertain.

In some advanced corporations, these global resource models will be used on a full-time, real-time basis to plan and run the business. I will discuss this topic further in Chapter 11.

The use of global resource modelers is just one of the tools necessary to maximize the global clout of the *corporation* over any one of its parts. Another such needed conceptual tool is the idea of corporate core competencies, discussed in Chapter 2. Many of today's corporations are no more than collections of small autonomous business units that achieve no *operating* synergy in product and process design, production, global sourcing, distribution, or information systems. Businesses operated in this manner are going to be too fat and unproductive to be world class competitors in the future.

Integrating MRP with JIT Thinking

With some background in MRP established, I shall return to a broader discussion of manufacturing planning and control systems (MP and CS) by bringing JIT into the picture. We will focus our application of JIT to fit the MP and CS environment. To do so, let's start with some definitions of commonly used but often misunderstood terms.

Kanban is the information system used to manage JIT production. A kanban, or sign, can range from a colored golf ball to a paper or metal sign on the side of a standard material handling container to a standard material handling container itself to a computer-printed and bar-coded paper sign on a container. Kanban is part of JIT production, which is a way to produce the necessary units in exactly the right quantities at the right time. JIT production is, in turn, a part of a much larger system—the Toyota Production System, initially developed and implemented by Taiichi Ohno and others at Toyota in the early 1950s, and continuously enhanced ever since. They originally described this system as a way to make products so that costs are reduced, quality is improved, and respect for humanity is enhanced.[7]

Many excellent books and articles have been written about JIT production in the last five to ten years, and I am not going to repeat those concepts and "how-to's" in this book. JIT is extremely simple conceptually, but it has proven to be inordinately difficult to implement in Western societies because it requires new management thinking and practices.

The one aspect of MRP and JIT that I want to explore involves the current "push-pull" thinking about both systems. For the past few years a number of consultants and college professors have been running around the country telling people that MRP is a failure—it's a "push" system that is inherently bad. On the other hand, JIT is a "pull" system, which is inherently good—in fact, right up there with cleanliness and motherhood. The not too subtle message is, "Throw out MRP and all those computers, implement JIT, and all of your troubles will be over." I suggest that one consider the situation more carefully.

First, recognize that JIT has been most successful in repetitive manufacturing—relatively high-volume fixed-routing manufacturing. At Toyota and many other places, to be most successful, it has also required that end-item demand be smoothed by a large finished goods inventory buffer (or backlog) so that plants can be run at a relatively fixed rate over time, usually with no more than 5 percent to 10 percent variance in short-term daily schedules. We have been able to learn a lot of important principles from JIT production that we can apply to all other manufacturing environments. But the primary use of and benefits from JIT production have been in repetitive manufacturing.

Recognize that both MRP and JIT are pull systems. Final assembly requirements expressed by some form of master production schedule pull products through the factory or supplier environment. Some JIT zealots espouse true "demand pull systems," wherein a customer order immediately triggers a factory order. If this is what is desired, with an MRP system the finished goods inventory and safety stock levels need only be to zero in the MPS, and the customer order will flow directly through to the factory—*if* the MRP system is run in real time or at least every night.

It is no inherent fault of MRP systems that they are push systems today. Instead, manufacturing people make them that way by operating them with a lot of "fat." How?

With regard to lead times, we make them too long in purchasing and manufacturing (final assembly and fabrication). If it takes two weeks to get a part from a supplier, we say "let's cover our tails and make that four weeks." If final assembly takes one week, we put a two-week lead time into the MRP system for a little protection, thus doubling WIP in final assembly. In a similar manner, most companies insert extra-long queue and move times in each product's routing.

Furthermore, the backscheduling algorithm in almost all MRP software uses fixed lead times that are lot-size independent instead of lot-size dependent. At a minimum, this implies a lot of lead time maintenance in the system if a company has a JIT program going and it is concentrating on reducing setups and reducing lot sizes on a continual basis. But ultimately, the company should be able to produce any required quantity— maybe as little as one unit—and have the MRP system schedule that properly. For most products, there is a big difference in lead time, depending on whether the lot quantity is 1, or 100, or 5000. Try a random sample of 10 of any company's products!

Now consider the netting algorithm that the MRP system uses. First, in the United States, safety stock is typically included as an inventory option. This is our wonderful American just-in-case system— keep a hundred on the shelf just in case!

Then MRP systems have many lot sizing algorithm options in addition to lot-for-lot. Lot-for-lot means that if ten parts are needed, only ten parts are built—no more and no less. In the United States, most MRP systems are run with economic order quantity (EOQ) lot sizing. At a minimum, this is likely to be wrong because the EOQ formula is based on an assumption of constant demand, which is rarely the case in manufacturing, especially two or three levels down in the bills of materials. Second, the costs used in the EOQ model are likely to be wrong because of the overhead allocation problems discussed in Chapter 5. In addition, scrap factors are often used in the MRP netting algorithm. The scrap factor reflects the fact that we might have to start 110 units to finally get 100 good ones. The Japanese are amazed by use of this feature. Their reaction is, "You (Americans) *plan* to build scrap?!"

Incidentally, this is as good a place as any to observe that many companies think they have a scheduling problem when they really have a quality problem. They never know when they are going to make a good part. Fixing the quality problem makes scheduling a lot easier and planning far more feasible and effective.

Consider a small lot sizing example. I'll leave out the safety stock, as it is the first thing handled by the netting algorithm anyway—and often is never consumed. Let's assume that in our MRP system we need ten parts, the inventory position is zero, the EOQ is 100, and the scrap factor is 10 percent. We therefore start with 110, hoping to net 100. We take our 10, and put the other 90 good parts in inventory. The Japanese or any well-run manufacturing operation would start 10 parts, make 10 good parts, not put any units in inventory, and not even need the shelf or inventory space, stockroom personnel, and so on. This represents an entirely new way of thinking for most U.S. manufacturers.

With respect to time buckets, we typically use large ones— quarters, months, or weeks. Why not days, or even shifts? The algorithm is the same and computing power is essentially free today.

Finally, we typically don't replan very often. MRP "runs" are made weekly, fortnightly, monthly, or even quarterly in some companies. One company I visited recently ran its MRP system all weekend to produce 16,000 pages of output that had to be analyzed before it could be run again! Oh, suffering horrors! Changes are happening on any manufacturer's shop floor and with customers and suppliers on a minute-by-minute basis. How can MRP that is run once a week or less mirror the reality of the daily manufacturing environment? MRP should be run at least daily so that its output is as close to reality as possible.

Companies often run their MRP systems in regenerative mode, wherein *all* the material requirements are replanned on every run, thus ensuring the greatest possible run time for any given computer. Many MRP systems can be run in net change mode, in which the only changes made to the plan reflect transactions that have caused changes since the last run.

So the fat creeps in, and a pull system gets changed into a push system. From a scheduling viewpoint, there is little or no difference between MRP and JIT. MRP is a computer-based scheduling and communication system. JIT is most often (in the United States) a paper-based communication and scheduling system. However, Yamaha's PYMAC system, developed over ten years ago in Japan, is a computer-based combination of a classical MRP system for job shop production and a single-card kanban system for repetitive manufacturing.[8] Interestingly, as the production environment in Japan gets more complex, many Japanese companies are now busy implementing MRP systems to handle the increased product diversity now required by today's customers.

Which Manufacturing Planning and Control System Should We Use?

Executives in many companies are puzzled as to which manufacturing planning and control system they should use—MRP, JIT, or maybe even this package called OPT that they heard so much about a few years ago, if it's still available. To answer that question, consider the historical development of each of these three systems or philosophies.

- MRP was developed in the United States, originally for use in job shops with its individual shop orders, material basis, backward scheduling, and infinite capacity planning.
- OPT came from Israel through Creative Output, Inc. This philosophy and package focused on identifying the bottleneck operation (at a given time) and forward scheduling from it, thus optimizing throughput given that specific bottleneck. It then backward scheduled all non-bottleneck operations. OPT was never sold as a complete package, as were most MRP packages, but rather was often sold as an adjunct to a full-blown MRP package.
- JIT, of course, came from Japan. Its goal is to eliminate waste (*muda*) in all forms from all business operations. It is more than an inventory reduction tool because inventory is just one form of waste. As we noted, JIT demands a relatively smooth schedule and therefore functions best in a repetitive manufacturing environment buffered by large finished good stocks. JIT may or may not be computerized.

Each of these systems or philosophies is capable of delivering powerful benefits to manufacturers that implement them effectively. The main thing to recognize about these three systems is that they are not mutually exclusive. Indeed, while developed from three different perspectives, manufacturing planning and control systems of the future will feature the best of all three philosophies.

Most companies need MRP as a base system to obtain control of operations. Some may not need to use all the modules of a full MRP package. Their product structures and production environments may be simple enough to use a good MPS and then a combination of spreadsheet scheduling and a pull system with visible feedback to execute on the shop floor, instead of the material requirements planning and shop floor control modules. JIT principles can be overlaid on a base MRP system in some areas after TQM and preventive maintenance systems are well established. TQM can exist without JIT, but not vice versa. For JIT (or MRP) to work effectively, a good part must be made every time, and production equipment to make the part must be available when required. Next, MRP capabilities can be enhanced with OPT-like features of forward scheduling from bottlenecks, optimization routines, and finite capacity planning. Finally, the MP and CS can be enhanced with simulation capability, expert systems, and color computer graphics for better reporting and improved user friendliness.

The point is not which "system" to use, but how to effectively blend the best features of MRP, JIT, and OPT into a flexible, real-time, and user-friendly system for planning and scheduling production and logistics within a company.

Combining JIT with MRP in Practice

In manufacturing environments that are simple, either because of the nature of the product or process or because they've been made simple, the traditional MRP/DRP system may only be needed as a planning tool to generate an MPS for the shop floor and time-phased procurement requirements for purchasing. The MPS requirements (possibly just dumped into a spreadsheet) will establish a daily line rate for each product or production line. The execution of this line rate for each product will then be accomplished by a kanban-led pull system through prior stages of production and supply.

Note that, operated as I have just described, bills of materials only have to be single-level (as opposed to indented, where a detailed product structure is articulated). In addition, routings, if used at all, can be crude bills of labor or machine usage used for planning purposes only, not for detailed shop floor dispatching. Shop floor data collection need only exist (for short-lead-time production) at the input to the production line (or out of material stores, if used, or receiving) and at the output of the production line into packaging (if variable) or distribution.

In more complex manufacturing environments with inherently longer production cycles, the MPS might plan material requirements in a conventional manner but drive a finite capacity planner to balance lines and optimize the use of shop floor resources. This environment would require a more traditional and detailed routing as a basis for the finite capacity planner. In addition, shop floor tracking of materials would have to be more detailed to provide the finite capacity planner with material and job movement data.

A northern California circuit board manufacturer has implemented a hybrid MRP/JIT system in its job shop.[9] Its MPS generates a kanban to initiate the production of a board when the board's finished goods level drops below a predetermined level. Standard containers on the shop floor serve as a kanban to trigger supplier orders electronically. The benefits this manufacturer has obtained from the system include the following:

	Before	After
Manufacturing lead time	6 weeks	1 week
On-time delivery	78%	100%
Productivity		up 30%
Purchase lead time	28 days	4 days
WIP reduction		90%

Getting Started with a Better
Manufacturing Planning
and Control System

Many manufacturers are kept by the way they operate their computer and MRP systems from making more progress toward integrating JIT principles with MRP along the lines I have mentioned. They say, for instance, that they could never run MRP every night—they don't have a big enough computer. Or, in the case of the example I cited earlier, they have to analyze 16,000 pieces of paper from their prior MRP run before they can run it again. What's needed here is to turn this kind of "logic" on its head and ask, "What do we have to do so that we *could* run MRP every night?" I offer the following suggestions:

• *Flatten bill of material structures.* If the production environment is simple enough, flatten them to a single level. Otherwise, look for areas, especially with purchased products, to order assemblies instead of parts from current suppliers, or consider finding new suppliers.

Unisys, in its Roseville plant, used to order all the sheet metal parts for a computer cabinet separately from many different suppliers (those providing lowest cost per piece) and assemble them itself. The cabinet assembly SKU therefore had several levels of SKUs in its product structure and required detailed MRP system-planner-buyer-expediter attention for each individual SKU in the assembly. New thinking about this process led Unisys to bid the job for the entire cabinet assembly to one sheet metal supplier. Several levels in the cabinet's bill of material were thus collapsed to one, MRP system and personnel overhead was markedly reduced, and, as a bonus, the cabinet's quality was dramatically increased.

• *Shorten the planning horizon.* The ideal way to accomplish this is to reduce cumulative manufacturing and supplier lead times. But even without doing that, some manufacturers force their MRP system to go out too far in too much time or product detail. I've seen three-year MRP planning horizons in some companies! Some manufacturers have purchased parts with long lead times. When this occurs, these manufacturers should put only these parts in the bill of material—not all the parts. Another alternative is to run MRP with a three- to six-month time horizon most of the time, and to run a longer time horizon only once per quarter or so. What really counts to most manufacturers is the next six months. All else is usually changeable after that.

• *Only track the high-value items in the MRP system*—not the "C" items that may or could exist as floor stock.

• *Tailor the MRP system to report more by exception,* but dampen the exception parameters so that insignificant details don't get reported.

• *Run the MRP system in net change—not generative—mode,* if possible, to reduce the aggregate amount of planning work it must perform.

• *Divide the company's plant into several "plants within a plant"* and give each its own LAN microbased MRP system (with integrated financials) to run their own businesses. If the company is currently running its plant on a mainframe, this step may drop information system costs by 30 percent to 50 percent, in addition to fostering a substantial operating improvement in manufacturing and customer service.

• *Buy faster computer equipment*—faster CPUs with more cache memory, larger data buses, and more input/output ports, as well as faster disk drives.

As an example of what will be commonplace in the future, Carp Systems International in Kanata, Ontario, sells software that, using either a parallel processing computer or IBM System/6000 or H-P 9000 Series 700 workstations, can run a master production schedule with 50,000 parts, 500,000 product structures, and 1,000,000 mrp requirements in under 30 seconds.[10] Real-time MRP is here today. But first, most manufacturers have to learn to effectively use an MRP system that runs once a day.

In this chapter, I've provided a critical overview of manufacturing planning and control systems. In the next chapter, I shall extend this perspective into the computer-integrated enterprise and demonstrate how all manufacturing companies will have to function by the turn of the century.

Chapter 8

1. For an especially learned and lucid discussion of the complexities of manufacturing scheduling, see H. Van Dyke Parunak, "Characterizing the Manufacturing Scheduling Problem," *Journal of Manufacturing Systems*, Vol. 10, No. 3, pp. 241–259.

2. Hal Mather, *Competitive Manufacturing* (Englewood Cliffs, NJ: Prentice Hall), 1988, pp. 31–35.

3. For an excellent discussion of planning bills of materials, see Dave Garwood, *Bills of Material* (Marietta, GA: Dogwood Publishing Co.), 1988.

4. A good discussion of master schedule lead time fences can be found in Mather and Plossl's booklet "The Master Production Schedule," 2nd ed., 1977, published by them in Atlanta, GA.

5. W. A. Hall and R. E. McCauley, "Planning and Managing a Corporate Network Utility," DEC Public Relations Brochure, 1991, p. 4.

6. M. A. Cohen and H. L. Lee, "Resource Deployment Analysis of Global Manufacturing and Distribution Networks," *Journal of Operations Management*, vol. 2, 1989, pp. 81–104.

7. For a good discussion of JIT nomenclature, see Yasuhiro Monden, *Toyota Production System* (Norcross, GA: Industrial Engineering and Management Press, Institute of Industrial Engineers), 1983.

8. Robert W. Hall, *Driving the Productivity Machine* (American Production and Inventory Control Society), 1981, Ch. 5.

9. Tony Baer, "Improvement Recipe: Combine 1 Part Kanban with 1 Part MRP II," *CIMWEEK*, 3–17 June 1991, p. 1. (Published in Norwalk, CT by Productivity, Inc.)

10. "Planning for Time-Based Manufacturing," *Managing Automation*, August 1991, pp. 16–18.

9

Establishing World Class Business Performance Measures

Establishing the right business performance measures is critical to becoming a world-class performer, for performance measures are one of the key ways to motivate people and measure progress against customer needs and competitors' performance. Yet there is ample evidence that a majority of Western culture–based manufacturers continue to operate with inadequate performance measures, as they have for decades. Consider a real-world example from my files.

A pipe company in the southern United States continues to suffer from a "foundry mentality" and looks at production from a weight and truckload viewpoint. A "good day" is one where 27 truckloads of pipe product roll out the door. And what happens when operations falls short of filling the 27 truckloads? They select products with the greatest positive cost variance, or the easiest, biggest, or heaviest product to make to fill up the 27 trucks, regardless of whether anyone *needed* those products. This fit in with their "keep the foundry operating to maximize utilization" and "absorb overhead" philosophy.

But, alas, customers don't order truckloads of pipe. They order specific SKUs—for example, ten each of 6-inch diameter by

8 feet long, four each of 6-inch diameter elbows, two each of 6-inch diameter tees, and so forth—and they want this exact order delivered next Monday morning at 10 A.M. Was anyone in the company tracking whether each customer got exactly what he ordered exactly when he wanted it, and at perfect quality? No. This manufacturer had acres of finished goods inventory and a fleet of over 200 lift trucks to move all that material around—hardly world-class, hardly customer-focused, and definitely measuring the wrong things.

What's Wrong with Today's Manufacturing Performance Measures?

How is it that manufacturers continue to operate with the wrong performance measures? What's wrong with the ones they're using?

We've seen that many manufacturing companies have not had an external focus in their performance measurements that considers the voice of the customer. This is most evident in the all-important customer order-to-delivery cycle, where many manufacturers don't start counting until the order is in their order entry system, and at the other end of the cycle when they stop counting time as soon as they've shipped the product—not when it arrives (in perfect condition) at the customer. Of course, failing to sufficiently focus on the customers' needs and desires makes it difficult to measure and ascertain how a manufacturer is doing on quality, since the definition of quality ultimately comes from an industry's customers.

We know that most manufacturers have not utilized world-class performance metrics and standards as a basis for measuring their performance. Indeed, most manufacturing company executives do not even know what these metrics and current performance standards are for their industry!

McKinsey & Co. has found that new product introduction lead times in world-class electromechanical product companies are 40 percent to 65 percent of those at typical companies, and manufacturing cost at world class performers is 30 percent to 50 percent lower than that at average manufacturing companies.[1] We also know that, historically, there's been too much focus on measuring costs instead of measuring time as a way to satisfy customers and improve business processes. Many managers can quote costs or cost variances to three decimal places, but have only the vaguest idea what their lead times are or how much time is wasted. In their book *Competing Against Time*, George Stalk and Tom Hout noted that a world class time-based competitor who can respond three to four times faster than its competitors "almost always grows three times faster than overall demand, at twice the level of profitability of the average competitor," among many other benefits.[2]

In addition, many of the measures we have traditionally used in manufacturing plants just don't apply in today's manufacturing environment. Consider labor utilization, for instance. When direct labor constituted 30 percent to 50 percent of manufacturing cost, it made some sense to have a group of industrial engineers perform time and motion studies, standardize motions employees made, and assign times in seconds for every standard operation. The creation of these standards caused much time to be wasted in non-value-added disputes between management and labor over their "correctness." The "standard" time for an operation was then utilized as a performance basis against which they could laboriously record actual times and compute a labor efficiency variance. Negative variances were investigated in arrears and "fixed." Somehow, positive variances never received the same amount of management attention, especially when some factories consistently ran at 135 percent to 150 percent of "standard."

None of this makes sense today. First, direct labor is (or could be) generally less than 10 percent to 12 percent of manufacturing cost in most industries. Its total cost is often outweighed by manufacturing overhead by a factor of five, even ten, to one in most modern companies, though this needn't be the norm. Second, variance information is about yesterday's problems. Few managers care about yesterday, compared with today's or tomorrow's problems. Third, the JIT concepts of work cells, multifunctional workers, and small lot sizes (potentially one item) make such detailed direct labor tracking somewhat antiquated. Furthermore, we want today's workers to be participating in simple preventive maintenance, workplace organization, group problem solving, and perhaps even customer or supplier visits, and in ad hoc as well as scheduled education and training programs. These activities don't fit in the classical industrial engineering time studies and methods environment.

It's unfortunate that a lot of companies spent a relative fortune on a huge staff of industrial engineers to set up and operate these complex labor reporting systems that many companies are still operating with today. They add no value to the product. World class manufacturers do not need them and cannot afford them. Much simpler labor estimates can be used to create a bill of labor for capacity planning and lead time offsetting in today's manufacturing environment.

Machine utilization is another old-fashioned performance measurement still utilized and overemphasized by many manufacturing companies. Rarely, though, is this measured on a 100 percent (24 hours per day, 365 days per year) time basis to reflect the amount of time companies pay for the equipment through ownership or leasing. Outdated absorption cost systems force many manufacturers to maximize machine utilization to absorb overhead with little regard to whether the parts the machines are producing are needed by customers. In manufacturing operations that are machine limited, it is important to have some appreciation for machine utilization—especially of the bottleneck machine—in order to have a handle on a plant's overall capacity for a given mix of products. But blindly maximizing overall machine utilization should not necessarily be the goal if the focus is on world class performance. High production equipment utilization should be a result of superb capacity planning, high quality, and effective scheduling—not a goal in itself.

Another major fault with today's performance measures is that, in many manufacturing companies, few people in a plant get to see the total picture. Indeed, in many operations I've been through, the total picture, as well as many of the details, is not available to the great majority of the workforce. This can be especially true with cost figures. If an employee doesn't know what a part or product costs, he or she cannot appreciate the consequences of scrapping one (or more!). If workers don't have some idea of an order's value, or how important a customer's business is to their company, then they can't appreciate what effect the order being late has on the customer and, ultimately, the company. How can their contributions to improving the product or the process be maximized if they are acting with anything less than full knowledge of current conditions?

To add further insult to injury, we know that in most cases manufacturers are using cost systems that don't provide the right answers today. As I noted in Chapter 5, our current cost systems were primarily designed for external reporting purposes, were designed when direct labor was a majority of manufacturing costs, and use a method of allocating overhead in a manner that often significantly distorts costs—overpricing high-volume standard products and underpricing the low-volume special products. Exhibit 9-1 is an example of such cost distortion from the printed circuit etch shop of a division of Hughes Aircraft Company.

Simply put, today's product costs rarely reflect accurately the direct or indirect activities that produced them. On a higher scale, we know that the kinds of numbers that Wall Street measures—earnings per share, return on equity, and the like— are not measures of manufacturing operations performance. As has been discussed in the press for years, these performance values, especially when emphasized in the short term, can work to keep a manufacturing company from ever becoming a world class performer.

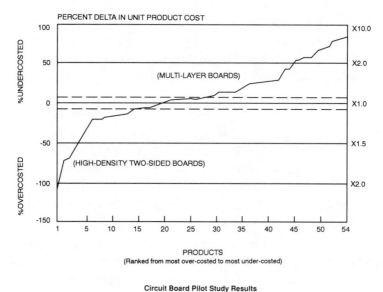

PERCENT DELTA IN UNIT PRODUCT COST

Circuit Board Pilot Study Results

Exhibit 9-1 Cost distortions caused by using traditional cost accounting concepts.[3]

This litany of things wrong with the performance measurement systems in many manufacturing companies only considers the performance metrics utilized and does not take into
account the cultural, political, and organizational factors that
can do so much to motivate (or demotivate) individuals or
groups of employees. The focus in this chapter is on establishing an integrated set of the right performance metrics that will
pull the company toward world class business performance.
These will augment the vision and positive cultural environment that management must also establish.

Measuring the Right Things

So what performance measures should a company use? We
know from the general principles of integration, TQM, CIM,

and JIT that several themes, listed in Exhibit 9-2, should dominate our new performance measurement system metrics. I have been somewhat redundant in this exhibit to make a point about certain specific subjects. A more sparse display would consider excess time a form of waste, as is low asset utilization, and would also consider customer satisfaction a part of quality. In like manner, we know from Chapter 5 that low cost is a highly probable result of achieving the other goals on this list.

What are the overall corporate measures I consider in evaluating at a "first cut" level the extent to which a manufacturing company is a world class competitor? Of necessity, they are ones primarily limited to publicly available information—annual reports, 10Ks (in the United States), research papers in various journals, and articles in the business and manufacturing press. Some world class competitors publicize meaningful data to demonstrate their considerable management and technical leadership. There are others, though, that reveal as little as possible about their performance in the hope of keeping the sources of their competitive advantage secret for the largest possible time.

I should emphasize that none of these measurements alone will denote a world class business performer, but the total pic-

	Minimization	Maximization
Time	✓✓✓	
Waste	✓✓✓	
Cost	✓✓✓	
Quality		✓✓✓
Flexibility		✓✓✓
Value-added		✓✓✓
Productivity		✓✓✓
Asset utilization		✓✓✓
Customer satisfaction		✓✓✓
Data and information integration		✓✓✓

Exhibit 9-2 World class business performance metric themes.

ture provided by the following metrics is a pretty good indicator of status for any given manufacturer. Furthermore, absolute value may not be as important as the trend in the numbers. Examining these numbers over time, for example, a ten-year period, often gives a valuable picture of how a company has improved or deteriorated over that period. More often than not, a ten-year company "numbers picture" will show roughly the same results year after year. This is deterioration in today's world of inflation, intense competition, and the need for continuous improvement.

Here are some of the major performance figures that I evaluate.

• *Sales per employee.* This is one of the easiest measures of productivity to obtain. The average for the Fortune 500 companies in 1990 was $152,000 per employee.[4] The top 200 U.S. electronics firms averaged $150,010 in 1990, and this number has risen an average of 5.2 percent annually since 1985.[5] Many clients that I have worked with have sales per employee of $60,000 to $90,000 per worker per year, with many having less than 50 percent of the average of the Fortune 500 companies. World class performance standards for this metric today are greater than $375,000 per worker per year. Apple, one of the world's best manufacturers, for instance, had sales per employee of $383,000 in 1990, compared with IBM's $185,000, Unisys's $134,000, and DEC's $104,000. Yamazaki's 1990 number is about $438,000 per employee—in the machine tool industry!

There are some caveats to be aware of when using this figure. First, sales are reported annually in current dollars. Thus, monetary inflation alone can raise the numerator (sales) while not affecting the denominator (number of workers). To solve this problem, one can either deflate the sales to constant dollars over a period of time or use payroll dollars to more equalize inflation's effect on both numerator and denominator. Payroll numbers are harder to come by, of course, for comparative purposes.

Second, sales per employee does not consider differences in industry structure and vertical integration. Less vertically integrated manufacturers generally have higher sales per employee. For instance, in electronics, desktop computer manufacturers (which are largely assembly operations of globally sourced components) had sales per employee averaging $263,000 in 1990, versus $169,000 for their more vertically integrated mainframe manufacturing cousins.[6] There is obviously a message here. A key to higher productivity, less asset investment, and more flexibility is less vertical integration. Some firms have the message. Some do not.

• *Sales per square foot* (total owned and leased reported in a company's 10K). This is a measure of overall space utilization and the use of physical assets to produce and sell products. Obviously, it is somewhat dependent on industry and product size (bulldozers vis-à-vis circuit boards) and vertical integration differences. But it can be used with some caution as a relative surrogate measure for how well plants are laid out and inventories are minimized. Exhibit 9-3 lists some companies' results (circa 1989) for comparison; I consider Apple a good world class benchmark. The highest sales per square foot figure I know of for a conventional manufacturer that does not subcontract all its manufacturing is for a $60 million Midwestern electronics manufacturer getting $1638 in sales per square foot.

Company	Sales per Square Foot
Apple	$752
Motorola	$355
Caterpillar	$248
General Dynamics	$239

Exhibit 9-3 Sample manufacturing companies' sales per square foot. (Reprinted from Summer 1991 *Target* "No More Peanut Buttering: Eye-Opening Activity-Based Costing (ABC)," Ralph Hoekstra, with permission of the Association for Manufacturing Excellence, 380 West Palatine Road, Wheeling, IL 60090, 708-520-3282.)

Sales per square foot is often useful to contrast against total space growth for a company over a ten-year period. Sales per square foot ought to increase every year with a good world class performance improvement program in place. Often it stays flat or decreases when companies are expanding too fast, when no such improvement program exists, or when one exists but is being implemented ineffectively.

• *Costs of poor quality* (percent of sales or defective parts per million). In Chapter 4, I cited current world class quality standards of less than 50 defective parts per million. Most manufacturers don't even track quality performance this way. In fact, most have only four numbers (if that many) regarding quality: scrap costs, rework costs, warranty costs (perhaps inflated by sales returns to entice new orders), and the cost of the company's quality control department. Typically, the first three of these figures alone add up to 5 percent to 12 percent of sales. The average company may also track failure rates at the end of the line, and these usually run 5 percent to 10 percent, or 50,000 to 100,000 defective parts per million. Experience and numerous surveys[7] have shown that companies with these kinds of numbers have total costs of poor quality in excess of 20 percent to 25 percent of sales and are running at a quality level of well over 100,000 defective parts per million.

Electronics producers usually have long burn-in procedures prior to final testing to weed out components or fabrication and assembly techniques causing poor quality. The longer the burn-in time, the worse the quality of the sourced components, the assembly, and the company's manufacturing process. In 1986 IBM was using a burn-in time of 10 hours in their Boca Raton PC plant[8] and working on reducing that. Many of its competitors were tying up over 1500 PCs at a time for three full days or more in their burn-in process.[9] An interesting statistic to examine, in addition to burn-in time and first-time failure rate, is the number of times a product has been reworked and recycled back through burn-in. It's not unusual in poor quality operations to find some products that have been reworked three or four times and may have spent a week or two in this test and rework mode.

• *Overall inventory turns* (cost of sales divided by average or year-end inventory). Inventory turns, of course, are one component of asset turns—a component that gives some idea of lead times and the effectiveness of the company's materials management function and systems. This indicator is sensitive to vertical integration and distribution channel differences, and world class performance is generally in excess of 20 total inventory turns per year, especially for companies with little finished goods or distribution inventory. It pays to look at the ten-year trends also.

• *WIP inventory turns* are sensitive to the kind of product being built, as one would expect. It's unreasonable to expect an airframe or submarine manufacturer to have the same WIP turns as an OEM automotive supplier or an electronics manufacturer. But for discrete part production, where more than a few products are being built per day, world class WIP inventory turn standards are in excess of 40 turns per year. In high-volume manufacturers, such as automotive and electronic assembly plants, world-class WIP turn standards are in excess of 80 turns per year. Nissan has been getting in excess of 150 WIP turns per year at its Muriyama plant in Japan for several years.[10] Even medium-volume job shop production environments should be able to turn WIP 15 to 20 times per year today using a combination of MRP and JIT techniques.

It's also somewhat more difficult to calculate or compare WIP turns because there's no convention for choosing a cost figure for the inventory, and companies vary widely on how much cost buildup detail their systems can provide at any given point in time or in the manufacturing process. Obviously, the cost figure must reflect the value added to the raw material and parts since they entered the work stream. But to value all the WIP as finished at full manufacturing cost would be wrong, too. What number to use depends heavily on the nature of the product and process, but for making a comparison within a company over a period of years, it will do no harm simply to pick a figure halfway between incoming and finished goods costs.

Particularly in companies with multiplant environments, where plants feed each other with components, it's important to see that inventory elements are defined properly to get the right focus on minimizing waste and improving throughput at a corporate level. One manufacturer I worked with often defined one plant's output as another plant's raw material. This was good at a plant level, but neglected the well-being and performance of the company as a whole. I suggested the following new corporate definitions of inventory levels for them:

- *Raw material:* material to which XYZ Company has added no value
- *Work in process:* any material between raw materials and finished goods
- *Finished goods:* goods ready for shipment to XYZ Company's customer with no more value to be added

Although the definitions above look rather fundamental, such basics are often lost in the complexities and pressures of day-to-day business. These definitions place a focus on total corporate material flow and eliminate a lot of game playing with inventory classification between plants.

- *Real sales growth* (in constant dollars). Is the company really growing and at what rate? Using any number of deflators (the U.S. government's producer price series will usually do, or one could use its GNP deflator), plot this over a ten-year period. World class companies almost always grow in real terms every year—because they're delighting their customers with world class products and services.

- *R and D as a percentage of sales.* Like MIPS for information systems, a crude measure (is it being spent effectively?), but you've got to start somewhere. The average for all U.S. industrial companies in 1990, according to *Business Week*, was 3.4 percent.[11] Industry averages can be obtained from the same listing to give a more relevant figure for any company in a specific industry. Unfortunately, this number doesn't tell you how the money is spent. As I noted in Exhibit 3-3, world class companies usually invest heavily in both product and process R and D.

• *Asset turns* (net sales divided by total assets). This measure gets at the amount of assets it takes to generate a given level of sales. Naturally, it will be lower for capital-intensive industries and for companies that are more vertically integrated. It's difficult to pin down a world class standard because of this, but more than one turn should be an absolute minimum goal. Again, a ten-year profile for a company is most instructive.

Beware of numbers games when looking at asset utilization. In some companies, smart CFOs who play to Wall Street will sell and lease back company buildings, for example, manufacturing plants, to get these assets off the balance sheet and make their return on assets look higher than it is. This may be OK for Wall Street, but it misses the entire point of becoming a world class performer—the maximizing of asset utilization, specifically buildings, equipment, systems, and people. One case where a client of mine had performed such financial engineering backfired when the client decided to become a world class manufacturer. Doing this involved rationalizing its production capacity and, for many different reasons, eliminating some current plants. But this couldn't be done optimally without severe penalties because the company had locked itself into long-term leases at nine of its manufacturing facilities. Oops— great finance, but poor operations management!

• *Education and training spending* per employee per year, or as a percentage of payroll. As I will demonstrate in Chapter 12, a minimum of $1000 per employee on a constant dollar basis is the standard for world class performance. This figure does not include the opportunity time loss from production when courses are held on company time. If a company's average cost per employee with fringes is $40,000 per year, then this spending on education and training is 2.5 percent of total payroll costs. In many small companies, where the average cost per employee figure is lower but the education and training need may be even higher, this performance standard could approach 3 percent to 3.5 percent of payroll costs for the first few years of an education and training program.

• *Information system (IS) spending* (including all engineering, manufacturing automation, personal computer, and telecommunication costs) as a percentage of sales. As noted in Chapter 7, this is a crude measure, but, in my experience with scores of companies over the years, an unfailing one. The companies spending 0.75 percent to 2.0 percent of sales for all ISs are always those with antiquated and incomplete information systems, and generally those with poor manufacturing and business performance. World class performance standards in this category call for a minimum of 6 percent of sales, especially for the "building" years covering the company's progression toward world class performance.

Even more interesting is to examine, in addition to a ten-year trend, the split of IS spending among business, engineering, and manufacturing automation or process control applications. One will often find that engineering-intensive companies don't devote an adequate share of the IS budget to engineering, given this function's strategic importance to the company.

• *Manufacturing cost structure* (labor, materials, and manufacturing overhead). This set of numbers is dependent on industry and degree of vertical integration. The manufacturing overhead number generally does not include selling, general, and administrative costs (SG and A), or R and D. The thing to look at here is the proportions between the factors. In some companies, overhead is over 50 percent of the manufacturing cost structure—prohibitively high for any manufacturing company today to be a world class performer. As we saw in Chapter 5, 20 to 25 percent is more of a world class standard for manufacturing overhead.

If direct labor is greater than 12 percent to 15 percent of manufacturing cost, this could be a red flag that highlights a company's lack of investment in manufacturing technology, poor materials handling and plant layout, improper design for manufacturability, or poor quality. The job is to find out where the people are and what they are doing in order to simplify things and improve throughput and productivity.

As I have stated, no one of these numbers above exclusively tells the tale. But taken collectively, they paint a picture of a company from two points of view. First, their trends over time (at least ten years) tell a story. Is the company's performance improving or deteriorating, and how fast? Can trend changes be tied to any one point in the company's history—for example, an acquisition, a new CEO, a new product, global expansion, or a new improvement program? In most of the companies I have observed, their performance has been flat (thus deteriorating invisibly) or visibly deteriorating. This generally means that management is unaware of how bad company performance really is (when compared to the real world) or what to do about it, that improvement programs either don't exist or are ineffective, and that current functional managers for a variety of reasons aren't accomplishing or can't accomplish anything more than maintaining the status quo.

Second, the numbers, viewed as a snapshot of current performance against general world class standards, give a valuable picture of overall company performance. Particularly when combined with an assessment of several of the company's plants, managers, and management information systems, they provide a clear picture of the company's performance and an opportunity to improve into a world class business performer.

Performance Assessment Through Competitive Advantage Tool Evaluation

We know that becoming a world-class business performer requires the use of concepts, philosophies, and tools from the world of TQM, CIM, JIT, and cost management. The extent to which these competitive advantage enablers are evidenced in a company is one indicator of the company's performance capability, assuming that enlightened management is guiding their implementation and utilization and is investing in manufacturing technology and in education and training for all employees. In most cases, interviews, data gathering, and plant tours can give a team enough information to map a company's status in these areas against what *is* in other companies or industries and what *could be* in the subject company. An example of this is shown in Exhibit 9-4, which is a summary view of the major tools and concepts.

Note that this company is weak and dangerously behind in implementing tools from almost every major category of competitive advantage tools. Also note that it's not necessary to be at 100 percent of the state of the art in every area, depend-

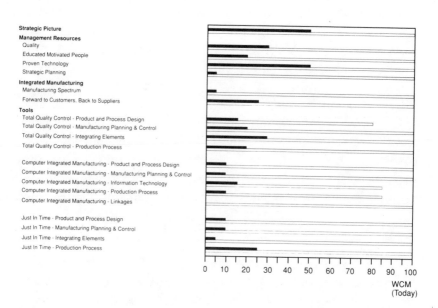

Exhibit 9-4 A sample manufacturing company profile against world class performance competitive advantage tool usage.

ing on the nature of the company's products, manufacturing processes, and production volumes.

A more detailed view of the use of CIM in the same company is shown in Exhibit 9-5. This picture shows the same state of affairs for the CIM-based competitive advantage tools—the company is using few of them to the extent they could be utilized to gain competitive advantage in the industry. I am sad to say that the two assessment pictures above are all too typical of many manufacturing companies today.

The competitive advantage tool assessments above are a subjective judgment call on the part of the assessor (often, and properly, an outside consultant), but they help to paint a profile of company performance and management competence that augments the numerical performance comparison discussed earlier.

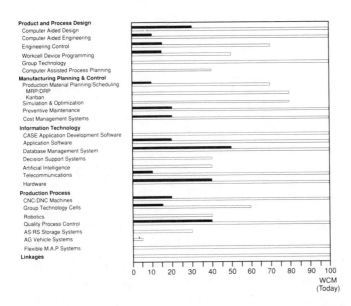

Exhibit 9-5 A real-world company status against CIM implementation in 1990.

Establishing Company Performance Measures That Pull the Company Toward World Class Business Performance

The goal of using performance measures to pull a company toward world class performance is to select a few—less than twenty will do—as overall measures to track at a corporate level over a three- to five-year period at a minimum. Some of these might change over time as the competitive situation demands—not all of them should be cast in concrete. These measurements should apply at a corporate and business unit level, and will comprise both aggregate measures such as asset turns and functional and business process measures.

Earlier in this chapter, we examined some indicators that, when viewed as a total picture, can show at first glance a company's overall performance level vis-à-vis several world class standards. I shall now list more—and more specific—performance factors that can be selectively utilized by managers to measure company functions or business process excellence. I have included those discussed earlier for completeness, and include comments where appropriate.

Financial

- Return on assets (ROA). ROA averaged 4.8 percent for the Fortune 500 during 1990.[12] World class for this measurement is in excess of 10 percent for discrete part electromechanical manufacturers. Pharmaceuticals (with the highest industry average of 13.1 percent in 1990), soaps, beverages, and food are at the high end of this list, so their world class goal should be higher, perhaps 20 percent. Again, beware the asset game mentioned earlier in this chapter. Also note that, when some companies are guided by only this figure, they will underinvest to keep the asset base low and raise ROA for any given profit level. This leads to run-down plants and equipment, obsolete technology, and poor quality—not to world class business performance.

- Total asset turns (net sales divided by total assets). This averaged 0.96 for the Fortune 500 during 1990.[13] However, this figure is very product/process dependent. Examples of world class from 1990 are Boeing (1.89), Apple (1.86), and General Mills (1.97).
- Sales per employee.
- Value-added per employee, or again, to level the effects of inflation, value-added per payroll dollar. Value-added is sales minus all purchases of goods and services.
- R and D spending as a percentage of sales.
- Sales per square foot.
- Units produced per payroll dollar. In the end, this may be the best single measure for a company to focus on, if its units can be measured consistently.
- Energy dollars used per year, or energy dollars used per end item unit of production.

Sales

- Customer order-to-delivery lead time. Minimize and continually improve.
- Number of customers retained per year. Here, as with sales and demand, the key is to know why the company lost a customer.
- Number of new customers per year. Beware—not all customers are good customers. It's likely that there is business you really don't want. (See the last item in this section.)
- Number of order entry errors per week.
- Number of orders entered per OE payroll dollar.
- Linearity of orders on a daily basis throughout the year.

- Number and value of orders lost because the company could not accommodate the customer. This is the critical difference between customer demand and sales that many companies do not know, in part because their order entry systems only track actual orders, and their order entry people may throw away the orders they cannot accommodate. Order entry systems should have a "bucket" for this category of orders so that the company will not lose sight of them. It is these orders that provide real value to a company concerned with customer satisfaction, continual improvement, and growth. Why didn't the company get the order? Was the cost too high? Couldn't the company deliver when the customer needed it? Wasn't there a sufficient quantity in stock in distribution? Did the last shipment to that customer have a quality problem? A Pareto analysis of the reasons for losing this business, plus the knowledge of the amount of business attempted but lost each year, would be most instructive to many companies.
- The cost of serving each different type of customer. ABC cost analysis can provide these figures, which are a great guide to doing business profitably and with an orientation toward growth rather than maintenance.

Engineering

- Product and process design lead time. Minimize and continually improve.
- Ratio of design to manufacturing engineers. This should be no more than three to one for world class new product and process development.
- Engineering (design and process) changes per week
- Engineering (design and process) changes per product. These can also be recorded against each product's life cycle to note where the bulk of the changes are made—for instance, before or after release to manufacturing.

- Engineering RFQ response time. The ability to respond quickly and accurately to RFQs (opportunities) is a hallmark of world class competitors and a capability that many companies in the build-to-order business often underemphasize.
- Number of engineering RFQ "closes." This should be better than 50 percent, or something is wrong.
- Design/manufacturing breakeven time. This is the time it takes to make a sufficient profit on a product's sales to fully recover the total investment (R and D, production ramp-up, sales and marketing expenses, and so on) in bringing a new product to market. The goal is to be continually reducing this time, both by minimizing design lead time and by maximizing product attractiveness and sales coordination.
- Parts count reduction per product. The number of parts in a product directly affects product cost, manufacturing complexity, and overhead—particularly transaction costs. Numerous companies' experiences have shown that parts count reductions of 30 percent to 50 percent can bring about product cost reductions of 20 percent to 30 percent or more, and have the potential to reduce overhead also.[14]
- Total product and process design lead time from product concept to release to manufacturing for volume production

Accounting

- Customer product receipt to received payment lead time. Use EDI and no invoicing here to save time and overhead as Ford and Mazda have.[15]
- Number of days to close the books at month or quarter end. World class is less than 5 days. Anything else is way behind. (Many companies require over a month!)
- Number of errors per line item billed

Information systems

In addition to traditional measures that I shall mention shortly, I have come to realize how essential information *value* is to an enterprise's competitiveness. I believe that there are ten primary critera by which to evaluate the information value an enterprise has available to effectively manage its business:

- *Completeness*—the extent to which electronically based information describes or captures each data element necessary for the enterprise's business processes and functional activities
- *Consistent definition* of data throughout the enterprise
- *Accuracy* of data used throughout the enterprise
- *Timeliness*—the extent to which the enterprise's information (or data) mirrors an event, with real time being the ideal
- *Responsiveness*—the time between request and receipt of desired information
- *Security*—the extent to which the enterprise's data and information systems are protected from accidental or deliberate alteration (by humans or a virus), misuse, theft, or destruction, as well as from decay or failure
- *Communicability*—the extent to which the enterprise's information (or data) can be shared electronically, sent or accessed at any time, across the distributed environment of the global enterprise, its global customers and suppliers, and its business information utility sources
- *Interpretiveness*—the extent to which the enterprise's electronic information can be quickly and easily interpreted by the human mind, with the use of summary color graphical output being the ideal
- *Integration*—the seamlessness of the information environment with a minimum amount of data and only one original entry occurrence for each data element
- *Span*—the extent to which information management reflects and integrates the three essential domains of busi-

ness (alphanumeric), engineering (geometric), and process control (real-time) data and systems

Information value is not directly quantifiable as are the other three business values of cost, quality, and time. It is far more subjective in nature and depends on the evaluator and evaluation scale having the broadest possible scope and state of the art thinking.

I suggest that initially the easiest way to characterize the information value chain for a manufacturing enterprise is on a subjective scale, perhaps from 1 to 10 (increasing in favorability) for each factor. Then the enterprise's performance for the information value chain could be grouped in classes such as these:

Ranking	Score Total
World class	90–100
Leading	75–89
Average	55–74
Trailing	40–54
Nonviable	0–39

The use of a matrixed checklist with stages of progress against world class performance for each of the ten attributes can be used to measure where a manufacturing enterprise stands with regard to its information value. The table can also show company-specific examples of world class performance from a variety of industries for each of the ten attributes. This assessment will paint a valuable picture as a basis for an enterprise's efforts to be a world class competitior.

More traditional measures for information systems deal with the following points.

- Number of workstations or terminals divided among the total number of employees. World class today is better than one for every two employees. (Motorola had 55,000 for 104,000 employees in 1990.[16]) The ultimate goal may be more than one per employee because some people will have a computer at home or may carry a portable to accompany them when they travel. The big question is whether shop floor workers each need a computer or terminal. Why not? They may need one to refer to assembly "drawings" or instructions, to query about tomorrow's schedule, to analyze quality information, to leave a special note to their night shift counterpart, to compare notes on an assembly procedure with another worker in another global plant making the same product, or to sign up for a new education and training class. The real criterion here is one of access capacity. Many, if not most, "knowledge workers" need quick access to information in various forms, and thus should possess their own terminals or workstations. Shop floor workers might only have a need to access information periodically, and thus could share a workstation or terminal with several other workers. The real need is for all employees to have quick access to a variety of information important to the effective conduct of their jobs.

- IS budget as a percentage of sales (see Chapter 7)
- System response time. Nobody today should be waiting more than 1 to 1.5 seconds for most common transactions and responses.
- Number of redundant data elements.
- Percentage of PCs and workstations networked as a percentage of the total installed. The goal here is 100 percent, as soon as practically possible.
- Number of engineering workstations as a percentage of the number of product and process engineers per shift. Today, 50 percent; as soon as possible, 100 percent.

Materials management and customer order-to-delivery

- Inventory turns, all categories: raw materials, WIP, finished goods, and total.

- Percentage of on-time delivery to customers' first required delivery date. *On-time* means plus one half-day, minus zero to a world class company. Get ready for on-time to mean within a one hour window.
- Percentage of on-time to the company's first commit date. Although it is currently different from the previous measure in many companies, this difference should disappear as a company becomes a world class performer.
- Master schedule changes per week. These should be minimized by the use of the available-to-promise function, by better (real-time, if possible) inventory knowledge and policies, and by working with customers to know (electronically) their requirements more accurately and earlier.
- Shipment linearity—percentage of quarter per week, and percentage of week per day. The world class goal is to have any one manufacturing day be as any other, thus ending the end of the month, end of the quarter, end of the year "hockey sticks" and craziness that pervade most companies today.
- Average number of levels in bills of materials. This should be less than five, with movement over time toward even fewer levels as JIT concepts are implemented on the plant floor.
- Customer order-to-receipt lead time.
- Percentage of customer order filled by line item and quantity.
- Number of forklifts in use. This in an inverse indicator; companies that have poor plant layouts and manufacturing processes and too much inventory have a lot of forklifts in use. The lower this number the better.
- Customer backorders as a percentage of total orders, by SKU and quantity.
- Inventory space (square feet) required as a percentage of total manufacturing space.

- Number of errors per order shipped. This refers to pick errors of either SKU number or quantity, not product quality problems.
- Number of long-term (two- to three-year) sole-sourced contracts with suppliers
- Percentage of supplier deliveries late. World class is less than 5 percent.
- Supplier parts defects. The same goals prevail for them as for the company.
- Percentage of certified suppliers.
- Percentage of buy with certified suppliers in dollars.
- Supplier lead times. This measure should decrease by a factor of at least 50 percent over a two-year period. It refers to total lead time from placement of the order (electronically, one hopes) through receipt of acceptable goods at the using facility.
- Number of suppliers per buyer. Five to ten is appropriate to really develop superb supplier partnerships and help suppliers lower their costs, improve their quality, improve their delivery accuracy, shorten their lead times, and contribute to the company's product and process design efforts.
- Total number of suppliers. This number should be reduced annually, with an overall goal of about an order of magnitude reduction over several years, for instance, from 2000 to 200. A company cannot afford to educate and train or deal with the extra 1800 suppliers.
- Percentage of orders or releases communicated by EDI.
- Money spent on helping suppliers to become certified. Most purchasing departments do not even have a budget for this activity. Honda of America's purchasing department had 40 engineers in 1990 who were completely devoted to helping their suppliers improve their productivity and quality, in addition to another 120 engineers in their quality department who dealt with purchased part and supplier quality issues.[17]

Human resources

- Education and training spending—percentage of payroll or dollars per employee per year.

- Employee turnover—percentage per year. Excess turnover costs many companies a fortune every year—not only to continually hire people to replace lost workers, but to educate and train them at least to the level of the employees who left.

- Employee absenteeism. Some European companies run 25 percent to 30 percent absenteeism each day.[18] In the United States, the worst companies run 15 percent to 20 percent. World class companies run less than 2 percent to 3 percent. Absenteeism represents wasted capacity, excess education and training time and costs, and wasted supervision time and costs.

Production

- Preventive maintenance spending as a percentage of sales. Many companies spend nothing in this area for preventive maintenance. Instead, they run a machine until it breaks, then patch it up again. A well-planned, ongoing preventive maintenance program lies at the heart of achieving JIT manufacturing and world class quality.

- Production machinery—mean time between failure and mean time to repair. Most companies don't even track these figures. World class performers do, at the individual machine level. They maximize the former and minimize the latter.

- Set-up time in hours. Minimization and continual improvement is obviously the goal here.

- Production space—square feet required as a percentage of total plant space. This is very product and process dependent. But given a constant or even mildly increasing production volume, it should be continually decreasing.

Quality

- Defect rate for *any* business or production process in parts per million. IBM and Motorola, among others, have been leaders in the U.S. quality movement. They have both done some interesting benchmarks of daily business processes, and have come up with the observation that most every-day processes like doctors' prescription writing, preparing restaurant bills, payroll processing, and customer order taking operate at levels around 6,000 to 10,000 defects per million. When IBM started measuring its quality levels this way in the beginning of 1990, its overall defect rate was about 66,810 defects per million operations.[19] This is a corporate average, because many of its manufacturing processes are meeting or exceeding world class standards today, and some have been for years. Leading world class companies are already performing at less than 50 defective parts per million and are shooting for less than 3.4 defective parts per million. The trick, obviously, is to have world class quality levels in every business and manufacturing process, not just one or two.
- Pounds material in compared to pounds material out.
- Number of customer complaints (about anything) per month.
- Elapsed time for first response to customer problem.
- Elapsed time to solution of customer problem.
- Number of rings to answer any telephone with a concerned human voice.
- All quality costs—prevention, appraisal, internal, and external as percentage of sales. I'd estimate that world class performance is about 3 percent to 5 percent of sales—a long way from most manufacturing companies' spending.

Note that all of these performance measures are designed to accomplish the overall performance goals outlined in Exhibit 9-2. There is nothing sacred about any one of them, and the reader may be able to think of many more, and even some more relevant to his or her manufacturing company and industry.

A Perspective on World Class Business Performance

Not only don't most executives realize what world class performance is and how far their companies are from it, but they remain unaware of the tremendous rate of change that is occurring in manufacturing companies with enlightened management that are combining today's technology with educating and training their people so that they continually improve. Let me cite two examples from the world of computer-aided design and engineering (CAD/CAE) as surrogates for this tremendous rate of change and what it portends for other manufacturers.

First, from the world of semiconductor design, we will examine application-specific integrated circuits, or ASIC chips. Consider Exhibit 9-6.

In 1988 Cypress Semiconductor required 30 engineers to work 18 months to design a 25 MIP RISC architecture chip. T. J. Rodgers, the CEO, said that if the CAD and CAE software and hardware available in 1982 had been used, it would have taken 45 engineers 36 months to design the same chip. In 1989, its engineers designed a chip three times as complex as the one just described using only ten engineers in nine months. What a phenomenal testimony to the power of technology and human learning! It doesn't require a lot of vision to see where this

CAE DESIGN SYSTEM AGE	TASK	NUMBER ENGINEERS	NUMBER MONTHS
1982	To design chip below	45	36
1988	25 Mip RISC Chip	30	18
1989	To design chip *3 times* as complex as above chip	10	9

Exhibit 9-6 ASIC semiconductor design using electronics CAD/CAE hardware and software, or electronic design automation (EDA).[20]

will lead, given today's dazzling increase in computing power and the further integration of electronics design tools under the CAD frameworks initiative. In the near future, two to four engineers are likely to sit at a workstation and design a chip of 10 to 100 times more complexity in a month or less.

On the process side of chip design and production, Intel has carefully tracked yield and defect density as a function of "time from first technology concept" of the last four generations of its chips. It has found that each generation of chips has cut by a factor of 2 the time required to achieve the same yield level as the preceding generation.[21]

In the mechanical world, consider Boeing's use of CAD/CAE hardware and solid modeling (Dassault's CATIA) software to design an engine to wing strut to fit Rolls Royce's engine to its 767 aircraft. Note, in Exhibit 9-7, the complexity of this design: 2350 detail parts, 360 installation standards, 46 major assembly tools, and the usual stacks of production, technical, quality, and safety documentation. The results are, for the aircraft industry, every bit as dramatic as those obtained by Cypress Semiconductor in the electronics industry. Lead time (for this first design effort on such a scale using solid modeling) was reduced by four months, or 16 percent. All design data was in digital form so that it could be directly used as a basis for programming downstream work cell devices such as CNC machine tools, coordinate measuring machines,

BOEING COMMERCIAL AIRCRAFT -- 767 ENGINE TO WING STRUT

DESIGN INCLUDED:

   2350 DETAIL PARTS,   360 INSTALLATION STANDARDS

   46 MAJOR ASSEMBLY TOOLS

   PRODUCTION, TECHNICAL, AND MAINTENANCE MANUALS

Exhibit 9-7 Mechanical design using CAD / CAE solid modeling software.[22]

and robots. Thirty thousand hours (at a rate of at least $50 per hour, I would estimate) were saved because no mockup was required. Over 70 interference points (for instance, where hydraulic tubing ran into a wiring harness or structural piece) were eliminated. Furthermore, the design was right the first time the parts were produced—saving an enormous amount of time and hand fitting on the production floor. Sixty-five percent fewer engineering changes were needed, and, in Boeing's industry, an engineering change costs on the average of $20,000 to $25,000.[23] This is another example of a tremendous rate of improvement. Boeing's new goal is to design its entire new 777 aircraft using this same technology. What does that imply for the companies who want to be their major suppliers of mechanical parts? What does that imply for their global competitors?

These are excellent examples of the rate of progress being made by many manufacturers that either are—or are vigorously pursuing becoming—world class manufacturers. They demonstrate what is possible as well as what their suppliers and other companies in their industry will have to do to keep up. Consider some other examples of world class business performance.

Digital Equipment Corporation implemented standard accounting and financial software on a global basis so that they can now close their books at the end of any accounting period in a mere seven to eight days.[24] With most companies, this process takes two to six weeks. Guess which company can respond more quickly to increasingly volatile global business conditions.

From the metal-cutting industry, let's look at Yamazaki Mazak, one of the two most advanced companies in the world (the other is Fanuc Ltd.). Exhibit 9-8 shows the three flexible manufacturing systems (FMSs) installed in one of their newest plants in Worcester, U.K.

Each machine tool in any of the FMSs has an 80-tool magazine. FMS #2 is capable of running 60 hours unmanned. All FMSs are manned only 12 hours each day. There is one operator for each FMS and two plant maintenance people in this

		Type	# different components machined	average machining time / piece
FMS #1	Rotational parts	3 Lathes	250	15 min
FMS #2	Small prismatic parts	7 Mach. Ctrs.	200	40 min
FMS #3	Large prismatic parts	4 Mach. Ctrs.	20	3.5 hours

Exhibit 9-8 Flexible manufacturing systems at
Yamazaki's Worcester, U.K. plant.[25]

section of the plant. Yamazaki's machining tolerances for its CNC lathes and machining centers produced in this plant are 2 to 20 microns (a micron is one-millionth of a meter), and assembly tolerances are 5 microns.

Yamazaki can show everyone what world class machine utilization is all about! The average cutting time of FMS #2 for two years on a 24 hour per day, 365 day per year basis, excluding three weeks of planned plant maintenance, was 94 percent. On this basis, the comparative percentage for most U.S. manufacturers, assuming that they, like Yamazaki, only made what they needed and didn't keep their machines running just to absorb overhead, would be 10 percent to 20 percent.

Two other stories serve to illustrate Yamazaki's world class performance. In 1983 I was one of the first Westerners to see its new Minikamo plant in Japan. Some of their stupendous performance figures from there are shown in my last book. At that point, Minikamo was just past start-up mode and they were busy ramping production up. The plant was only running one shift unmanned then. Now, eight years later, they are producing more products there and in far greater volumes than before. In the spring of 1991, they had just changed to running two shifts unmanned in this plant. Yamazaki has one of the highest sales per employee figures I know of in manufacturing, especially in the metal cutting industry. Its global sales in 1990 were about $1.4 billion with just 3200 employees, thus generating $438,000 sales per employee. Not a bad target to shoot for, but an almost impossible number to successfully compete against.

How many examples will manufacturing executives have to hear about, from different industries in all parts of the world, before they take action in their company? One of the arguments I often hear from recalcitrant executives is that you have to be a big company—an IBM, a Boeing, a John Deere, or a Toyota— to be or become a world class performer. Nothing could be further from the truth. Consider these examples.

United Electric Controls Company was a $30 million manu-facturer in Watertown, Massachusetts, in 1989. Using primarily a combination of JIT and SQC in a program that started around 1988, it was able to achieve the benefits shown in Exhibit 9-9: lead times were reduced by a factor of ten, total inventory came down by 40 percent, and WIP was reduced by 75 per-cent. On-time deliveries went from 65 percent to 95 percent, while in-process inspections were cut from 2,700 to 300. A parts standardization program took 43 percent of parts out of production. It now uses one building, not three, thus reducing its space requirements by 60 percent. Sixty percent of its orders are shipped in three days or less. Lot sizes that used to aver-age 200 now average 10. The number of stockroom employees went from 26 to 5. The former 30-person production and in-ventory control department merged with the former 20-person sales and order department to create a 12-employee customer

	BEFORE	EARLY 1990
LEAD TIMES (Average weeks)	10	1
TOTAL INVENTORY (Index)	100	60
WIP INVENTORY	$1,200,000	300,000
ON TIME DELIVERIES	65%	95%
IN-PROCESS INSPECTIONS	2,700	300
ACTIVE PARTS (Standardization)	14,000	8,000

Exhibit 9-9 JIT/SQC results at United Electric Controls Company.[26]

service and scheduling department. (How do we reduce over-head?)

United Electric is only a $30 million company, with about 375 employees (they're not world class in productivity *yet*). But this is what can be achieved in a short amount of time with almost no capital investment—only enlightened management and education and training were needed. Still to come is the entire world of CIM, Taguchi methods, and other critical competitive advantage tools for becoming a total world class business performer. United Electric won the Shingo Prize for Manufacturing Excellence for Small Business in 1990 for its great efforts toward world class performance.

Now examine Exhibit 9-10, which shows the progress that Tokai Rubber in Japan has made toward world class performance using just a combination of JIT, TQC, and preventive maintenance. Tokai manufactures rubber parts for automobiles, but not tires. Note that its inventory turns were either 25 or 37 back in 1980, depending on whether 250 days or 365 days is used as a base. In 1988, it was about either 110 or 160 inventory turns per year. Note the in-process reject rate drop, although I cannot explain the lack of progress since 1986. (I speculate that it is caused by not using Taguchi methods sufficiently). Note the tremendous effect of its preventive maintenance program. Tokai Rubber's sales were about $180 million in 1988—a small company, and sales per employee that year was

	1980	1985	1986	1987	1988	
INVENTORY TURNOVER (Days)	10	3.6	2.8	2.5	2.3	JIT
REJECT RATE - IN PROCESS	0.9	0.53	0.28	0.29	0.30	TQC
NUMBER MACHINE BREAKDOWNS (Cases/month)	185	7	3	2	2	TPM

Exhibit 9-10 Historical world class performance progress at Tokai Rubber.[27]

approximately $413,000. Not too bad for a small company—world class, in fact.

So there is no doubt that a company can become a world class performer even if it is a small one. It's a matter of attitude—believing in a vision and the will to win—and effective management. Each manufacturer has the money, for the money each wastes today as a percentage of sales is about the same regardless of company size. The money to become a world class performer is lying right out there on the shop floor (and in the offices) as the cost of poor quality, long lead times, employee ignorance, and lack of management will.

Implementing performance measures that pull a company toward world class business performance is relatively easy compared to the rest of the tasks that lie before most manufacturers. The measurement definitions and starting point measures need to be established, and information systems (manual or computer-based) need to be put in place to gather the right data on a timely basis. The absolute value of the measurements at the starting point matter little. What does matter is for the company's management to establish the discipline to make progress against the selected performance measures every day. To this end, bonus and other incentive plans must be changed to be based on progress toward world class business performance goals as well as customer satisfaction.

Where you start is irrelevant. Where you can end up against these targets is unknown. The important thing is to get started now. Do it.

Chapter 9

1. Walleck, et al., " Benchmarking World Class Performance," *The McKinsey Quarterly*, No. 1, 1991.
2. George Stalk Jr. and Thomas M. Hout, *Competing Against Time* (The Free Press, New York), 1990, p. 36.
3. Ralph Hoekstra, "No More Peanut Buttering: Eye-Opening Activity-Based Costing (ABC)," *Target*, Association For Manufacturing Excellence, Summer 1991, p. 47.

4. "The Fortune 500," *Fortune*, 22 April 1991.

5. L. Stallman and E. B. Baatz, "The Electronic Business 200," *Electronic Business*, 22 July 1991, pp. 32–68.

6. Ibid. pp. 56 and 58.

7. Two such studies are KPMG Peat Marwick/ Illinois Manufacturers Association, reported in *American Machinist*, January 1991, p. 17; and The Willimantic Division of Rogers Corporation, reported in *Quality Progress*, July 1986, pp. 21–24.

8. Gunn Associates, Inc. files.

9. Gunn Associates, Inc. files.

10. Oliver Wight Company Newsletter, 1986.

11. "R & D Scoreboard," *Business Week Innovation*, 1990, p. 157.

12. "The Fortune 500" *Fortune*, 22 April 1991.

13. Ibid.

14. Several examples: Andrew Lee-Mortimer, "Designing For The Future," *Total Quality Management*, April 1991, pp. 99–104—NCR ATM money cassette: 58% parts reduction, 44% cost reduction; Deby Venziale, "Design To Excellence At Beckman Instruments," *Target*, Spring 1990, pp. 30–33—41% parts reduction, 26% cost reduction; Therese R. Walter, "Design For Manufacture and Assembly," *Industry Week*, 4 September 1989, pp. 79–82—Texas Instrument Defense Systems and Electronics Group redesign of a reticle assembly; Therese R. Walter, "Motorola Gets A Charge Out Of DFMA," *Industry Week*, 3 September 1990, pp. 75–76; and Peter Dewhurst and Geoff Boothrayd, "Computer-Aided Design For Assembly," *Assembly Engineering*, February 1983, pp. 18–22—Xerox latch, 73% parts reduction, 36% cost reduction.

15. Michael Hammer, "Reengineering Work: Don't Automate, Obliterate," *Harvard Business Review*, July–August 1990, pp. 104–112.

16. William Wiggenhorn, "Motorola U: When Training Becomes An Education," *Harvard Business Review*, July–August 1990, pp. 71–83.

17. "Honda," *Industry Week*, 19 March 1990, p. 19.

18. Robert Taylor, "Spoon-feeding A National Malaise," *Financial Times*, 30 August 1989, p. 12.

19. Bruce C.P. Rayner, "Market Driven Quality: IBM's Six Sigma Crusade," *Electronic Business,* 15 October 1990, p.70.

20. T.J. Rodgers, *Harvard Business Review,* Jan–Feb 1990.

21. "Intel Focuses On The Customer," *Electronic Business,* 19 March 1990.

22. Robert H. Johnson, "Reaching New Heights with Solid Modeling," *Computer Graphics World,* December 1989, pp. 65–72.

23. Gunn Associates, Inc. estimate.

24. Digital Equipment Corporation public relations materials and conversations with Peter E. Brown, DEC's corporate telecommunications manager.

25. Yamazaki material and Gunn Associates, Inc. files

26. See Cathi Rossi, "Japanese Techniques Yield Both Results and Recognition," *Metalworking News,* date unknown, pp. 4 and 22; and Michael A. Verespej "The Self Education of Bruce Hamilton," *Industry Week,* 1 April 1991, pp. 16–22.

27. Ludo F. Gelders, "Shop Floor Performance Indicators," *Logistics Information Management,* March 1990, pp. 45–47.

10

Developing a
Winning Strategy

Most manufacturers must undergo a tremendous amount of change if they are to survive, grow, and prosper in the future. The change necessary in their companies is a direct result of the change, uncertainty, and risk they must cope with as competitors in the general manufacturing business environment and as players in the larger social, economic, and political global environment. Before discussing how to develop a winning strategy, consider the complexity of the modern manufacturing business environment. What are some of the forces manufacturers face today?

Reviewing the Change,
Uncertainty, and Risks Around Us

Weather variables are a considerable influence, affecting not only consumer demand for things like clothing, snowblowers, lawn mowers, and farm equipment, but also manufacturers' operations. Snow and rain can affect JIT deliveries of material from suppliers or deliveries to customers. Severe heat can cause power brownouts that can affect production machinery and computers in a factory.

Legal issues and new rulings on old subjects such as environmental regulations and the transfer of data between countries in Europe can wreak havoc on a company's business plans and implementation costs.

Political issues can keep business in a constant state of change. Changes in the minimum wage rate, import duties and tariffs, capital investment tax treatment, corporate tax rates, and lobbying laws are a constant concern for businesses.

Currency volatility in global financial markets can be disastrous to company earnings if a company lacks the skill to hedge properly against such threats. Allied with currency rate changes are changes in interest rates that influence global financial market swings.

Changes in government spending can have a large influence on manufacturers, whether these changes are in the country's defense budget or its information systems for federal agencies.

Changes in the use of conventional materials and their sources can radically affect sourcing costs and modes of transportation for the materials. Then too, transportation changes can occur because of deregulation of the truck and airline industries, for instance; these changes have radically affected how manufacturers use these services.

Customer expectations change about what constitutes good quality, and about fashion—what kind of clothes, cars, or houses are desirable. In good part these changes are a function of new social trends, such as single-parent families or young people living with their parents longer.

Demographic changes, while reasonably predictable, regularly affect markets as age groups move through their life cycles. As societies continue to age, new products and services are needed for the care of older people, such as diapers for adults.

Change regularly occurs as variations in the business move some industries through **boom and bust periods.** Oil, construction, autos, and heavy equipment are examples of cyclical industries. Historically, patterns of expansion and contraction have occurred in the United States regularly every 50 years or so following the Kontradieff wave.[1]

Changes in the performance of some of a manufacturer's suppliers not only create pressure for the rest of their suppliers to improve, but make possible changes inside the manufacturing company such as discontinuing incoming inspection or reducing inventory.

Changes in the organizational structure of companies create both opportunity and fear for employees. Examples of this are recent trends toward fewer levels between CEO and shop floor workers, and toward the use of ad hoc cross-functional teams to solve business process problems whose solutions were formerly left to functional managers.

Coupled with the organizational structure changes are **changes in organizational culture** that empower people with the learning and tools to get their jobs done and push decision making further down in an organization. This is most threatening to foremen and supervisors because they must change from being the source of knowledge and authority in their arena (a command/control style) to being coaches and inspirational leaders who allow their work teams to make most of the decisions.

Employee demographics continue to change—in age, education, race, gender, and expectations about what is desired from the job and life in general. Maintaining excellent labor relations, whether the company's workforce is unionized or not, will be far more demanding in the future.

Competitors are a major source of change in industry. Not only are competitors coming from new places, such as Korea, Thailand, and Brazil, but they are coming into the global business environment with a new degree of sophistication and competitive zeal. Furthermore, their learning curve to attain competitive parity, or even superiority, as manufacturers is remarkably short today.

The globalization of business introduces even more complexity into our business lives. There are new languages, customs, laws, and cultures to understand. New geographical territories are intermixed and overlaid upon current ones. Communication and coordination become more complex when spread across more time zones and cultures.

The pace of business and life—or is it life and business?—continues to accelerate. We now know how important time-based competition is for world class business performance superiority. Everything must be just in time today, and all signs point to an even faster business pace in the future. Product life cycles continue to shorten, driven by an ever faster rate of technological change.

Then there's the **trend in business toward less vertical integration**—toward more global sourcing—as a way to reduce a manufacturing company's asset base and to ensure greater flexibility in the marketplace.

Computerization has also made it possible to move from economies of scale to economies of scope. Instead of large plants dedicated to high-volume runs of products in large lot sizes, we can now have software-based flexible factories that can handle lot sizes of one economically.

Ultimately, **technology continues to change** rapidly as our accumulated knowledge grows exponentially in three important areas: materials, processes, and, of course, computing.

New materials are added to our design arsenal daily. These can range from smart fluids to memory metal alloys to super-conducting materials to plastics that conduct electricity. How will these open up entirely new ways of making products? Ford has produced an experimental Taurus with five major glass-fiber-reinforced molded plastic parts that replace over 400 sheet metal parts that have to be precision aligned and fastened together.[2] A Japanese air conditioner manufacturer uses memory metal alloys to automatically have louvers point one way when cold and the other when hot.[3]

New manufacturing processes, such as flex forming,[4] are sometimes developed to manufacture new materials, but they are more often dedicated to using conventional material to make old things in new ways. Lasers have been used for years in manufacturing to cut, drill, and heat treat metal. Now Maho in Germany has found a way to control the depth of the laser "cut" with its Lasercav so that the machine can be used to machine metal.[5] New optical interferometry surface measuring devices will allow better knowledge and control of manufacturing processes by capturing surface finish variation to less than 10 angstroms (one angstrom is one-ten-billionth of a meter).[6]

Improvements in computing technology continue to dazzle us and outstrip the average person's or company's ability to absorb and use them. New architectures such as massively parallel processing make older standards of measuring computer performance, such as MIPS, nearly meaningless. Neural networks give us computers that can learn as they accumulate experience, just as humans do. New advances, far beyond any silicon-based device capabilities mentioned previously in this book, will foster undreamed-of applications. For instance, researchers in the emerging field of molecular electronics have already demonstrated the ability to store data in three dimensions in a protein molecule. Just six one-centimeter cubes of this material could store all the information in the entire U.S. Library of Congress—about a terabyte (one trillion bytes) of information.[7]

Advances in information technology such as this reinforce Intel president and CEO Andrew Grove's statement that

> The history of this industry proves that greater computer performance brought to the world by the progress of technology is exactly what pulls new applications out of thin air, as if by natural law.[8]

Ten Generic Strategies for Coping with the Future

Thus change is all around us. With change comes uncertainty regarding both direction and rate, and risk—the risk of being too far ahead, or worse yet, too far behind. The following are ten generic strategies necessary for your company to win in business, given the sea of turmoil I've described. Implementing these strategies alone will not make your company a world class business performer. But ignoring them will likely seal your company's fate as a mediocre also-ran.

1. Monitor global data, create information, and make it available to the widest possible array of people in your company on a real-time basis. Companies that are world class performers know the importance of searching for new information—about new technology, market trends, social trends, and the like—to add to their accumulated learning. This demands not only an aggressive search routine, but also the modern information systems to capture and move the information from and to a variety of global areas quickly, accurately, and in different media forms at an appropriate level of detail.

2. Foster ongoing education and training for all employees. The goal here is to establish an environment of continuous learning in the corporation. I shall discuss this topic in more detail later in this chapter.

3. Learn to adapt quickly to new conditions. This strategy has several components. First, people must have open minds and attitudes that welcome (or at least don't fight) change. They have to be receptive to new ideas, no matter where they originate—from outside the company, or from inside the company from a different plant or office or culture, or from a different level in the organization. Second, the company's information systems (person-to-person, paper-based, and computer-based) have to be flexible enough to quickly be reconfigured to new business opportunities and conditions. Third, the company's organization structure must be flexible when the situation demands it.

4. Pursue speed and responsiveness in all activities and business processes. The customer, remember, is the ultimate judge of your company's speed. Stalk and Hout's book *Competing Against Time*[9] provides example after ex-

ample of how companies that focus on doing things quickly enjoy greater profits, market share, and growth.

5. Encourage innovation and entrepreneurship in all employees. Seek out employees who have a "start up" mentality, who enjoy implementing new ideas and growing new business. Open up your company's culture to the flow of new ideas. Don't shoot the messengers. Encourage people to take initiative in improving business processes and adding value for your company's customers.

6. Promote prudent risk taking from a basis of possessing the facts and careful planning. This strategy is closely allied to the one above. Experience provides a great basis for learning. Nothing ventured, nothing gained.

7. Use information technology in every possible place to gain competitive advantage and build in value-added for your customer.

8. Build global value-added partnerships. No one company can afford to be everything to its customers or to develop new product or process technology all by itself. The careful selection of global partners to add to your company's overall capabilities and product and service offerings can considerably strengthen your competitive advantage. This strategy takes hard work, totally open communication, and years of mutual cooperation for payoffs to materialize for both companies. Don't look to this as a quick solution or as a way to avoid having to create operations that perform in a world class manner.

9. Exploit new organizational configurations. In this day and age, where is the boundary of your organization? For instance, your company could have several of its manufacturing engineers permanently on-site, helping key suppliers overcome cost, quality, or delivery problems. Your sales people could be permanently assigned to work on-site at one of your largest customers, as Procter and Gamble's are now with a permanent office in Walmart's headquarters.[10] Your information systems could

allow your customers or suppliers to access your company's order or quality data bases. The point is that the organizational boundary of your company is no longer its four walls. In fact, increasingly, organizations are organized around business processes that include customers and suppliers, not only internal functions. Seek innovative ways to deploy your people to add value for your customers and suppliers.

10. Become a product services company, not just a product company. The point here is to look beyond the tangible physical products your company manufactures to also include the services that you do or could offer with the tangible product. Instead of just thinking of your company as a machine tool manufacturer, for instance, think of yourselves as a machining services company—offering machining advice, the machine tool itself, custom software for machine tool control, special tooling configuration, machine tool installation advice, and so on. Customers want fast, effortless results. Intensely focus on how your company can give its customers the greatest possible assistance in achieving their desired results.

What Is Left to Do?

Once a manufacturer has accomplished all the essential things that I've covered to this point that must be done to turn a manufacturing company into a world class business performer, what is left to do?

If any single word says it all, I believe that word is *integration*. What things must management focus on integrating?

- Strategies—both vertical and horizontal—to move a united company toward common goals
- Improvement programs that bring effectiveness and efficiency to key business processes and move the company toward world class business performance.

- Information systems—the data, applications, processing infrastructure, and telecommunications networks necessary to effectively run the business
- Corporate culture—to unlock the tremendous potential inside every one of your company's employees
- Key corporate functions—critical to building and maintaining the core competencies needed for competitive success
- Corporate performance measures—vital to promoting customer satisfaction and pulling operating improvements to world class performance levels

Second, management must find ways to generate higher added value (sales minus purchases) for its customers. A key to accomplishing this is to develop the ability to read and stay close to your company's customers. They have many of the new product ideas your company needs, if only you aggressively seek them and listen to what they are saying.

Another key to generating higher added value for your customers is to develop world class product and process design capability—both mechanical and electronic—to create robust new products in a minimal amount of time. For any manufacturer to accomplish this, CAD/CAE, group technology, computer-aided process planning (CAPP), and concurrent engineering are imperatives today to even be in the game—this is the price a manufacturer must pay today to be a viable competitor in the global economy. In addition, future survival, growth, and prosperity demand that your company also be using Taguchi methods, design for manufacture methods, and quality function deployment as product and process design enablers.

Clearly, manufacturing companies must increase their level of business sophistication in the future. This means more analysis, better planning, the implementation of expert systems where appropriate, and better focus on their customers and the world around them. But the same companies also must ensure that the basics are in place first. This means, for instance, that product structure taxonomies must be logically thought out and rigorously applied across the board, and that fundamental inventory management skills methods must exist throughout the corporation. As unbelievable as it may seem, many manufacturing companies currently do not measure up because they are missing the basics.

Consider the case of a $10 billion computer company that did not have the most fundamental inventory control methods in place at the right level in their product structure taxonomy. Customers ordered stock keeping units (SKUs) at the lowest level in the product structure taxonomy. Yet inventory was managed in the system at one level above the SKU level, which I'll call the product level. Thus, a planner would look at the on hand (not at the available-to-promise—but that's another story) inventory for a given product number and conclude that enough was on hand to satisfy the quarter's (not the week's— but that too is another story) requirements. But the inventory system and planner had no visibility into the SKU level. The inventory figure might have shown 1000 of a specific product number in stock. But there was no SKU level information to show how much of that stock was black or white, 110 or 220 volts, 50 or 60 hertz, with or without power cord, and so on. This lack of fundamental inventory management information created havoc with distribution, suppliers, and of course, the company's customers. Business school students and many experienced business people take it for granted that large multibillion dollar companies have had all these basics solved and under control for years. Nothing could be further from the truth in many companies.

I have seen several companies wrestling with 15- to 30-digit part numbers because they have attempted to place product or process intelligence about the part into the part number. Thus part numbers become harder to memorize, write, or enter on a keyboard without making a mistake. Field sizes in application software have to be laboriously expanded, and management reports and bar code labels become cluttered with large part number fields. As noted earlier, part numbers are for identification: group technology is for intelligence.

Another clear mandate for manufacturers is to provide an environment where their employees are proud to work for their company, and where their personal growth, by whatever measure the employee defines it, is encouraged. For the former, good companies to look to are those that make *Fortune's* annual list of America's Most Admired Corporations.[11] This award is given to companies for the quality of their management as well as their ability to attract, develop, and retain people. Companies like Merck, 3M, Phillip Morris, and Walmart regularly make this prestigious list.

Ensuring Employee and Corporate Intellectual Capital Growth

Personal growth is often closely tied to the amount of education and training the employer provides and the culture in which people are allowed to put this education and training to work. Note that I always use both words—education *and* training. Education is the "why." Training is the "how." In the long run, neither is sufficient without the other.

The facts about employee education and training in manufacturing, as I am able to discern them, have not changed much in the last few years. Leading U.S. businesses are spending anywhere from $1150 to $3500 per worker per year on education and training. Here's a list I have developed over the years:

General Electric	$3500	
IBM	2000	
Xerox	2000	
AT&T	2000	
Hewlett-Packard	2000	
Litton Defense Systems	2000	
Motorola	1150	(about 3% of payroll costs)
U.S. public education (grades K–12)[12]	3500	

All these numbers except Motorola's are estimates of spending gleaned from various public documents, articles, and executive's speeches. In evaluating these numbers, part of the problem is that there is no consistent way established by today's FASB accounting standards to account for corporate spending on education and training. Does a company include room and board, travel to and from courses, the cost of the facilities and equipment, the cost of outside speakers brought in to teach, the cost of lost employee time on the job, and so on? As with the use of MIPS to measure computer power, these numbers are crude measures that assume that each company's spending is producing comparative results. Moreover, we're assuming these reported figures are actually spent, not just budgeted and used against negative variances in other areas at the end of the operating year. Regardless of these definitional problems, the same high-performance companies seem to spend at least the amount mentioned in the table above year after year to keep their people up to date and provide a base level of learning and competence in the organization.

One could say that some of the education and training money spent, for instance by IBM, was for technical sales training to explain to customers immensely complex technical products and ideas. OK, granted. So maybe the "right" amount to be spending is more similar to Motorola's figure or even about $1,000 per worker per year. Unfortunately, this is still about an order of magnitude more than most companies in the United States and Western Europe spend to educate and train their people.

Most manufacturing companies do not spend over $200 per worker per year on education and training, and I've found many companies that don't even come up to $100 per worker per year. Of course, you've got to be careful here; a few companies will *budget* education and training dollars higher than this, but will never *spend* it—instead holding it as a reserve against the negative performance variances they will accrue over the year. Such tiny education and training budgets today do not even cover the cost in most companies of providing basic English language and simple mathematics literacy to the workforce. Even worse, I invariably find in companies spending this little that the money spent is devoted to executive-level education and seminars (often in warm far-away places near golf courses) and very infrequently on the lower-level workforce.

What's the payoff from such education and training? Motorola, whose program was described in the *Harvard Business Review*,[13] has documented (subject to an outside independent audit) that they received $33 back for every $1 they put into their education and training program in the form of better quality, higher productivity, less waste, and other improvements. A key thing Motorola has learned during its program is that it was far better off retaining and retraining its older workers, rather than firing all of them and starting with new employees. Allen Bradley, a division of Rockwell Corporation, states that it has gotten back $13 for every $1 it invested in an education and training program far less sophisticated than Motorola's.[14]

Interestingly, the top companies listed have been spending at those levels for some years. With their sophisticated management, if that kind of spending didn't pay, do you think they would continue the spending, especially under the competitive pressure some of them have been under in the last few years? They must know something the average manufacturer doesn't—that education and training pay for themselves many times over. Indeed, from these public results, it appears that investing in your own company's people gives about the best ROI possible—easily passing any company's financial hurdle rate. Why aren't more companies doing it?

The average CEO, when he or she hears that the company should be spending even $1000 per worker per year, says, "There's no way we can afford that kind of spending!" Yet, as we pointed out in Chapter 4, these companies and executives are precisely the same ones who have willingly paid out annually 20 percent to 30 percent of sales for the cost of poor quality for years, if not for decades.

A 400-employee manufacturer with average productivity should have about $60 million in sales. If its cost of poor quality is only 20 percent of sales, it throws $12 million down the drain every year with little or no employee and organizational learning taking place. If this manufacturer spent $2000 per worker per year, that's only $800,000 in total, or 6.7 percent of the $12 million. At $1000 per worker per year, it would spend $400,000 annually. Either of these numbers spent on gaining any level of organizational knowledge is a pittance compared to blowing $12 million with little or no learning occurring every year. So the money for the education and training and most everything else needed to be a world class business performer is lying right out there on the shop floor or in poor business and management practices within the company.

One reason for the CEO's reluctance to get started on any substantial education and training effort is the financial shock of going from near nothing today (about $150 per worker per year) to even $1,000 per worker per year. The average CEO can't see the return (particularly short-term, while he or she is there) and knows the company can't lay out that kind of money immediately. The trick is to gradually ramp up the spending on education and training while accruing the payback results with savings from increased quality, greater productivity, better return on assets, and so on. World class performance enablers such as JIT, SQC, and improved purchasing always produce quick results and a financial payback that can be used to fund longer-term, more technical solutions and improved education and training needed to achieve world class business performance. Manufacturing executives must break the cycle of poor performance with an investment in the most fundamental asset of all—their company's people, from board level right down to clerical and maintenance workers. For most companies, it makes sense to build up to the $1000 per worker spending figure over a period of two or three years, since it will take that amount of time to establish an effective education and training program for all the company's employees.

Understanding
Manufacturing as a Science

At a minimum, there are two more tasks that manufacturing companies must attend to. The first is to understand manufacturing as a science, not as an art. Manufacturing as a science is the same in any industry. The late Joe Harrington showed this eloquently in his second book, *Understanding The Manufacturing Process*.[15] His book reinforces what we've seen when we apply data flow modeling to manufacturing companies. You have to get down three or four levels in these diagrams before significant differences show up across different manufacturing industries.

But manufacturing as an art is different everywhere — between industries, in one industry, between countries, and even between plants in a single company. In how many companies have you heard proud statements such as, "Only we understand the *art* of rubber molding. You can't analyze that — that's a black art." This attitude changes when companies use Taguchi methods for the first time. After their first experiment is over, they inevitably comment, "You know, we've been making that product for 30 years and we now realize that we've never understood what we were doing, what the critical process parameters were, and what process capabilities we needed." The principles of the science of manufacturing (including product and process engineering) are the same everywhere. If semiconductor manufacturers can control material properties on an almost atom-by-atom basis, why can't rubber molders do at least as well?

Finally, companies have to zealously pursue continuous improvement — the idea that they have to be just a little bit better every day. A 0.1 percent improvement every work day would amount to about a 30 percent improvement over a 260-day work year, and would bring about a 44 percent improvement over a 365-day work year.

Americans typically spend their management time looking for the silver bullet or magic wand or big hit — one improvement in one narrow area that will give them a 30 percent or 40 percent gain. But these are few and far between, and they often take years to implement. In contrast, the Japanese style is to improve one thousand things 1 percent each and compound that over many days and years.

Western cultures also tend to set goals that turn into limits. The scenario goes like this: your boss comes to you, the materials manager, and says that your goal for the year is to reduce WIP inventory by 10 percent by the end of the year. You know you could achieve a 20 percent reduction this year, but you are afraid the boss would ask for that (or more) again the following year, and you may not know how to achieve that so easily. In addition, you know you've got to do better than his or her 10 percent bogey to get a bonus and show your capabilities for promotion—but you want to leave yourself some slack for next year. So you achieve a 13 percent inventory reduction, tucking some more inventory reduction potential in your back pocket for next year. Thus goals end up becoming limits in our culture.

The Japanese don't care where they start, and don't know where they will end up. Their overriding concern is to improve continuously, a little bit every day, constantly searching for new and better ways to do things. In that way they achieve performance gains over time they never could have envisioned when they started.

There's no question that U.S. manufacturers need to set dramatic improvement goals in order to alert their employees to the fact that they aren't going to achieve those improvements by doing business as usual. But experience shows that the best way to attain those dramatic improvements is through a program of continuous improvement in all business processes.

Another thing we all do as human beings is to fall in love with our problems. Routine runs our life and makes us comfortable. Think of how many manufacturing companies have a Monday morning (or even worse, daily) production meeting, where each departmental manager goes to "solve" the problems of the day or week or minute. Many people love these meetings; they can play the hero, jumping into the fray, shouting, pointing fingers of blame, ordering people around, and making things happen. If you went to these people and told them that you had a magic wand that would solve all their daily problems, their first reaction would be, "Well then, what would I do?" And quickly following that question would come a second, more paralyzing one: "Then why would the company need me?" Both questions arise because people don't realize that another set of new and more sophisticated management problems would arise for them to solve. So part of a continuous improvement environment is to keep the environment from settling into a routine, and keep people in love with improved performance—not with complacency and comfort.

Business Challenges to Come

In one sense, the journey to world class manufacturing business performance is never finished. Just as we conquer today's challenges, different ones arise to challenge us anew. Consider just a few new technologies and challenges on the horizon today:

- Superconducting materials
- Object-oriented programming
- Desktop manufacturing
- Genetic engineering
- X-ray lithography
- Micro- or nano-manufacturing
- Manufacturing in outer space
- Neural networks
- Digital video interactive (DVI) technology
- Computer voice input and language translation
- Optical computing and holographic memory

All these and many more constitute enormous challenges and opportunities for manufacturers to use them to add value for their customers and to improve their management and operations.

But then consider some other developments in global markets we can expect. The wiring of the world with fiber optics—both homes and businesses—will open huge untapped markets for manufacturing companies in terms of both stimulating demand and allowing interaction directly with home consumers around the world. This will revolutionize current marketing and distribution channels and will most likely remove one or two levels from today's distribution chain.

In addition, the current business environment in the world for the Japanese, United States, and Western European triad really only has about one-half of the world for a marketplace. The recent dramatic opening up of the Eastern European markets, and the prospect of markets opening up in the USSR, China, and India could more than double our current markets for consumer and industrial goods and services.

The real question is whether a company will be prepared to compete in and prosper in the global business of manufacturing during the next 25 years. How will your company differentiate itself competitively in future years? Once every surviving company is a world class manufacturing performer, this will mean they all have about the same levels of quality and manufacturing cost, since the same technology and manufacturing principles will be used to manufacture each company's products. Thus, the major way manufacturing companies will be able to distinguish themselves will be through the services they offer with their tangible products. Start thinking about how your company will compete successfully in this fashion. But don't take your management eye off the ball. The first goal is to become a world class manufacturing performer, or your company won't be around to tackle its value-added opportunities.

Chapter 10

1. J. W. Forrester, "Innovation and the Economic Long Wave," *Planning Review,* November 1980.

2. Stephen E. Plumb, "E Pluribus...Five," *Ward's Auto World,* November 1989, p. 91.

3. J. Kurtz, "Metals That Memorize A Shape," *New York Times,* 19 May 1991.

4. "Volvo Installs A 90,000-ton Press For Prototype Work," *Production,* August 1987, p. 34.

5. "Report From EMO Hannover," *American Metal Working News,* 25 September 1989.

6. G. M. Robinson, et al., "Optical Interferometry Of Surfaces," *Scientific American,* July 1991, pp. 66–71.

7. Amal Kumar Naj, "Bacteria Protein May Help To Miniaturize Computers," *Wall Street Journal,* 4 September 1991.

8. Andrew Grove, "Debate — Should The U.S. Abandon Computer Manufacturing?" *Harvard Business Review,* September–October 1991, p. 141.

9. George Stalk, Jr. and Thomas M. Hout, *Competing Against Time* (New York: The Free Press), 1990.

10. B. J. Feder, "Moving The Pampers Faster Cuts Everyone's Costs," *New York Times,* 14 July 1991.

11. "America's Most Admired Corporations," *Fortune,* 11 February 1991, pp. 52–79.

12. "Why We Should Invest In Human Capital," *Business Week,* 17 December 1990, pp. 88–90.

13. William Wiggenhorn, "Motorola U: When Training Becomes An Education," *Harvard Business Review,* July–August 1990, pp. 71–83.

14. "World Class Quality: The Challenge of the 1990's," Special Section, *Fortune,* 23 September 1991.

15. Joseph Harrington, Jr., *Understanding The Manufacturing Process* (New York: Marcel Dekker, Inc.), 1984.

11

Envisioning the Computer–Integrated Enterprise

The extent to which a manufacturing company can integrate its information will play a dominant role in determining its competitiveness in the foreseeable future. As I have noted in Chapter 7, integrated information systems can improve the quality of data and resulting management information, the speed at which a company can communicate within its four walls and to its outside constituencies, the productivity of the company's employees, and the flexibility of its operations. In this chapter we'll consider how a truly computer-integrated enterprise could function from the viewpoint of the three major business processes discussed in Chapter 3, as well as from some other considerations.

It is the year 2001, and the hypothetical company of our discussion produces a variety of electromechanical equipment for both industrial and consumer markets. Its plants and offices are scattered around the globe, as are its customers and suppliers.

Computer–Integrated
Product and Process Design

A normal work day, that is, any of 365 per year, will show that 575 of the company's 700 engineering workstations (combinations of today's personal computers and engineering workstations) are in use, and scores of design team members will be working using the engineering network from remote sites (usually their homes). A manufacturer's engineering network will contain a large variety of engineering software for both electronic and mechanical design. It will be centered around a top CAD vendor's base software package that includes both capabilities. This package, an outgrowth of the CAD Frameworks initiative that started in the late 1980s in the United States, allows engineers to move (and move data) seamlessly between applications in both the mechanical and electronic design worlds. This is particularly important because a majority of any manufacturer's products will be a combination of mechanical and electronic devices. Therefore, semiconductor engineers can design ASICS, ASWs (new kinds of application-specific wafers), and complex multilayered circuit boards with the electronic design software, while their mechanical design counterparts use the latest variational geometry-based solid modeling design and analysis software for their mechanical designs.

Design teams composed of engineers from around the globe will work on the company's new products. In many cases these teams will be made up of contiguous workers grouped physically in the same work room around a circular bank of engineering workstations. Here, representatives of various company functions such as design engineering, manufacturing engineering, purchasing, quality, and marketing will work concurrently to bring their product to market in the shortest possible time. In some cases where special skills are needed from other company facilities, these people—no matter where they are located around the globe—will electronically share the same design work on their workstations. Because of competitive business conditions, some design teams will function on a 24 hour a day basis 7 days a week. Staffing teams both this large and this dedicated will be considered quite normal. Most team participants will have access to the engineering network from home, although sometimes on less sophisticated equipment than they have at their office. In addition, at the completion of the design and pilot production cycle for their new product, they will have a one–month break, during which two weeks is to be devoted to vacation and two weeks is to be devoted to continued education and training before returning to another product design team assignment.

Members from the design team can access a variety of data from different sources. For instance, the company's U.S.–led team members designing an industrial product to be used as a component in their customer's mechanical product can access and download from their customer in Australia the latest engineering (geometric) data representing the solid model of the part of the customer's product where its product has to mate and function. The company's engineering software will automatically check its latest design for proper fit and engineering tolerance stackup. In a similar fashion, the company's engineers will send another product's geometry to one of its key suppliers in Italy to be used as a basis for the plastic injection molds this supplier will design and machine for them.

Design specialists can refine the design of complex parts on the company's CAD and CAE system. This system—a combination of the CAD/CAE industry's best software packages and hardware along with some highly proprietary company-designed applications—is of standard configuration on a global basis. The company had long ago learned that the strategic benefits of everyone using the same CAD/CAE software far outweighed the chaos of allowing plants to "optimize" their local CAD/CAE capability. Additionally, this standardization minimizes education and training costs and reduces errors in communicating data.

A design engineer can call up a part she has to examine out of an assembly—for instance, a complex part of an aircraft landing gear—call for the necessary finite model to be automatically generated, and run the company's mechanical design optimizer on it. Given her familiarity with both the part and her working analytical tools, she estimates this optimization can run for about 20 minutes while she looks up some other data from a material properties data base run by a materials science company in Germany. At the end of 20 minutes, the design optimizer will have run through about 25 simulations of the part design, each time homing in on the optimal solution for the design of the part—its dimensions, the shape of its supporting webbing, the radius of critical fillets, and the diameter and wall thickness of its tubing. (Each one of these simulations would have required a full day in 1990.)The optimizer will automatically compare the initial design with the last iteration using both a printout of relevant engineering numbers as well as color views of both stress and strain. Given the incremental improvement from iteration to iteration, the model will also suggest whether further simulation time would be beneficial.

At the end of this design optimization, the engineer can store the final design data or go on to have a prototype made in a variety of materials as an outgrowth of the stereolithography process developed in the early 1990s. The design team's manufacturing engineer, who has had access to the product design since its inception, will describe its features for the company's group technology software. This description will be the basis for creating a process plan for the product using the company's generative computer–aided process planning (CAPP) software.

The company's CAPP software will first ask the designer about several important criteria as a basis for its decision making. The first of these will seek the target manufacturing cost of the product, which will be based upon its target market price—a key constraint in determining possible manufacturing processes. Other questions will follow. Will the part be manufactured on a least–cost or least–time basis? Will material substitutes be allowed? What are the likely production quantities per day, and what is the life cycle production unit forecast? What kind of nondestructive testing will be utilized in the manufacturing process? Are there any limitations on which plant the product has to be produced in? All of the company's manufacturing plants for this product are configured with identical production equipment, but at one plant the company is starting to install new process equipment that might be applicable to this part.

After considering these assumptions and conditions (at a minimum), the CAPP software will develop a manufacturing process plan based on the company's globally standardized tooling and process machinery. This process plan will be complete with all cost figures relative to the manufacture of the product.

Taguchi methods—what the Japanese just call quality engineering—are an integral part of any product and process design effort at the company, and they are available in the form of sophisticated and highly integrated quality design software found in the company's engineering toolbox. Taguchi method software especially focuses on parameter design to make the company's products robust and therefore as insensitive as possible to noise factors that are difficult and expensive to control. The company's manufacturing process data base includes each production machine's up to date process capability. The company's standard design process ensures that products are not approved for production until their product and process design engineers have achieved Cpk ratios (the product specification range divided by the process capability range) of greater than two, but more often than not four or five. This gives some room for the process shift that inevitably occurs because of noise factors while eliminating the need for checking every product produced with SPC techniques.

Other sophisticated tools are also available on the engineering network. Design for manufacturability or assembly software is available to analyze product design with the aim of minimizing parts count and the amount of handling a product requires through fabrication and assembly. This software plays a key role in minimizing complexity in the company's products and manufacturing operations, thus helping to ensure its position as the low-cost manufacturer in its industry.

Quality function deployment software is another integrated tool used extensively by the company's engineering teams to ensure that the voice of the customer is translated into the entire set of product and services (bundled or unbundled) desired by the marketplace. This software, developed by leading companies in the late 1980s and generally available in the marketplace in the early 1990s, had been enhanced by the company's engineers to represent an expert system for product and service design. Any changes in customer requirements ripple through the QFD system to show the resulting changes necessary in engineering specifications and manufacturing process, at a minimum. This tool is a key factor in allowing the company to respond quickly to rapidly changing customer desires and competitor moves.

The company has a variety of work cell devices that can quickly be programmed based on a part's geometry and features stored in its CAD/CAE data base. CNC machine tools, robots, coordinate measuring machines, and vision systems are examples of machines that share the need to have their programs based on the part's geometry in the company's engineering data base, and in the case of some vision and robot applications, even the work cell geometry stored in the company's facilities engineering data base.

Electronics design engineers in the company occasionally face a difficult problem involved with the design of a leading edge ASIC or ASW. After probing the company's global engineering resources for an answer, they can look outside the company for help. One of their design engineers will enter the design problem (adequately coded to describe the source) into the worldwide university research network (URN) to see if any professors and researchers in the world's top 300 colleges and universities are performing work in that area and would have the interest and time to help the company with its design problem. URN is set up as a free market system where interested professors and researchers can identify themselves, send information about their qualifications, and even bid for work on the system. Thus URN is a brokering service to match engineering and scientific talent to industrial need for subscribing companies.

The company's network manager can also note the extent to which its geometric product catalog (GPC) data base had been accessed during the previous 24 hours by customers, especially those in the consumer products division. This CAD system-based product catalog is a key feature of the company's sales strategy that gives it enormous competitive advantage in the consumer products marketplace. The company established this feature to be used by three primary groups: customers, distributors, and salespeople.

Individual customers can access the geometric product catalog data base directly from their homes given a certain level of technical sophistication in their home workstations and local network capacity. The company's market research had found that by the year 2000, more than 40 percent of its consumer products customers had workstations of such performance in their homes, and another 25 percent of these individuals could access its GPC through a workstation they had access to where they worked. Customers can browse through the company's product catalog, stopping to examine products—from different angles, or perhaps in different colors, or with different options. These customers often want to personalize the company's product design with their name or perhaps create a personal color scheme for it. In other cases, they might want some dimension altered to better fit their body size, or the place in their home where the product is to be used or stored.

After they make their personal alterations, the company's product and process design order filter screens the product to see if it is still producible, estimates the delivery date to the customer's home within a two-day window, calculates a new price if the requested work is outside of a standard price envelope, and asks whether the customer would like to place his order. If so, the order entry information will be stored in the company's order entry system with a note to reference the customer's personal design now stored separately in its engineering data base. As a final step, the company electronically sends its order confirmation to its customer at the time of order placement.

Almost the same capability is available to the company's distributors to design their variations of the company's standard products. But here, in addition to product design, packaging design is frequently important to a distributor who might want his own private-label packaging. The company thus makes an entire packaging design module available to its distributors, who can easily operate it to tailor their packaging to their individual needs. Furthermore, distributors' order sizes can run from quantities of one to tens of thousands. In this instance, therefore, additional interfaces to the company's order entry, distribution, and master production scheduling systems are used to check whether the company will be able to handle the distributor's order in the time period the distributor wanted it, and to consider special quantity discounts for whatever quantity the distributor specified.

The company's salespeople are another big user of the GPC described above. Working in their local sales offices or even from a potential customer's location, they can go through the same process of working with the customer to custom-design a standard product for him or her. They have the additional advantage, however, of being able to work directly with an entire multifunctional design team on-line to help address the customer's needs. This feature is only a prearranged special option for their distributors and individual customers.

Once the company's product and process designs are complete and authorized for production, all product-related engineering and technical data is directly used as a basis for the company's technical publishing function. Here, geometric data is combined with the appropriate text material as the input for parts and service manuals, bids to customers, and design quality documentation material.

The company has found that its engineering network allows it to electronically move its engineering resources around to compensate for the inevitable peaks and valleys in different groups' engineering workloads. No one group could afford to staff for its peak periods or hire a complete range of specialized technical expertise. The engineering network, with its standard applications software, standard engineering procedures, access to standard component and materials data bases, and proprietary capabilities was a key source of competitive advantage for the company.

Another big advantage of the company's engineering network is that the total engineering resources of the company were available electronically to solve difficult product and process engineering problems. Any engineer needed only to type, write, or talk in a problem, perhaps with a drawing or simple sketch, and answers or suggestions would soon start appearing from its engineers around the world. This synergy and ability to tap an enormous range of talent and experience is another tremendous source of competitive advantage for the company. In addition, its engineering network is a great tool for fostering a global team spirit and high esprit–de–corps for its engineers and new product and process design teams.

New products are carefully tracked in their design and development cycles by the company's engineering project management system. Their release to production is only allowed when all relevant geometric data for product, tooling, and packaging is complete and all manufacturing process data established. In addition, no part can go into production with a Cpk ratio of less than two at expected production volumes. This system is especially valuable in managing the company's overall product and process design efforts with a minimum of resources. In addition, it plays a major role in keeping the company's design lead times at a more than competitive minimum.

Computer-Integrated Logistics

The company realized early in the 1990s that it would need to build a highly integrated set of business information systems if it was to attain sustained competitive advantage in its manufacturing operations. In doing so, it concentrated on two critical business processes to simplify and integrate with information systems: the customer order-to-delivery process and the materials management process, both a part of the company's overall logistics process.

Part of their decision making early in their strategy formulation was, as it is for any company, at what level to "center" the entire materials management system—at the corporate, group, division, or plant level. This is most often a function of corporate size, organizational structure, and management style. This company decided to center logistics at the division level, which means that customer orders are to be collected and schedules driven from the divisional level down, and that information is aggregated from the divisional level up to the company's group and corporate levels. This decision was governed by the many products the company produces and the many different markets in which it competes. One of its competitors, a much less diverse company, used similar software to receive orders and schedule its plants from a corporate level.

The company's overall system is based on a top MRP/DRP software system, with the company's enhancements integrated in modular fashion so that it can easily update its software as the vendor does. The system runs daily and uses daily time buckets, although the company's executives are considering moving to a shift–oriented approach (a run every eight hours using a new massively parallel architecture computer) on their way to what they all know will be real-time replanning MRP within another year or two. The system is on-line so that transactions on a global basis update various data fields in their data bases on a real-time basis. Furthermore, the system follows the net change approach of only changing those portions of the plan whose data change. Almost all company employees, of course, have their own workstations (of various levels of technical sophistication), with over 75 percent of the employees also having access to the company's system through one or more home or travel computers. Any employee can access the company's system, with system security controlled by employee and need to know.

Customer orders come in at a division level by various means, but most often directly by computer through a real-time computer–to–computer communication that had its roots in the Electronic Data Interchange (EDI) systems developed in the mid–1980s. Most early EDI systems were of the mailbox variety with the actual computer information transfer occurring once a day. This was far too slow for a company to be competitive in the year 2000. Almost all industrial customers (manufacturers and distributors) order via computer after selecting products from the company's product data base, which include a product's geometric description if desired, as well as text information to describe any product or part number desired. In one or two of the company's consumer divisions, over 50 percent of home customers also ordered directly by computer.

Other orders still come by phone on occasion, but since the company gave customers electronic access to their distribution information, this practice—which was necessitated in earlier days by a "we need this, do you have it in stock before I order it, or can you get my order to us in a week" oral request—was no longer necessary. Still other orders come from the company's salespeople by computer, most often directly from a customer's office while the salesperson is there.

Most of the company's regular industrial customers provide it with daily or weekly outlooks of their requirements by part number for up to a six–month time horizon in various time buckets from daily to monthly. Normal customer orders come to each division from regions served by the company's distribution centers through its DRP system, with national account orders coming directly by computer into divisional headquarters.

Sales forecasts are developed for each product, either by rolling up from the lowest level product or by using a planning bill and a sales percentage developed from historical usage. Either way, this forecast is updated every other week by the sales force. In all cases, the company's financial forecasts are based on the unit sales forecasts, so there is never a mismatch between forecasted units and dollars anywhere in the company's systems.

Orders that can be filled from stock go directly to the company's highly automated warehouse and are generally picked within three hours by a combination of robotized pickers and humans. All orders of make–to–stock items are guaranteed to be shipped from stock no later than five hours from time of order receipt. Depending on location, some customers receive their orders on the same day, most within two days.

For larger inventory replenishment orders or particularly for industrial products that require more than a few days' design and production time, the incoming orders flow into the division's master schedule customer demand line. In the division's operations control room, the division master schedule, often at an aggregated level, shows divisional data as well as the suggested plant schedule breakdown for manufacturing each unit required. Plant production is bucketed within a day, and it is up to each plant to fulfill its daily schedule in the best way it sees fit. This practice has only been in effect for two years at the company. Before that, the plant MPS at the divisional level was in a weekly bucket, with the plant having the freedom to vary its daily schedule within a five- or seven-day period as long as it executed the week's requirements successfully. Now, competitive pressure no longer allows that kind of slack. The division operations people can call up any plant's daily schedule and note real-time progress against it, since all products and material are tracked with radio-frequency bar code or smart tags through the factory and in the distribution pipeline. Product master schedule information is aggregated by product family and made available to group and corporate executives who want either the unit or financial information for planning purposes or for checking actual shipments against gross production forecasts.

For new products or product lines and for particularly large or complex customer orders, the company routinely uses its global resource modeler (GRM) as a tool to decide where a given order should be produced, or whether global capacity needs to be expanded and where, or where to source raw materials and components. This modeler uses a variety of data bases for its raw data such as currency status (real–time or forecasted), export or import tariffs and duties, shipping costs and distances by a variety of transport globally, and the like. One of the keys to the company's manufacturing flexibility is that it uses globally standard product and process designs. Products produced in more than one plant are therefore produced with exactly the same equipment in exactly the same manner. Thus, production can be shifted from a U.S. plant to anywhere else in the world by duplicating the tooling and software instructions for both the workcell devices involved and the human workers.

The GRM can evaluate tradeoffs in capacity, costs, and time in evaluating the best way to satisfy all of the company's customers. It can evaluate each order to see where the optimal source of supply is and where to produce the product, given each plant's proximity to the order's customer.

One of the interesting things the company found as it put its global manufacturing strategy together is that its global production capacity was directly related to its tooling capacity. This is especially so in its plastic-injection-molded and metal-stamping product lines. If the tooling wasn't available at the right plant and in top condition, nothing could be produced. Although it had initially put great effort into modernizing its product-oriented MRP systems in the late 1980s, it totally neglected its tooling information system and left it a patchwork of old batch systems until about 1992. These batch systems considered tooling only on a local basis, did not capture and locate all the company's existing tooling on a real–time basis, and, worst of all, gave no information about the tooling itself—which outside company or internal shop had produced it and when, what condition it was in, how many parts it had produced, and what the quality of the parts produced were. To its surprise and horror, when the company finally got its arms around its total tooling, it realized that it had more money tied up in tooling inventory than it had in total product inventory and yet had no modern information to manage its tooling base and subsequent operating capacity. Its current tooling system tracks on a real–time basis the company's global tooling inventory, its condition, its repair or replacement schedule, and the cumulative quantity and quality of the parts it produces.

The company's sourcing and procurement systems play a major role in its overall competitiveness. Requirements from the company's MRP/DRP (DRP for service parts) systems are rolled up by major product and commodity from all plants to a corporate level, where the corporation could take advantage of its purchasing clout and volume requirements to arrange for blanket contracts and JIT delivery to each using plant. Many products continue to be purchased locally at each plant when there is no advantage to sharing the corporate system.

Purchasing decisions are made using an on-line vendor rating system that considers each vendor's quality, delivery performance, cost, and contribution to the company's product design efforts. Every effort is made to ensure long term harmonious relationships with vendors and to help them improve their competitiveness so that they can continue to supply the company with parts and materials. Many of the company's largest and most important suppliers provide it with real-time access to their inventories, master schedules, and quality data, just as the company does for its major customers.

With regard to global sourcing, the company is a member of the globe's largest worldwide parts and materials network (WOPAMN). Similar to the University Research Network mentioned for engineering, companies can place material requests for products—especially standard items, but even custom ones, whereby the interested company downloads the company's design data electronically to see the product needed—on WOPAMN's global real–time network. Companies from all over the world are then free to bid on the purchase requirement, but of course must submit substantiation of their design and manufacturing capabilities, their quality capabilities, their price, and other qualifications, in addition to an estimate of the time needed to deliver the order in the customer's desired facility. The WOPAMN network is a brokering service that matches global buyers with sellers; it ensures a high degree of competition among all suppliers.

Tracking materials from global supplier to and through the company's plants and distribution facilities and on to each customer is no longer a problem for any company to achieve. The company can, at the touch of a few keys, track any material in real time anywhere in the world, thanks to satellite-based tracking. This capability is essential to ensuring the integrity of the entire logistics chain and maximizing customer satisfaction.

Accounting and Financial Systems

All the company's accounting and financial systems are in real time, and they post results as electronic financial transactions occur. Management thus can check a real–time set of financial statements or any supporting account detail at any time during the day. When the company's management proposed to its auditors that they create this advanced system, there was, of course, the usual reaction of "that's impossible." But the company asked the question in a new way—"What would have to be done so that we could create such a real time system?"—and persevered. The handling of accruals was the most daunting challenge in creating the new software, but the company built an expert system specific to its accounting practices and financial strategy that enables the system to work with a high degree of accuracy.

The company has several hookups to information utilities that sell financial information and, of course, has real–time access to all financial markets for trading purposes to hedge against the world's currency fluctuations.

Sales and Marketing Systems

The company's sales systems also work in real time, driven by transactions as they occur. Company sales data is continually shown in graphical form on six- to eight-square–foot panel color displays in many offices throughout the corporation. Ad hoc inquiries to the company's sales data bases can generate new or more detailed information for these color displays within seconds.

The company's salespeople each have several computers by which they can access any of the company's data bases on sales history, product history, customer history, competitive product line information, sales call route optimizers, and other productivity and knowledge tools. Of course, their ability to utilize the company's engineering network and geometric product catalog gives them a substantial leg up on their competition. Given the sophistication of the company's order and tracking systems, its salespeople never have to waste their valuable time tracking down customer orders or shipments, or finding out whether the company can handle a customer's order either from a quantity or timing viewpoint.

In its marketing division, the company routinely uses data available from several large information utilities, such as demographic and psychographic data and economic forecasts. It routinely scans the larger consulting firms' market and technology study offerings which, of course, are available electronically at the push of a button. More importantly, marketing pays close attention to its electronic hotline, seeking problems or suggestions from customers who have free access there from their home computers. Another feature of the marketing system is an algorithm that periodically sends an electronic survey to a customer's location, polling the customer about his or her satisfaction with the company's products and services. In short, the company's customers are repeatedly reminded that the company is interested in their satisfaction with its products, and their ideas for product or service improvement as well.

Human Resource Systems

The company's real–time human resource system is a vast repository of relevant data about each employee—all their normal health care, payroll, tax, and job record and performance ratings. In addition, each employee has a career track clearly identified in the system, complete with various company executives' comments and a thorough documentation of the individual's education and professional development history. At any time, an executive can obtain a complete suggestion list of qualified candidates from anywhere in the corporation for a job opening, along with a profile of each employee. In particular, those employees who form a vital part of the company's core competencies are so noted in the HR system, and the system flags them for frequent reviews and to promote their being used on a rotating basis by many business units in the corporation.

The Trend in Information Integration

The picture I have painted in this chapter represents no great leap forward in information systems applications, but is really a continuation of what's been going on for the past 25 years or so. Information technology was first used to perform one small task in a company. Then its use was expanded to serve an entire function, several functions, then a complete facility. Now it is being used to connect facilities within a corporation, and to tap into information utilities and financial markets. The final step is the integration forward to global customers (industrial plants and individual consumers) and back to global suppliers—beyond the four walls of the corporation.

The world and its people, whether in business or in their personal lives, are on their way to being connected by wire, by fiber optic cable, and by broadcast technology. The important question for manufacturing management is whether it can integrate its company into this emerging global network fast enough, and with a seamless suite of application software and data base management systems that give its company at least parity, if not competitive advantage. Manufacturing companies need the ability to "plug and play" in tomorrow's electronic world. Will your company be there *and* be successful?

12

Bringing It All Together

Manufacturing Trends
with a New Perspective

Let's pause to catch our breath a bit, and review some of the key trends in manufacturing that we've examined.

• On *the people front*, manufacturing managers are trying to build a new culture in their companies—one of open communication, continuous learning and improvement, and of teamwork toward a shared vision. Part of the challenge is to retain and retrain the company's older, more experienced workforce. It is they who have an intimate knowledge of the company's products and often even its customers and suppliers. Doing this—providing people with growth and new futures that they thought were neither possible nor probable—goes a long way toward building the kind of esprit de corps and loyalty that a world class performing company needs from its employees.

World class manufacturing performers have employees with winning attitudes. The hard job is to find people with the right attitudes and reinforce their attitudes every day through a winning company culture. Herb Kelleher, Southwest Airlines' chief executive and the leader and sparkplug behind their phenomenal success, comments on finding the right "raw material":

> We draft great attitudes. If you don't have a good attitude,
> we don't want you, no matter how skilled you are. We
> can change skill levels through training. We can't change
> attitude.[1]

Given management and employees with the right attitudes, manufacturing companies are awakening to the tremendous investment in the company's intellectual capital they must
make to ensure its competitive success. This job is expensive
and time-consuming. But it pays for itself many times over.
McKinsey studied 39 West German machine tool producers to
find out what separated the winners from the losers. One of
their conclusions was that the winners spent six times more on
educating and training their employees than did the others.[2]
The correlation of high levels of education and training with
leading performance is high and has been demonstrated by
leading companies around the world. Why do most manufacturing companies ignore such a proven path to better performance?

• *Supplier reduction* is a trend in almost every industry as
companies find that, among other things, they cannot afford to educate and train their current quantity of suppliers to be world class suppliers to them. Two examples suf-
fice. Considering only metal stamping companies that supply the Big Three in the auto industry, Ford has reduced its
stamping suppliers from 300 to 110 in the past three years
and plans to eliminate 50 more in the next two years. General Motors has cut its stamping supplier base by 50 percent
in about the same period. Chrysler is moving in the same
direction.[3]

Just seven companies mentioned in a *Wall Street Journal*
article[4] —Xerox, Motorola, DEC, GM, Ford, Texas Instruments,
Rainbird, and Allied Signal Aerospace—have over the past
several years reduced their total number of suppliers by 49.3
percent or up to 32,440 companies, assuming that no supplier
supplied more than one of those seven companies. Even allowing generously for multiple supplier coverage, more than
16,000 companies were shut out of selling to large and good

customers! This is just the tip of the iceberg if we consider the top 1000 manufacturing companies in the United States, not just the seven mentioned in the article. Every company is someone's supplier. How do you ensure that your company isn't one of the ones cut out of the picture? Only by transforming your company into a world class performer.

• There is a universal move afoot leading companies to *implement computer-integrated manufacturing* (CIM) and then the *computer-integrated enterprise* (CIE). There are several forces behind this trend. One is to integrate the organization electronically into one virtual organization independent of time and geography. Another is to integrate the flow of information and to eliminate inefficiencies of labor and lost time in its use. Yet another is to reap the benefits of the software-driven factory, with its demonstrated ability to improve quality, productivity, speed, and flexibility. Once the characteristics of the product design and manufacturing process are captured in software, it's critical that the plant have the software-driven tools downstream to allow a seamless flow of information—both alphanumeric and geometric—throughout the rest of the manufacturing environment. Finally, as noted in Chapter 11, integration spreads as naturally as the ripples produced when a stone is dropped in a pond. Integration always produces benefits, and the benefits of integrating forward to customers and backward to suppliers are obvious to world class manufacturing aspirants who are thinking strategically.

Most U.S. and European executives err on several fronts with regard to CIM or CIE. First, they claim that no one knows what CIM or CIE are. Some people don't know, or don't have an appreciation of the total CIM or CIE vision. But more than a few people do share the vision and knowledge of these concepts and are moving with great dispatch to implement them in their companies. Or these executives claim that CIM (like MRP) was a failure in the 1980s. Yes, in many companies it was—because the companies' management didn't understand it, didn't think big enough, got too far ahead of the technology or human learning curves, or failed to invest sufficiently in planning or their employees' education and training. In addition, many vendors oversold it. Other executives think that CIM can't be financially justified, at least using traditional U.S. financial measures. This is generally indicative of thinking too narrowly about CIM, or of ignoring its strategic benefits — CIM's role in establishing and maintaining the company's overall competitiveness. Perhaps most damaging, though, is that many of these executives think that the Japanese don't believe in CIM ("You don't see any computers when you go through a Japanese plant, do you?"), and that computers play little role in the land of JIT, TQC, and continual improvement. Their misperception lulls them into a sense of complacency and a feeling that CIM can't be important if the Japanese aren't implementing it. Both of these are fatal errors in judgment.

It's true that Japan initially focused on the three enablers mentioned above and was slow to wake up to the U.S.-originated concepts of CIM and CIE. During the 1980s, the Japanese moved through the conceptual stages of mechatronics and factory automation (FA) before finally coming to the CIM and CIE concepts. But now Japan's leading companies have the message. A survey of 282 leading Japanese companies conducted by the Japan Management Association in July 1990 showed that 32.6 percent were introducing CIM in their companies then, with another 18.4 percent planning to introduce CIM within one or two years (of 1990). To quote from the article describing this survey, "It is thus clear that as many as 225 [of 282] companies are treating the installation of CIM systems as a subject of major importance."[5] Even more instructive is to note the three leading reasons for the Japanese to be introducing CIM in their companies:[6]

- "To reduce lead time" (73.9 percent)(in the land of JIT, no less!)
- To enhance the communication between production, sales, and technical [engineering] divisions (58.4 percent)
- To cope with the large-variety, small-lot production (52.2 percent)

Describing the forthcoming environment for manufacturing in Japan, Professor Jinichiro Nakane of the System Science Institute of Waseda University in Tokyo comments,

> This post-JIT environment places an emphasis on information systems—not only those that communicate customer design orders, but also on electronic production-control systems.[7]

Don't sell the Japanese short on their understanding of the benefits of information technology and their skill in implementing the computer-integrated enterprise. They are attacking the CIE challenge with their usual strategic long-term perspective, hard work, and tenacity. As successful as they already are in manufacturing, they know they need information technology, CIM, and CIE, just as any successful manufacturing competitor will, as soon as possible.

• There has been a trend of *increasing outsourcing* among manufacturers lately, with an even greater trend toward consideration of outsourcing (typically of the company's information systems function or "data centers") by manufacturing managers whose bosses are looking for lower costs and "more focus." But there's a smart way and a not-so-smart way to go about outsourcing, and the latter produces the wrong results for manufacturers. An unpublished Boston Consulting Group study of more than 100 manufacturers in the United States, Japan, and Europe found that in many Western companies that had outsourced various parts of their operations for a few years, costs often went up—not down; some companies felt that they were losing their technological edge in product and process design; and some felt that their product quality was slipping. Why? According to an article in *The Economist*,

> Part of the answer is that most western firms start using subcontractors simply because they want to cut overhead.... Exactly which bits of their manufacturing

processes are subcontracted out is decided by which will save most on overheads, not by which makes [the] most long run sense.[8]

If Western management followed the teachings of Professor Brian Quinn (at the Amos Tuck School at Dartmouth College) and others,[9] and the example set by leading Japanese manufacturers, it would outsource far more strategically. The Japanese outsource their low value-added operations—those that are commonplace and add no particular advantage to the product. The goal of their outsourcing is to improve their overall manufacturing process, not to cut labor and overhead costs. In addition, when considering which company to outsource from, they consider as criteria quality and reliable, timely delivery long before low cost as a basis for selecting their partners.

Outsourcing can deliver many benefits if it is performed in the context of a strategic program to increase the overall competitiveness of a manufacturing company. But if used only to reduce costs and only to carry out the same routine operations as previously performed, outsourcing adds little competitive benefit to a company, especially in the long term. And it adds another relationship to manage. Looking back after two or three years of outsourcing, the CEOs of companies that have outsourced some major operation such as their information system function sometimes reflect, "All we did was replace our people and equipment with their people and equipment. And now, because our transactions have increased by 50 percent, we're back at the same total cost we were before. So what's changed—we haven't gained any real or new competitive advantage."

Companies that sell outsourcing services must realize that their opportunity and the value they can bring to their customers is not in preserving their customers' status quo for 3 percent a year less cost, but in helping their customers to achieve lasting business performance improvement more quickly, economically, and competently than they could have done by themselves.

• There's no question that *companies' organization structures are becoming flatter*—necessitated by the requirements of lower overhead costs and speedier decision making, and made possible by the use of improved information systems. Stalk and Hout report,

> on average, Japanese overheads are one third the overheads of U.S. and European competitors.[10]

John Deere, a leader in world class manufacturing, produced the same tonnage output in 1990 as it did in 1980 with one-third fewer employees.[11] Many leading Japanese and U.S. companies (for example, Chaparral Steel, Nucor Steel, Walmart) operate with only four levels of management from top to bottom. The average U.S. company has at least double that number, and some have three to four times that many levels in their management structures.

As manufacturers *achieve dramatically lower manufacturing cost*, distribution costs become a higher percentage of their total costs. Toyota provides a dramatic example of this:

> About ten years ago Toyota's manufacturing capability in Japan enabled the manufacturing of a car in 2 days. It took 15 to 26 days to get the order to the factory, get the car made, and deliver the car to the customer in Japan. The cost associated with selling and distribution was higher than the variable costs of making the car. . . . By 1987, Toyota reduced turnaround to eight days, including the time for making the car.[12]

I believe that, as I write this in September 1991, this cycle is now down to five days! Distribution-intensive companies might look to the leading frozen and perishable food companies or the mail order firms like Land's End and L. L. Bean as benchmarking candidates to help them lower their distribution costs and lead times.

• Another trend is the *movement of production closer to the customer* so that the customer enjoys the fastest service and, in the case of food, the freshest taste. Lenscrafter moved its eyeglass lens grinding and fitting into their stores and now promises a customer his or her eyeglasses in one hour or they are free. Mrs. Field's cookies are baked in the store right in front of customers. Some pizza services are now baking their pizzas in ovens in their trucks as they are being delivered. Many manufacturers are renting space from their major customers and putting their production line right in their customers' plants, thus saving inventory, reducing lead times, and obtaining quicker quality and design feedback from their customers.

• Manufacturing companies are *learning to be more flexible.* Hewlett-Packard has carried quick setups to an even higher level by applying the concept to its entire manufacturing facility. Their "cheap to change" philosophy allows H-P to reconfigure production equipment and process flows over a weekend if necessary to achieve the kind of flexibility it needs as well as to increase the return on their facilities assets.[13]

• Certainly, there is a need for manufacturing companies to *demonstrate a greater sense of urgency* in two areas. They first must speed their rate of performance improvement if they are to become or remain competitive. The second area where a greater sense of urgency is needed is in managing their customers instead of their preoccupation with managing the (short-term financial) numbers. The right customer focus will go a long way toward "pulling" the right financial numbers along.

Remember, it's not only absolute change but the *rate* of change that counts, especially in the customer's eyes. In addition, the goal can't just be to catch up—"me too" imitation of today's world class performers (although that's a fair place to start for most companies). You've got to play the game to win, to beat the competition. Hal Edmondson, Hewlett-Packard's vice-president and corporate manufacturing director, says that to accomplish this "requires a vision for the business, a plan of constant improvement, and a stomach for change." [14]

• We see a glimmer that indicates *some manufacturing executives are starting to realize that many forces and activities in their business are related and dynamic in nature.* Therefore, effective solutions to today's business problems cannot be solved by old models that treat each function or even each business process separately and from a static viewpoint. Peter Senge's book *The Fifth Discipline* elaborates on this theme and asserts that only systems thinking will solve the complex interrelated problems inherent in today's business environment. He defines the new approach needed thus:

> The essence of the discipline of systems thinking lies in a shift of mind:
> • seeing interrelationships rather than linear cause-effect chains, and
> • seeing processes of change rather than snapshots. [15]

When more manufacturing managers start to think this way, and to use today's powerful PC-based systems dynamics modeling packages such as "think"™ [16] initially to model parts of their businesses, and eventually the entire business, more effective solutions will be possible in a shorter time period with a fuller understanding of the likely implications of the solution or its alternatives.

• *An appreciation of systems thinking, when coupled with the trend toward the computer-integrated enterprise—and the computer integrated business world—*gives rise to another concept that is raising the anxiety level of forward-thinking manufacturing executives. We are on a rush toward real-time management. Gone are the days when managers have weeks or months to gather facts, analyze data, and make decisions. Gone are the days when committees and task forces could take months to form and then to study a problem and recommend a solution to another level of management, who would then take even more time to approve a course of action or send the original team back to consider several more alternatives. Gone are the days when manufacturers could routinely tell customers "give us a couple of days and we'll get back to you with the information about when and if we can produce that order." All signs point to increasing speed and momentum toward real-time management. Any customer would be foolish not to want real-time, dependable answers.

This trend means that manufacturing management must have all the facts possible at its fingertips. This can only be done with information systems that have the right data defined and instantly accessible and that have powerful applications and modeling software that provide answers and sensitivity analysis at the push of a button. It can be done only if the manufacturing company can plug and play in the global information market, and if everyone in the company can communicate with each other in real-time from anywhere around the globe—whether people are at home, in one of the company's offices, or traveling. It can be done only if the company's people and its culture are educated and geared to fast decision making and can implement changes quickly and smoothly. It can be done only if the manufacturing company's management is closely and personally linked to its customers and suppliers. In the interim period until this state of affairs represents a universal condition in the business world, the advantage will always go to the manufacturing company that is closest to real-time management, all other things being equal.

Reviewing the Game Plan to Win

My prescription for progressing toward world class business performance has been straightforward and certainly easier to describe than to accomplish.

- We started with a vision—for the business and science of manufacturing, as well as for the company's strategy for market success.
- We made sure we had an objective and factual understanding of where a manufacturing company stands in performance—against its global competitors and against current world class performance standards.
- We made sure that a proven planning process and the cultural support for it was in place before embarking on the long journey to world class manufacturing performance.
- We brought together the learning and skills to improve the company's performance along the cost, quality, and lead time activity chains while intensifying its focus on its current and potential customers.
- We captured the energy and intellectual contribution the company's employees could make to its performance improvement by empowering them under the company's vision and performance improvement goals, while educating and training them to increase their capability to contribute to the company's success as well as to their own personal growth and success.
- We created performance measures that measured the right things and fostered the company's movement toward world class business performance.
- We created a long-term improvement program designed to dramatically improve the company's manufacturing and business performance. The program was focused, justified as a total program, and prioritized for greatest strategic leverage, and it covered the core of the company's business activities.

Implementation of the world class business performance program demands management commitment, reward systems that reinforce its implementation, and the commitment of sufficient resources in money, skills, and numbers of people to get the task accomplished. Above all, its implementation demands perseverance in pursuit of the overall goal of being a winning manufacturing competitor.

Understanding the Real Challenge

The real challenge for world class performance aspirants is to build and sustain a winning organization. As usual, it all comes down to people. Manufacturers have the same challenge as sports teams. They first have to recruit the best people. Then they must provide them with superb coaching and instruction and an environment that encourages their personal growth. Then they must infuse them with a vision of what they can do and must do to become winners in the game. They must establish appropriate reward systems that cater to the collective team need as well as to each player on an individual basis. They must provide them with the equipment and the best play book (plan) to succeed. Finally, the team's management must provide all-encompassing support during the game (or implementation) itself.

Look at all the great sports team dynasties that have prevailed over the years—the Boston Celtics under Bill Russell or Red Auerbach, the Green Bay Packers under Vince Lombardi, and the auto racing teams of Roger Penske, to name a few. How is it that these teams were able to dominate their sports year after year? Their leaders built great organizations.

It has been no different in business. In Japan, it's been accomplished by leaders such as Akio Morita at Sony, Soichiro Honda at Honda, and Seiuemon Inaba at Fanuc. In the United States, Tom Watson built IBM into the world's largest computer company, Fred Smith created Federal Express and the overnight package delivery industry, John Young has steadily built Hewlett-Packard into a winning company, and Jack Welch has reinvigorated General Electric. In Europe, Heinz Nixdorf created a nimble and highly successful Nixdorf Computer AG under his leadership, and Percy Barnevik is transforming Asea Brown Boveri into a global electrical engineering giant.

In the end, the challenge in manufacturing continues to be one of leadership—exerting the leadership to build and maintain a world class organization. Leaders appreciate the enormous capabilities of educated, motivated people working as a team toward a common vision. Leaders have the ability to inspire people to united action and to achieve tasks they never dreamed possible. Leaders can instill their will to win in their organization.

Most of today's manufacturing companies around the world are in desperate need of leadership toward world class business performance and survival, growth, and prosperity. How and when will you exert the leadership to move your organization toward this goal? I have told you how. It's time to get started.

Chapter 12

1. S. N. Chakravarty, "Hit 'Em Hardest with the Mostest," *Forbes*, 16 September 1991, pp. 48–51.
2. "Less Is More," *The Economist*, 25 May 1991, pp. 75–76.
3. *The Detroit Free Press*, 8 August 1991.
4. John R. Emshwiller, "Suppliers Struggle to Improve Quality as Big Firms Slash Their Vendor Rolls," *Wall Street Journal*, 16 August 1991, pp. B1–B2.
5. "CIM Fever Still Shows No Signs of Cooling," *METALWORKING Engineering and Marketing*, May 1991, pp. 48–53.
6. Ibid.
7. John Teresko, Factory Automation Special Report, *Industry Week*, 2 September 1991, p. 50.
8. "The Ins and Outs of Outing", *The Economist*, August 31, 1991, pp. 55–56.
9. J. B. Quinn, et al., "Beyond Products: Services-Based Strategy," *Harvard Business Review*, March–April 1990, pp. 58–67.
10. George Stalk, Jr. and Thomas M. Hout, *Competing Against Time* (New York: The Free Press), 1990, p. 57.

11. S. Weiner, "Staying on Top in a Tough Business in a Tough Year," *Forbes*, 27 May 1991, pp. 46 and 48.

12. Paul A. Strassman, *The Business Value of Computers* (New Canaan, CT: The Information Economics Press), 1990, p. 167.

13. Harold E. Edmondson and Steven C. Wheelwright, "Outstanding Manufacturing In The Coming Decade," *California Management Review*, Summer 1989, pp. 70–89.

14. J. Teresko, "Hewlett-Packard Keeps Reinventing Itself," *Industry Week*, 19 August 1991, pp. 44–52.

15. Peter M. Senge, *The Fifth Discipline*, (New York: Doubleday Currency), 1990, p. 73.

16. "think"™ software available from High Performance Systems, Inc., Hanover, NH, 603–643–9636.

Appendix

GENERIC MANUFACTURING

Product &
Process
Design

Planning &
Control

Integrating
Elements
• Information
• Culture
• Customer
  Orientation

Production
Process

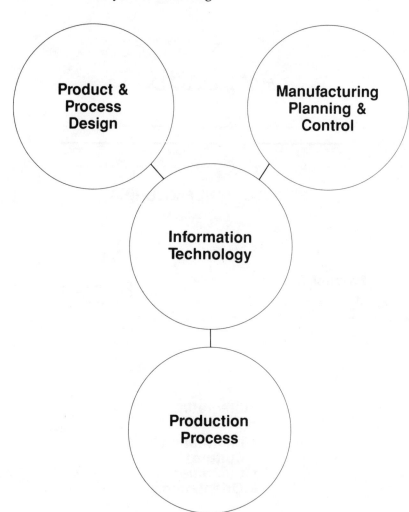

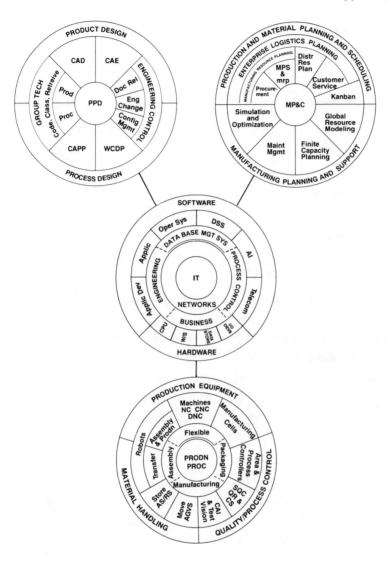

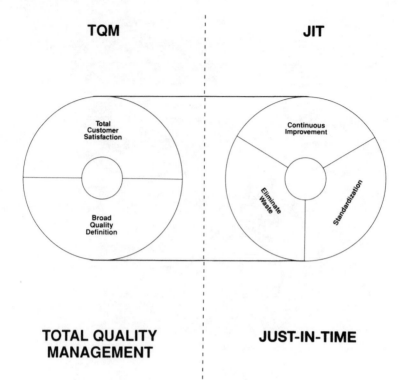

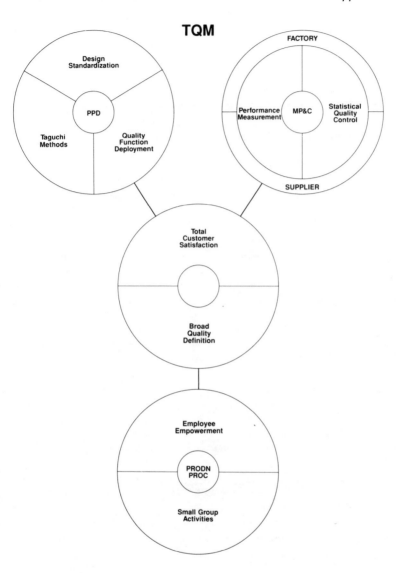

JIT

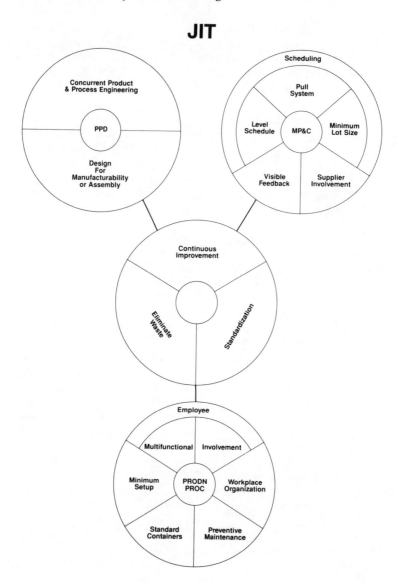

COST MANAGEMENT

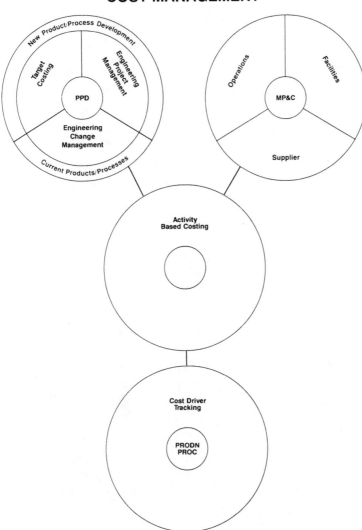

GLOSSARY

ABC analysis A method for grouping inventory by decreasing order of annual dollar usage according to Pareto's law. Typically, the inventory is divided into three classes—A, B, and C—in which approximately 20 percent of the items account for 80 percent of the annual dollar volume (A items), 50 percent of the items account for 5 percent of the annual dollar volume (C items), and all other parts are B items.

back scheduling Scheduling backward from the order due date by the time each operation takes, in order to arrive at an order start date.

bill of labor A listing of all labor operations that are involved in making a part, usually with set up and run times for every operation. These can be created in various degrees of accuracy for either rough–cut or detailed planning.

bill of material A listing of all parts that make up a product. This listing can show materials, parts, or subassemblies and can be created in various degrees of accuracy for either rough–cut or detailed planning.

bit A binary digit, either 0 or 1.

burn-in A test method in which electrical/electronic components are run under electrical power at normal or elevated operating temperatures to ascertain whether they operate correctly.

business process The complete set of activities necessary to execute a major element of business, such as customer order–to–delivery.

byte A group of bits of binary computer data. There are eight bits to a byte.

CAD computer–aided design   The use of a computer to capture the design geometry of a part or product. This design is then stored electronically in an engineering data base.

CAE   (computer–aided engineering) The use of a variety of computer-based analytical software to analyze a part's design, for example, finite element modeling analysis to analyze for mechanical stress and strain.

CAPP   (computer–aided process planning) Variant CAPP is computer-based process or routing planning that can take advantage of standard sequences of manufacturing operations for part families classified under the group technology concept. Generative CAPP selects operations based on part features (geometry) and other specifications.

CASE (computer–aided software engineering)   A computer-based set of methods and disciplines to engineer and produce software. One of its major components is a repository that contains all object definitions and relationships. "Upper CASE" refers to front-end analysis and design tools. "Lower CASE" refers to back-end code generators. CASE tools cover the entire software design process from strategic planning and system planning through data modeling, system analysis, logical design, physical design, code development, and documentation.

CIE (computer–integrated enterprise)   The use of information technology to fully integrate the flow of data and information within an enterprise, as well as outside of it, to its customers, suppliers, and information utilities. CIE implies a minimum of logical data bases and data entry limited to once per data element.

CIM (computer–integrated manufacturing)   The integration of all information (engineering, business, and process control) involved in the total spectrum of manufacturing activity.

clock speed   The rate at which a microprocessor completes one switching cycle.

Cpk ratio   The product specification range divided by the process capability range, adjusted to center the process on the target value.

cross functional A process cutting across more than one internal function, for example, from sales through manufacturing.

data element A single defined entry in a file or data base, for example, a part number.

data base management system (DBMS) The application software that manages data in an information system. It usually includes a data dictionary or repository used to define the data and the relationship of each data element to another.

DRP (Distribution Resource Planning) A software package that is used to determine inventory replenishment needs at branch warehouses in a distribution network, and to aggregate those needs in a time-phased manner back to their supplying sources as input to their master production schedules. The resource planned can also be, at a minimum, warehouse space, shipping mode (truck or rail or airplane space),or manpower.

economic order quantity (EOQ) A method of calculating order quantity (lot size) that relates ordering cost to holding cost given the assumption of constant demand for the product. Specifically, the economic order quantity equals the square root of [(two times the annual demand times the ordering cost) divided by the annual holding cost].

electronic data interchange (EDI) The direct transfer of information between computers according to standardized information formats and communication protocols.

Feigenbaum quality model A quality cost model proposed by Armand Feigenbaum that considers prevention, appraisal, internal, and external factors as the total cost of quality.

file server A computer that serves as a data storage and management device in a local area network.

finite capacity planning Loading a factory or work center only to its capacity. This process automatically schedules lower–priority items into the next available time period if the current time period's capacity is fully utilized.

flexible manufacturing system (FMS)   A group of more than two computer-based machine tools combined with integrated material handling and quality control equipment to produce a family of parts with similar product or process attributes. Two machine tools or less would constitute a flexible manufacturing cell.

forward scheduling   Scheduling a process from a start date forward by operation time to arrive at a finish or ship date.

full factorial experiment   An experiment where all possible combinations of factors are evaluated. If there are two levels for each factor and seven factors, for instance, 128 trials (2^7) would have to be performed.

graphical user interface (GUI)   A user interface displayed on a computer CRT screen that is rich in its use of graphics and point–and–click methods that utilize icons, pull–down menus, and pop up windows. The Apple Macintosh was the first commercial example of a GUI-based computer. Other examples today are Microsoft Windows 3.0, X Windows, Motif, and Open Look.

group technology   The use of a coding and classification system to group products or processes into families with similar attributes.

holistic   Emphasizing the importance of the whole and the interdependence of its parts.

infinite capacity planning   Loading a work center or plant without regard to its capacity. Used to show where overloads exist so they can be corrected by planner intervention.

inventory turns   How often in a period of time the inventory "turns over" or is used, calculated by dividing sales at cost by the average inventory dollar amount.

just in time (JIT)   A manufacturing philosophy developed by the Japanese that seeks to eliminate all waste in manufacturing business processes.

kanban   The information system used to run JIT production. A kanban is a sign that can be a simple as a colored box, a metal tag on a parts container, or a computer–printed bar code label or ticket.

linear programming models Computer-based models that solve resource allocation problems with one or more (often hundreds of) constraints.

logical A view of a system without regard to physical location of its elements.

Lot-for-lot A lot sizing algorithm where the quantity to be produced exactly reflects the amount needed in the time period with no considerations for safety stock or producing any overstock.

lot–sizing algorithm The algorithm that determines the quantity to be produced after taking into account in a variety of ways supply and demand for a given time period.

make–to–order A manufacturing environment where products are only manufactured when a firm customer order is in hand. This may be due to policy, or more often to the fact that each product is custom-specified by a customer at the time of order.

make-to-stock A manufacturing environment where standard products are produced and often stocked in a distribution network that starts with a finished goods warehouse.

manufacturing The complete spectrum of activity starting with product and process design and going through manufacturing planning and control, production, distribution, and after-sales service and support.

manufacturing resource planning (MRP) The complete application software package that contains modules including forecasting, order entry, master production scheduling, capacity planning, material requirements planning, procurement, shop floor control, and cost accounting. MRP II packages contain integrated accounting and financial reporting functions as well.

master production schedule (MPS) A statement of the products a manufacturing enterprise will produce in a given time period, after taking into account the products' supply and demand.

materials requirements planning (mrp) An order–scheduling mechanism that sets and maintains order priorities for manufactured or purchased parts. The basis for the scheduling is the explosion of required product quantities (determined by the time-phased master production schedule) through each product's bill of materials to determine gross part requirements, and then netting these requirements against parts on hand and due in (scheduled receipts).

mean   The arithmetic average of a set of observations, usually denoted by the Greek letter mu (μ).

mega   A prefix meaning one million.

meter   A unit of measure equal to 39.37 inches.

metric   A standard of performance measurement, for example, speed, time, yield, and so forth.

metrology   The science of measurement.

micron   One–millionth of a meter.

microprocessor   A complete mainframe computer-equivalent on a chip. Microprocessors have arithmetic, logic, register, control, and memory functions necessary to work as a self–contained computing unit.

MIP (Millions of instructions per second)   A crude measure of computing power. In 1980, a DEC VAX minicomputer was rated about one MIP.

molecular electronics   The use of biological molecules (protein molecules today) to store data as an optical memory device.

Monte Carlo sampling   The random selection of one or more data points from a given probability distribution.

nano   A prefix meaning one–billionth.

nanoelectronics   The design of electronic devices that are measured in nanometers (billionths of a meter) and are grown as clusters of atoms rather than being etched in silicon as are most of today's semiconductor chips.

net change   Transaction–driven MRP, where the portion of the production or materials plan updated is only that affected by transactions such as inventory receipts or withdrawals, engineering changes, work completion, and so on.

netting algorithm   The algorithm that determines the steps used to aggregate demand and calculate net requirements after considering available supply.

noise factors Factors that influence the response of a process but cannot be economically controlled, such as dust, weather conditions, vibration, machine wear, and so forth.

object code The actual program in machine language that is executable by a computer. It is the result of running source code through a compiler.

operating system The software that coordinates the operation of the essential parts of a computer—CPU, memory devices, internal data management, and so on.

orthogonal array A mathematical device based on Latin squares, developed by Genichi Taguchi to identify factor and level combinations that allow less than full factorial experiments. An L8 array would call for 8 trials on a seven–factor two–level experiment, instead of 128 for the full factorial experiment.

parameter design The optimization process in Taguchi methods that makes a design as robust as possible—as insensitive to uncontrolled or expensive-to-control variations of noise factors in the factory or field.

pareto analysis The cumulative analysis of items, wherein the results usually are split into three classes (A, B, and C), with the A class items being 20 percent of the items responsible for 80 percent of the results.

physical The actual physical arrangement of system devices, as opposed to the logical arrangement. A logical view might show data storage as one conceptual element whereas, the physical view might split this into two disk drives in two locations, and one tape backup unit.

planning bill of materials A bill of materials that uses percentages to quantify option usage based on historical demand.

planning horizon The amount into the future a given method or system considers when planning, for instance, six months, one year, three years.

ppm Parts per million.

process shift The shifting of a process with given characteristics from one mean to another.

product   The physical item produced along with a set of value-added services that do or could accompany it.

product structure taxonomy   The hierarchy from topmost grouping such a group down to individual stock keeping units at the bottom, for example, group, family, class, style, SKU.

quality loss function   Genichi Taguchi's statement that losses mount exponentially the further a given characteristic is from its target value.

quality function deployment (QFD)   A quality engineering method for developing a design quality aimed at satisfying the consumer and then translating the consumers' demands into design targets and major quality assurance points to be used throughout the production stage.

quantum transistor   A transistor utilizing quantum mechanics theory. A switching signal triggers an atom's band gap differences in energy level to allow the conduction of electrical signals. Such transistors switch at speeds at least twice as fast as today's fastest silicon-based devices, and may be 1000 times as fast in the future.

regen(erative)   A form of materials planning where, at each run, all the previous plan is thrown away and a completely new plan is developed. This contrasts with net change MRP, where usually only a portion of the old plan is ever thrown away.

RFQ   Request for quote; also RFP—request for proposal.

return-on-management™ (R–O–M)   Paul Strassman's term representing management value-added divided by management costs.

six–sigma   A term used as a measure of quality, wherein good parts will represent plus and minus six standard deviations within a normal distribution, and thus bad parts will equal 2.2 per million with no process shift, and 3.4 parts per million with a 1.5 standard deviation process shift.

solid modeling   Computer–aided design that captures the complete mathematical description of a part, and thus defines it unambiguously.

source code The code, expressed in a high–level language, originally used to write a software program.

standard deviation A measure of dispersion or variance about the mean of a distribution of numbers, normally denoted by the Greek letter sigma (σ).

Statistical Quality Control / Statistical Process Control (SQC/SPC) The use of variation analysis to ensure a process capability that will produce parts within a given set of specification limits.

stock-keeping unit (SKU) A part or product kept in stock as a uniquely identified item.

Taguchi methods A quality engineering tool that uses the quality loss function as a way to explain quality issues to top management and emphasizes parameter design to design products and processes of robust quality that are insensitive to expensive-to-control noise factors.

tera A prefix meaning one trillion.

time buckets The size of the time segments in which a planning system groups events, for example, days, weeks, months, quarters, or years.

time fences Future time periods when, based upon manufacturing lead times, master production schedule changes are feasible and allowable, troublesome but to some extent allowable, and infeasible and therefore not allowable.

total quality management / total quality control (TQM/TQC) A complete philosophy of company-wide quality control that includes the use of many lesser quality tools such as quality function deployment, Taguchi methods, and statistical quality control, among others, to achieve world class quality performance.

transportation network analysis The use of linear programming models to analyze the quantity and locations of distribution warehouses and plants given a unique combination of sources, customers, and transportation modes and costs.

variation A measure of dispersion about a central value.

Recommended Readings

Abegglen, James C. *The Strategy of Japanese Business*. Cambridge, MA: Ballinger, 1984.

Abegglen, James C., and George Stalk, Jr. *Kaisha: The Japanese Corporation*. New York: Basic Books, 1985.

Abernathy, William J., Kim B. Clark, and Alan M. Kantrow. *Industrial Renaissance*. New York: Basic Books, 1983.

Adler, Paul S., Henry E. Riggs, and Steven C. Wheelwright. "Product Development Know-How: Trading Tactics for Strategy," *Sloan Management Review*, Fall 1989, pp. 7–17.

Akao, Yoji, ed. *Quality Function Deployment*. Cambridge, MA: Productivity Press, 1990.

Berliner, Callie, and James A. Brimson, eds. *Cost Management for Today's Advanced Manufacturing*. Boston: Harvard Business School Press, 1988.

Brown, Robert G. *Materials Management Systems*. New York: John Wiley & Sons, 1977.

Camp, Robert C. *Benchmarking*. Milwaukee: ASQC Quality Press, 1989.

Clark, Kim B., and Takahiro Fujimoto. *Product Development Performance*. Boston: Harvard Business School Press, 1991.

Cohen, Stephen S., and John Zysman. *Manufacturing Matters*. New York: Basic Books, 1987.

Crosby, Philip B. *Quality Is Free*. New York: New American Library, 1979.

Davenport, Thomas H., and James E. Short. "The New Industrial Engineering: Information Technology and Business

Process Redesign," *Sloan Management Review*, Summer 1990, pp. 11–27.

Dertouzos, Michael L., Richard K. Lester, and Robert M. Solow. *Made in America*. Cambridge, MA: The MIT Press, 1989.

Drucker, Peter F. "Japan's Choices," *Foreign Affairs*, 65 (5), 1987, pp. 923–941.

———. *The New Realities*. New York: Harper & Row, 1989.

Ealey, Lance A. *Quality by Design*. Dearborn, MI: ASI Press, 1988.

Eureka, William E., and Nancy E. Ryan. *The Customer Driven Company*. Dearborn, MI: ASI Press, 1988.

Foster, Richard N. *Innovation*. New York: Summit Books, 1986.

Garvin, David A. "What Does 'Product Quality' Really Mean?" *Sloan Management Review*, Fall 1984, pp. 25–43.

———. *Managing Quality*. New York: The Free Press, 1988.

Gilder, George. *Microcosm*. New York: Simon & Schuster, 1989.

Goldratt, Elijahu, and Jeff Cox. *The Goal*. Croton-on-Hudson, NY: North River Press, 1984.

Gunn, Thomas G. *Computer Applications In Manufacturing*. New York: Industrial Press, 1981.

———. "The Mechanization of Design and Manufacturing," *Scientific American*, 247 (3), September 1982, pp. 43–49.

———. "The CIM Connection," *Datamation*, February 1, 1986, pp. 50–58.

———. "Integrated Manufacturing's Growing Pains," Electronic Engineering Manager, *Electronic Engineering Times*, February 10, 1986, pp. 1–8.

———. *Manufacturing for Competitive Advantage: Becoming a World Class Manufacturer*. Cambridge, MA: Ballinger, 1987.

———. "U.S. Global Players Win," *Managing Automation*, July 1987, pp. 42–43.

———. "Process-Oriented Management: A Fresh Perspective," *Managing Automation*. August 1990, p. 6.

Hammer, Michael. "Reengineering Work: Don't Automate, Obliterate," *Harvard Business Review*, July–August 1990, pp. 104–112.

Harmon, Roy L., and Leroy D. Peterson. *Reinventing The Factory*. New York: The Free Press, 1990.

Harrington, Joseph J. *Computer Integrated Manufacturing*. Huntington, NY: Krieger Publishing Company, 1978.

———. *Understanding the Manufacturing Process*. New York: Marcel Dekker, 1984.

Hayes, Robert H., and Ram Jaikumar. "Manufacturing Crisis: New Technologies, Obsolete Organizations," *Harvard Business Review*, September–October 1988, pp. 77–85.

Hayes, Robert H., and Steven C. Wheelwright. *Restoring Our Competitive Edge*. New York: John Wiley & Sons, 1984.

Hayes, Robert H., Steven C. Wheelwright, and Kim B. Clark. *Dynamic Manufacturing*. New York: The Free Press, 1988.

Henderson, Bruce D. *The Logic of Business Strategy*. Cambridge, MA: Ballinger, 1984.

Ishikawa, Karou (trans. David J. Lu). *What Is Total Quality Control?* Nagaya, Japan: Central Japan Quality Control Association, 1979.

———. *Guide To Quality Control*. Tokyo, Japan: Asian Productivity Organization, 1986.

Jacobsen, Gary, and John Hillkirk. *Xerox: American Samurai*. New York: Macmillan, 1986.

Japanese Management Association (trans. David J. Lu). *Kanban: Just-In-Time at Toyota*. Stamford, CT: Productivity Press, 1986.

———. (trans. Alan T. Campbell). *Canon Production System: Creative Involvement of the Total Workforce*. Cambridge, MA: Productivity Press, 1987.

Johnson, H. Thomas, and Robert Kaplan. *Relevance Lost: The Rise and Fall of Management Accounting*. Cambridge, MA: Harvard Business School Press, 1987.

Kanter, Rosabeth M. *The Change Masters*. New York: Simon & Schuster, 1983.

———. *When Giants Learn to Dance*. New York: Simon & Schuster, 1989.

Kaplan, Robert S. *Measures for Manufacturing Excellence*. Boston, MA: Harvard Business Press, 1990.

Kogure, Masao, and Yoji Akaro. "Quality Function Deployment and CWQC in Japan," *Quality Progress*. October 1983, pp. 25–29.

Leebaert, Derek, ed. *Technology 2001: The Future of Computing and Communications*. Cambridge, MA: The MIT Press, 1991.

Martin, Andre J. *Distribution Resource Planning*. Englewood Cliffs, NJ: Prentice Hall, 1983.

Mobley, Lou, and Kate McKeown. *Beyond IBM*. New York: McGraw-Hill, 1989.

Monden, Yasuhiro. *Toyota Production System*. Norcross, GA: Industrial Engineering and Management Press, Institute of Industrial Engineers, 1983.

Moden, Yasuhiro, and Michiharu Sakurai, eds. *Japanese Management Accounting*. Cambridge, MA: Productivity Press, 1989.

Ohmae, Kenichi. *The Mind Of The Strategist*. New York: McGraw-Hill, 1982.

———. *Triad Power*. New York: The Free Press, 1985.

———. *The Borderless World*. New York: Harper Business, 1990.

Parasuraman, A., L. Berry, and V. Zeithaml. "Understanding Customer Expectations of Service," *Sloan Management Review*, Spring 1991, pp. 39–48.

Peters, Thomas J., and Nancy Austin. *A Passion for Excellence*. New York: Random House, 1985.

Peters, Thomas J., and Robert H. Waterman. *In Search of Excellence*. New York: Harper & Row, 1982.

Porter, Michael E. *Competitive Strategy*. New York: The Free Press, 1980.

———. *Competitive Advantage*. New York: The Free Press, 1985.

———. *Competition in Global Industries*. Boston, MA: Harvard Business School Press, 1986.

———. "Changing Patterns of International Competition," *California Management Review*, 28 (2), 1986, pp. 1–40.

———. *The Competitive Advantage of Nations*. New York: The Free Press, 1990.

Prahalad, C. K., and Gary Hamel. "Strategic Intent," *Harvard Business Review*, May–June 1989, pp. 68–76.

————. "The Core Competencies of the Corporation," *Harvard Business Review*. May–June 1990, pp. 79–91.

Quinn, J. Brian, Thomas L. Doorley, and Penny Cushman Pacquette. "Beyond Products: Services-Based Strategy," *Harvard Business Review*, March–April 1990, pp. 58–67.

Rappaport, Alfred. *Creating Shareholder Value*. New York: The Free Press, 1986.

Ross, Phillip J. *Taguchi Techniques for Quality Engineering*. New York: McGraw-Hill, 1988.

Schlesinger, L. A., and J. L. Heskett, "Breaking the Cycle of Failure in Services," *Sloan Management Review*, Spring 1991, pp. 17–28.

Schonberger, Richard J. *Japanese Manufacturing Techniques*. New York: The Free Press, 1982.

————. *World Class Manufacturing*. New York: The Free Press, 1986.

Scott Morton, Michael S., ed. *The Corporation of the 1990s*. New York: Oxford University Press, 1991.

Senge, Peter M. *The Fifth Discipline*. New York: Doubleday Currency, 1990.

Shingo, Shigeo. *Study of Toyota Production System*. Tokyo: Japanese Management Association, 1981.

Smith, P. G., and D. G. Reinertsen. *Developing Products in Half the Time*. New York: Van Nostrand Reinhold, 1991.

Stalk, George, Jr., and Thomas Hout. *Competing Against Time*. New York: The Free Press, 1990.

Strassman, Paul A. *The Business Value of Computers*. New Canaan, CT: The Information Economics Press, 1990.

Sullivan, Lawrence P. "The Seven Stages in Company-Wide Quality Control," *Quality Progress*. May 1986, pp. 77–83.

————. "Quality Function Deployment," *Quality Progress*, June 1986, pp. 39–50.

Suzaki, Kiyoshi. *The New Manufacturing Challenge: Techniques for Continuous Improvement*. New York: The Free Press, 1987.

Taguchi, Genichi. *On-Line Quality Control During Production*. Tokyo: Japanese Standards Association, 1981.

Taguchi, Genichi, and Yu-in Wu. *Introduction to Off-Line Quality Control*. Nagaya, Japan: Central Japan Quality Control Association, 1979.

Thomas, Philip R. *Competitiveness Through Total Cycle Time*. New York: McGraw-Hill, 1990.

Turney, Peter B. B. *Common Cents: The ABC Performance Breakthrough*. Hillsboro, OR: Cost Technology, 1991.

Walleigh, Richard C. "What's Your Excuse for Not Using JIT?" *Harvard Business Review*, March–April 1986, pp. 3–8.

Wantuck, Kenneth A. *Just In Time for America*. Southfield, MI: KWA Media, 1989.

Waterman, Robert H., Jr. *The Renewal Factor*. New York: Bantam Books, 1987.

Wiggenhorn, William. "Motorola U: When Training Becomes an Education," *Harvard Business Review*, July–August 1990, pp. 71–83.

Womack, James P., Daniel T. Jones, and Daniel Roos. *The Machine That Changed the World*. New York: Rawson Associates, 1990.

Zuboff, Shoshana. *In the Age of the Smart Machine*. New York: Basic Books, 1988.

INDEX